Maxine Hong Kingston was born in Stockton, California, in 1940. She now lives in Honolulu with her husband, Earll Kingston, an actor, and their son, Joseph.

The Woman Warrior was first published in 1976, and won the National Book Critics Circle Award in the USA.

China Men is her second book.

Also by Maxine Hong Kingston
in Picador
The Woman Warrior

Maxine Hong Kingston

China Men

PICADOR
Original
published by Pan Books

First published in Great Britain 1981 in Picador
by Pan Books Ltd, Cavaye Place, London SW10 9PG
© Maxine Hong Kingston 1977, 1978, 1979, 1980
Portions of this book have been published in
different forms in *Bamboo Ridge*, *Hawaii Review*,
the *New York Times*, the *New Yorker*, and *Seattle Weekly*
Grateful acknowledgement is made to the University
of California Press for permission to reprint from
The State of the Language, edited by Leonard Michaels
and Christopher Ricks, 1980
ISBN 0 330 26367 6
Made and printed in Great Britain by
Cox & Wyman Ltd, Reading

for Tom, George, Norman, and Joe Hong
and Earll and Joseph Kingston

Contents

On discovery

Once upon a time, a man, named Tang Ao, looking for the Gold Mountain, crossed an ocean, and came upon the Land of Women. The women immediately captured him, not on guard against ladies. When they asked Tang Ao to come along, he followed; if he had had male companions, he would've winked over his shoulder.

'We have to prepare you to meet the queen,' the women said. They locked him in a canopied apartment equipped with pots of makeup, mirrors, and a woman's clothes. 'Let us help you off with your armour and boots,' said the women. They slipped his coat off his shoulders, pulled it down his arms, and shackled his wrists behind him. The women who kneeled to take off his shoes chained his ankles together.

A door opened, and he expected to meet his match, but it was only two old women with sewing boxes in their hands. 'The less you struggle, the less it'll hurt,' one said, squinting a bright eye as she threaded her needle. Two captors sat on him while another held his head. He felt an old woman's dry fingers trace his ear; the long nail on her little finger scraped his neck. 'What are you doing?' he asked. 'Sewing your lips together,' she joked, blackening needles in a candle flame. The ones who sat on him bounced with laughter. But the old women did not sew his lips together. They pulled his earlobes taut and jabbed a needle through each of them. They had to poke and probe before puncturing the layers of skin correctly, the hole in the front of the lobe in line with the one in back, the layers of skin sliding about so. They worked the needle through – a last jerk for the needle's wide eye ('needle's nose' in Chinese). They strung his raw flesh with silk threads; he could feel the fibres.

The women who sat on him turned to direct their attention to his feet. They bent his toes so far backward that his arched foot cracked. The old ladies squeezed each foot and broke many tiny bones along the sides. They gathered his toes, toes over and under one another like a knot of ginger root. Tang Ao wept with pain. As they wound the bandages tight and tighter around his feet, the women sang footbinding songs to distract him: 'Use aloe for binding feet and not for scholars.'

During the months of a season, they fed him on women's food: the tea was thick with white chrysanthemums and stirred the cool female winds inside his body; chicken wings made his hair shine; vinegar soup improved his womb. They drew the loops of thread through the scabs that grew daily over the holes in his earlobes. One day they inserted gold hoops. Every night they unbound his feet, but his veins had shrunk, and the blood pumping through them hurt so much, he begged to have his feet re-wrapped tight. They forced him to wash his used bandages, which were embroidered with flowers and smelled of rot and cheese. He hung the bandages up to dry, streamers that drooped and draped wall to wall. He felt embarrassed; the wrappings were like underwear, and they were his.

One day his attendants changed his gold hoops to jade studs and strapped his feet to shoes that curved like bridges. They plucked out each hair on his face, powdered him white, painted his eyebrows like a moth's wings, painted his cheeks and lips red. He served a meal at the queen's court. His hips swayed and his shoulders swivelled because of his shaped feet. 'She's pretty, don't you agree?' the diners said, smacking their lips at his dainty feet as he bent to put dishes before them.

In the Women's Land there are no taxes and no wars. Some scholars say that that country was discovered during the reign of Empress Wu (AD 694–705), and some say earlier than that, AD 441, and it was in North America.

On fathers

Waiting at the gate for our father to come home from work, my brothers and sisters and I saw a man come hastening around the corner. Father! 'BaBa!' 'BaBa!' We flew off the gate; we jumped off the fence. 'BaBa!' We surrounded him, took his hands, pressed our noses against his coat to sniff his tobacco smell, reached into his pockets for the Rainbo notepads and the gold coins that were really chocolates. The littlest ones hugged his legs for a ride on his shoes. And he laughed a startled laugh. 'But I'm not your father. You've made a mistake.' He took our hands out of his pockets. 'But I'm not your father.' Looking closely, we saw that he probably was not. We went back inside the yard, and this man continued his walk down our street, from the back certainly looking like our father, one hand in his pocket. Tall and thin, he was wearing our father's two-hundred-dollar suit that fit him just right. He was walking fast in his good leather shoes with the wingtips.

Our mother came out of the house, and we hung on to her while she explained, 'No, that wasn't your father. He did look like BaBa, though, didn't he? From the back, almost exactly.' We stood on the sidewalk together and watched the man walk away. A moment later, from the other direction, our own father came striding towards us, the one finger touching his hat to salute us. We ran again to meet him.

The father from China

Father, I have seen you lighthearted:

'Let's play airplane,' you said. 'I'll make you a toy airplane.' You caught between your thumb and finger a dragonfly. You held it by the abdomen. Its fast wings blurred, but when its motor paused, I saw that the wings were networks of Cellophane. Its head bulged with eyes, below which the rest of its face was crowded. 'You hold it,' you said. Around its belly, you slipped a lasso of thread, which you tightened, crinkled its shell, pinched a waist, and the tail bent downward slightly. Then you tied the other end of the string around my finger and said, 'Let go.' The tying hadn't hurt it one bit; the dragonfly whirled up and flew in circles at the extent of the string, which I pulled towards me and cast away, controlling my pet airplane. It flew lower, and I turned with it not to get entangled. Suddenly the dragonfly dropped and dangled, but all we had to do was shake it, and it flew again. After a while, though I poked and prodded, it did not go any more. You watched for five more dragonflies to alight until each sister and brother had had a turn.

Upon hearing about the sage of the Ming period who shook himself and turned into a red dragonfly, I remembered our airplane, which was not red. The sunlight had iridized the black into blues and greens.

On summer nights, when we picked new routes home from the laundry through the Stockton streets, crickets covered the sidewalks and the lighted windows. Bats flew between the buildings, and some got hit by cars; we examined them, spread their wings, looked at their teeth and furry countenances. The bats wafted like burned paper in the searchlights, which lit up tightrope walkers who had strung wires from the tallest rooftops and walked with no nets to and from the courthouse dome. On garbage nights, we children ran ahead and rummaged the department

15

store bins for treasures; in trade, you left our garbage, a bag here and a bag on the next block. But usually we didn't walk the long way on Main Street; we went through Chinatown, Tang People's Street, grey and quiet except for the clicking of gamblers who had left a window open. Then we passed the Japanese's closed-up house, nobody home for years, and the Filipino Lodge, where we sat on the benches that were held up by tree bark growing over their edges; the Filipinos had gone in for the night. On our own front porch, you snapped on the light, and the moths came swarming. 'It's a Hit-lah,' you said, swatting one with your newspaper. 'Hit-lah,' we shouted, and attacked the moths, killed them against the walls and railings, '*Hit*-lah!' and a hit on the first syllable. They were plain no-colour butterflies. We killed Hitler moths every summer of The War. It was interesting to grow older and find out that only we called them that, and outside the family, things have other names.

But usually you did not play. You were angry. You scared us. Every day we listened to you swear, 'Dog vomit. Your mother's cunt. Your mother's smelly cunt.' You slammed the iron on the shirt while muttering, 'Stink pig. Mother's cunt.' Obscenities. I made a wish that you only meant gipsies and not women in general.

You were tricked twice by gipsies. One unwrapped her laundry right there on the counter. She shook out her purple and rose cloths, held them up, and said, 'You've torn my best dress. Oh, look. And the blouse, too. Nothing left but rags. And the skirts. Torn to pieces. Mangled. You'll have to pay for them, you know. Replace them. Oh, my new expensive tablecloth. You're going to have to give me money for new clothes. A wardrobe. Come on. Pay up now. Pay. Pay.' She wiggled her fingers through the holes. She had brought dustrags, of course.

'No,' you said. 'Your clothes be old,' you said.

The gipsy strewed her clean, pressed rags and rushed out, but she returned with a sister gipsy – and a cop. The two gipsies talked hard, their earrings leaping with the movements of their jaws. The fan and air-conditioner circulated the smell of their winged hairdos. The policeman, whose navy blue bulk expanded to fill the room, metal and wood clunking, kept saying, 'Small claims court.' Deportation. So you paid, rang up the No Sale on the cash register and paid. Twice.

16

'I knew she was up to something,' MaMa shouted. 'Remember when I sorted her bag, I said, "How do the gipsies afford to have rags laundered?" I could tell that that Romany demoness was up to no good. She and that other one who acted as witness concocted a big story in English for the police. And you couldn't speak English well enough to counteract it. Fell for it twice. You fell for it twice.'

'Kill your Romany mother's cunt,' you said between your clenched teeth. 'Kill your Romany demoness mother's cunt dead.' There is a Cantonese word that sounds almost like 'grandmother', *po,* and means a female monster that looms and sags. In the storeroom were a black bag and a white bag, which we never opened. They were big enough for us children to climb like hills and we called them Black Bag Po and White Bag Po. You called the gipsies those names too. 'Old bags,' you muttered. 'Gipsy bag. Smelly pig bag. Sow. Stink pig. Bag cunt.'

When the gipsy baggage and the police pig left, we were careful not to be bad or noisy so that you would not turn on us. We knew that it was to feed us you had to endure demons and physical labour.

You screamed wordless male screams that jolted the house upright and staring in the middle of the night. 'It's BaBa,' we children told one another. 'Oh, it's only BaBa again.' MaMa would move from bed to bed. 'That was just BaBa having a dream. Bad dreams mean good luck.' She would leave us puzzling, then what do good dreams mean?

Worse than the swearing and the nightly screams were your silences when you punished us by not talking. You rendered us invisible, gone. MaMa told us to say Good Morning to you whether or not you answered. You kept up a silence for weeks and months. We invented the terrible things you were thinking: That your mother had done you some unspeakable wrong, and so you left China for ever. That you hate daughters. That you hate China.

You complained about holiday dumplings: 'Women roll dough to knead out the dirt from between their fingers. Women's fingernail dirt.' Yet you did eat them. MaMa said, though, that you only lately began eating pastries. 'Eating pastries is eating dirt from women's fingernails and from between their fingers.' As if women had webs. Finger jams.

MaMa pays you back, with her tomato and potato wages, the money she sends to China. 'They're my relatives,' she says, 'not his.'

You say with the few words and the silences: No stories. No past. No China.

You only look and talk Chinese. There are no photographs of you in Chinese clothes nor against Chinese landscapes. Did you cut your pigtail to show your support for the Republic? Or have you always been American? Do you mean to give us a chance at being real Americans by forgetting the Chinese past?

You are a man who enjoys plants and the weather. 'It's raining,' you said in English and in Chinese when the California drought broke. 'It's raining.' You make us inordinately happy saying a simple thing like that. 'It rains.'

What I want from you is for you to tell me that those curses are only common Chinese sayings. That you did not mean to make me sicken at being female. 'Those were only sayings,' I want you to say to me. 'I didn't mean you or your mother. I didn't mean your sisters or grandmothers or women in general.'

I want to be able to rely on you, who inked each piece of our own laundry with the word *Centre*, to find out how we landed in a country where we are eccentric people.

On New Year's Eve, you phone the Time Lady and listen to her tell the minutes and seconds, then adjust all the clocks in the house so their hands reach midnight together. You must like listening to the Time Lady because she is a recording you don't have to talk to. Also she distinctly names the present moment, never slipping into the past or sliding into the future. You fix yourself in the present, but I want to hear the stories about the rest of your life, the Chinese stories. I want to know what makes you scream and curse, and what you're thinking when you say nothing, and why when you do talk, you talk differently from Mother.

I take after MaMa. We have peasant minds. We see a stranger's tic and ascribe motives. I'll tell you what I suppose from your silences and few words, and you can tell me that I'm mistaken. You'll just have to speak up with the real stories if I've got you wrong.

*

My father was born in a year of the Rabbit, 1891 or 1903 or 1915. The first year of the Republic was 1911. In one of his incarnations, one of the Buddhas was a rabbit; he jumped alive into a fire to feed the hungry.

BaBa was the youngest and the smartest of four brothers. They put their ears to the door of the room where he was being born. At midday the midwife came out carrying a basin of blood; and they did not understand how a baby could be constructed with so much blood left over.

The oldest brother, Dai Bak, Big Uncle, said, 'Get some boxes and chairs and come with me.' The brothers balanced the teaks and pines in a stack under their parents' window and climbed it like acrobats. By the time they reached the curved sill, the baby had been born. They saw its foot sticking out of a bundle tied to the hook of the rice scale. The baby's bottom plumped out the white cloth. Their mother and father were laughing, and laughed harder when they saw the boys at the window. 'BiBi has arrived,' their father announced, and simultaneously they heard a baby's cry come from the dumpling, the *dim sum*, the little heart. The brothers clutched one another, they cheered, jumped up and down. ' "Jump like a squirrel," ' they sang. ' "Bob like a blue jay, tails in the air, tails in the air." A baby is born. A baby is born.' They scrambled down and ran inside to have a look at him. They hung over the headboard, knelt by the bedside, put their heads next to the baby's on their mother's pillow. All day the brothers smiled when they saw one another and the baby.

Grandmother, Ah Po, said, 'Your little brother is different from any of you. Your generation has no boy like this one. Come. Look.' She unwrapped the baby to show how skinny he was. She uncurled his fists, and his brothers touched the wrinkles inside, looked at their own wrinkles. 'Look at the length of his hands and fingers,' said Ah Po. 'This kind of hand was made for holding pens. This is the boy we'll prepare for the Imperial Examinations.' The other boys were built like horses and oxen, made for farmwork. Ah Po let them each sit on the bed and hold the baby in his lap. They felt big and important. Dai Bak, the oldest, remembered also holding the other two; curious how each brother had felt different in his arms, this one so light. 'Now when you go out to play, you have a baby to strap on your back,' he said to the brother who, up to then, had been the youngest. Grandfather stood at the foot of the bed and was dumbfounded that he had four sons, all in his old age.

At the baby's one-month birthday party, Ah Po gave him the Four Valuable Things: ink, inkslab, paper, and brush. The other children had only gotten money. She put the brush in his right fist. Villagers and relatives praised the way he waved it about. Eating bowls of chicken-feet-and-sweet-vinegar soup and pigs'-feet-and-sweet-vinegar soup, they said good words for the future. Ah Po shaved her baby's head except for the crown, though it was only baby fuzz he had growing on his head. The house was ashine with lights and lucky with oranges.

Third Uncle, Sahm Bak, waited until the baby was tucked away in his parents' bedroom for a nap. Then he ducked into that room and pressed himself against the wall so as not to be spotted from the guest hall, the doors never shut in this house. He dropped to his knees, crawled quickly behind and under furniture, and reached the bed. He grabbed two handfuls of the quilt and hoisted himself up, his chubby legs kicking. He saw the baby asleep, curled in a nest of blankets in the middle of the bed. Sahm Bak delighted in drawing the curtains and hiding inside the layers of canopy and mosquito netting; this high bed was his flying boat to the moon, a secret room, a stage for plays, night in the middle of the day. He stood up, captain of his flying boat, and walked over to his baby brother. His feet sank into the quilts. He was wearing a pair of leather shoes his father had brought back from the Gold Mountain. The shoes were too big for him, but he had stuffed the toes. He pushed and pulled the baby free of the blankets, then he jumped on its stomach. The baby was not as soft as the quilts. The unexpected bones and the oversize shoes made Sahm Bak fall. The baby began to cry. Sahm Bak got to his feet quickly. He had to hurry before the noise brought the adults running. He jumped up and down, up and down on the baby's stomach, so bouncy. The baby let out a squeal each time the shoes depressed his stomach. When the adults arrived, the baby was not squealing any more, but was blue. Since being hit and scolded on a birthday would be bad luck, Sahm Bak had to wait until the next day for his punishment; Dai Bak, who should have been more alert watching his brothers, would have to be punished too. The adults sent the guests hastily home with red eggs and ginger to 'fill their hands'.

For years afterwards, Ah Po would say, 'You were so bad, you stomped on him for hours.'

'I don't remember doing that,' her third son said. 'Do you remember my doing that?' he asked you, BaBa.

'No,' you said. 'I don't remember either.'

Sometimes Sahm pretended he was a baby, quietly nudging himself on to his mother's lap, but when she noticed him, she put him on the floor and picked up BaBa, her BiBi, her lap baby. She loved him so much, she licked the snot from his nose.

Grandfather, Ah Goong, ploughed fields hour after hour alone, inching along between earth and sky. To amuse himself, he sang girls' songs in an old man's falsetto. He wished for a happy daughter he could anticipate seeing in the evenings after work; she would sing for him and listen to him sing. He tied his ox near some water and took a walk about the village to find out what the neighbours were doing. One family he often visited had had a baby due at the same time as our family. After seeing what he himself had gotten, he went to find out what they'd gotten. His mouth and throat, his skin puckered all over with envy. He discovered why to be envious is 'to guzzle vinegar'. Theirs was the loveliest dainty of a baby girl. She lay ignored in a yam basket. He gazed at her and sang to her until he had to leave, should he fall farther behind in his ploughing. The next time he visited, he brought her a red ribbon, which he fashioned into a bow and arranged by her ear. He laughed at the air it gave her. She wore rags, which sent waves of delicious pity coursing through him. 'Poor girl,' he said. 'Poor, poor girl.'

The day his third son stomped on the baby, Ah Goong sneaked away from the commotion. He scooped up party food on the way out. He went to the girl's house. He tucked red packets of money in her faded shirt, no special red dress for her today, no new red jacket, no tiger shoes nor hat with eight boy dolls for tassels. Her family offered him shredded carrots, scant celebration. How sorry he felt for her, how he loved her. She cried, squeezing bitty tears out of her shut lids. His heart and his liver filled with baby tears. Love filled his heart and his liver. He piled grapefruits and oranges in a pyramid for her. He tarried so long that he had to use the outhouse, but he carefully weighed his shit on the outhouse scales so that these neighbours could return a like amount to his fields.

He cut a reed from the New Year narcissus and blew tunes between his thumbs. Though the snowpeas would be fewer at harvest, he brought the girl their blossoms, pinks with purple centres, light blues with dark blue centres, the vine flowering variously as if with colours of different species. She chewed on the flowers and pulled the tendrils apart in her chubby hands. Extravagance. In the summer he fanned her with a sandalwood fan; he rubbed its ribs with sandpaper, and with one pass, the air thickened with memories of Hawai'i, which is the Sandalwood Mountains. In the autumn the two of them would rattle dry peapods.

'It's only a girl,' her parents kept saying. 'Just a girl.'

'Yes,' said Ah Goong. 'Pretty little sister. Pretty miss.'

Away from her he detached a fuzzy green melon from its nest and tucked it for a moment inside his sweater next to his heart. Whenever he had to leave her, he felt the time until he would see her again extend like an unploughed field, the sun going down and a long country night to come. No, he would not endure it.

He went home and put on the brown greatcoat that he had bought in San Francisco. 'Where are you going with that coat in this weather?' asked Ah Po, who did not follow him about the house because of her bound feet; the three maids who fanned her and helped her walk were working in the kitchen. When she walked unassisted or with one maid, she touched the walls gracefully with thumb and little finger spread, index and middle fingers together, fourth finger down. 'I'll just take a peek at the baby,' he said, 'then go out.' He picked up his wife's baby and hid him inside his greatcoat. If you had been a little older, BaBa, you might have felt proud, singled out for an excursion that made Ah Goong dance down the road, a bright idea in his head.

He ran into the neighbours' house and unwrapped the baby, first the greatcoat, then the diapers to show the family that this doggy really was a boy. 'Since you want a boy and I want a girl,' he said, 'let's strike a bargain. Let's trade.' The family was astounded. They would have let him buy the girl if only he'd asked. They would have had to give her away eventually any-

22

how. And here was this insane man who did not know the value of what he had. What a senile fool. Take him up on it before he comes to his senses. As if his son's boyness was not enough, he pointed out his attributes. 'This boy will be very intelligent,' he said. 'He's got scholar's hands. And look what a smart forehead he has. He'll win a name for you at the Imperial Examinations. He's very skinny and eats hardly any food.'

'Yes, we'll take him,' said the neighbours. Ah Goong placed the girl inside his greatcoat. He did not remove the boy's fancy clothes, the gold necklace, the new shoes, nor the jade bracelet that signified that you would not have to do physical labour. He hurried out before her family could change their minds. His heart beat that they would reclaim her at the last minute. The girl wore no jewellery, but with his soul he adopted her, full diapers and all.

He walked slowly, adoring the peachy face. He sat by the side of the road to look at her. He counted her pink toes and promised that no one would break them. He tickled her under the chin. She would make his sombre sons laugh. Kindness would soon soften the sides of their mouths. They would kneel to listen to her funny requests. They would beguile her with toys they'd make out of feathers and wood. 'I'll make you a doll,' he promised her. 'I'll buy you a doll.' And surely his wife would get used to her soon. The walk home was the nicest time. He showed her, his daughter, how the decorative plants grow wild and the useful plants in rows. 'Flower,' he said, pointing. 'Tree.' He rested by the stream for her to listen to its running.

At home, he walked directly to the crib and tucked her in. He drew the quilt over her as a disguise. Then he hung up his greatcoat and returned to the crib, gave the quilt a pat. She was a well-behaved baby and made no noise. He kept strolling past the crib. His happiness increased in her vicinity. 'My heart and my liver' he called her. (*Sweetheart* is an English word that emigrants readily learn.)

Ah Po heard the sniffing and squeaking of a baby waking up. She swayed over to the crib. The baby noises sounded unfamiliar. She screamed when she saw the exchanged baby.

Ah Goong came running. 'What's wrong? What's wrong?' he asked.

'What is this? Where's my baby?' Ah Po yelled.

'It's all right.' He patted the baby. 'Everything's all right. He's at the neighbours'. They'll take good care of him.'

'What neighbours?' she yelled. 'What's he doing at the neighbours'? Whose is this ugly thing?'

'Oh, no, she isn't ugly. Look at her.' He picked her up.

'Where's my baby? You crazy old man. You're insane. You idiot. You dead man.'

'The neighbours have him. I brought this one back in his place.' He held his little girl. 'All we have are boys. We need a girl.'

'You traded our son for a girl? How could you? Who has my son? Oh, it's too late. It's too late.' She thrust her arms as far as she could reach; she bent her torso from side to side, backwards and forwards, a woman six feet tall on toy feet. 'Take me to that family,' she cried. 'We're trading back.' Lunging her weight at Ah Goong, who hunched his shoulders and caved in his chest to protect the baby, she pushed him out the door. She walked in back of him, shoving him while hanging on to his shoulder. She was not used to dashing about on the roads. 'I'm coming to rescue you, BiBi. Your mother's coming.' Ah Goong clung to his baby as if she were holding him up. 'Dead man,' Ah Po raged, 'trading a son for a slave. Idiot.' He led her to the neighbours' house, weeping as he walked. 'Dead demon.' The villagers lined the road to look at Grandfather and Grandmother making fools of themselves.

Ah Po scolded the girl's family. 'Cheating the greedy pig, huh? Thieves. Swindlers. Taking advantage of an idiot. Cheaters. Trying to catch a pig, are you? Did you really think you'd get away with it? Pig catchers. A girl for a boy. A girl for a boy.' The family hung their heads.

She pulled the girl out of Ah Goong's arms and shoved her at an older child. Her own baby she snatched and held tight. She sent for her sedan chair and waited for it in the road. She carried her son herself all the way home, not letting Ah Goong touch her baby, not letting him ride. He hardly saw the road for his tears. Poor man.

Perhaps it was that very evening and not after the Japanese bayoneted him that he began taking his penis out at the dinner table, worrying it, wondering at it, asking why it had given him four sons and no daughter, chastising it, asking it whether it were yet capable of producing the daughter of his dreams. He shook his head and clucked his tongue at it. When he saw what a disturbance it caused, he laughed, laughed in Ah Po's irked face, whacked his naked penis on the table, and joked, 'Take a look at *this* sausage.'

When BiBi was walking upright instead of 'in cow position' on all fours, his second brother, Ngee Bak, walked him to the fields. 'Come on, BiBi,' he said, taking his hand. 'Let's go look at what shoots came up overnight.' He slowed his steps for the toddler, but walking the veering way children walk, the two boys often turned around and went back the way they came, each one following the other here and there, lifting rocks, prodding bugs, squatting to part the grass and thrill at the small live movements. But a plan kept reappearing in Ngee Bak's mind so that they did eventually arrive at the rice field, which looked like a lake on fire with rows of doubling green flames.

'Isn't it beautiful?' said Ngee Bak, who threw a pebble at the water in front of BiBi. Waterdrops spattered his knees, and laughter gurgled up inside his chest like ripples and like the waterdrops. With both hands, he plucked stones out of the dam. He threw one rock after another and loved the giggles that splashed happily out of his mouth. Then he pushed the mud and rice straw and rocks aside and jumped into the water, kicked it, watched the rings spread and fade. He touched the shoots, grasped them, and pulled, such a satisfying loosening and snapping of roots from the earth. He collected the green rice in his pockets.

Meanwhile, Ngee Bak ran tattletaling to the house, 'Come quick. Hurry. Look. Look. Look at BiBi.'

Grandfather and Grandmother lifted him out of the water and ordered their oldest son, 'Go cut a switch.' Dai Bak did not climb a tree for a fresh switch; he hunted in the faggots for a brittle branch that had fallen during a winter storm. He trimmed off the twigs. He knelt at his parents' feet and knocked his forehead on the ground.

'Please beat me, Father and Mother, to teach me a lesson,' he requested.

They took turns hitting him across the back and shoulders,

not his head because they did not want to damage his brains. 'This – will – teach – you – to – teach – your – younger – brother – to – watch – his – younger – brother,' a switch with each words. They administered what Tu Fu called 'the beating by which he remembered his guilt'. There was sap in the branch yet.

'Thank you, Father and Mother,' he said when they were done whipping. BiBi and Ngee Bak stood near by and watched. The two of them listened, thankful he wasn't the oldest, who has the duty of setting a good example. (We American children heard too, and resolved not to 'return' to China.)

Instead of acrobatics and shuttlecock, he liked studying. Ah Po kept her boy close. She sewed little scholar's caps and scholar's gowns. She used the left over black scraps for knee patches on her other sons' pants. Even before BiBi could talk, she fed and lodged itinerant scholars, who stayed the night or week to read to him. They drew giant words and held them over his crib. 'How intelligent he looks,' they told her. When he was old enough for regular lessons, his brothers sometimes came inside from their chores to rest on the floor at the tutor's feet. Ah Po did not stop them, did not chase them back out. If they overheard some learning, all the better; they would have it to ponder during the years in the fields. Soon the farming brothers' heads nodded; when they suddenly jerked awake, it embarrassed them that the tutor might have seen them bored. One by one they withdrew to slop pigs, draw water, feed chickens before it grew too dark for chickens to eat, dumb fowls.

BaBa was also very good at gambling, but he won so often that his brothers would not play with him. 'It's not fair,' they complained. 'He memorizes the cards and tiles.'

'He's lucky,' Ah Po bragged, her eyes and her rings glittering as if she were sweeping in the winnings herself. 'Lucky.'

So instead of gambling in the evenings, BaBa 'hummed' poems. He practised his handwriting at his own corner of the gambling table, which was also the dining table. The words he wrote were as large as his chest, the word *heart* bigger than his own heart, the word *man* almost as big as himself. He had to stand on a chair to write so big, 'playing with big words' like the nine-year-old Tu Fu, who wrote enough words 'to fill a hard-bottomed bag'. A humming came from him continually.

The three older brothers founded a clubhouse inside a grape arbour. By excluding one, they made a secret society. Under the jagged leaves, the three brothers peeked at their little brother kneeling in the dirt. He was scratching the ground with a stick. 'He's writing,' they whispered. 'Even outdoors he's writing. Let's torture him.' They scurried out of the vines and circled him while they sang 'The Song of the Man of the Green Hill'. They schemed that if their mother saw them from the house, she'd think they were only playing with him. ' "Poetry addict, poetry addict",' they sang. ' "Poetry addict won't work for rice, shoulders a hoe but forgets to till. Poetry addict won't comb his hair, defends his home with a rusty sword. Poetry addict rude to guests, out of food and forgets to eat. He won't loosen tongue to bring about the fall of seventy cities." ' He scribbled on the ground until his brothers wearied and left him alone.

One autumn morning, when he was about fourteen years old, he left the village to take the qualifying test for the last Imperial Examination ever given. Instead of taking a boat, he walked beneath the trees, useful for inspiration, their branches like open arms forking smaller and smaller until the topmost branches spread into fingers reaching and gesturing, posing and pointing in the wind. The branches formed words too, as did the skeins of geese. 'The snow goose of ambition stirs its wings,' Tu Fu had said on his way to the tests. 'I ride the great snow goose of my ambition.' The geese flew with wingtips pointing. The farther BaBa walked from the village, the larger the world grew. He sat by a stream at noon and hummed a poem that ordered the sounds of water.

Towards evening he passed a hermitage with door open and no hermit inside; he passed an inn, and farmhouses where rich families were lighting lanterns. The owls flew with fanning wings into the twilight. He spread his bedroll in a reaped field. The wooden pillow under his neck lifted his thick braid, which Grandmother had woven tight to last for days, and it trailed on the ground. No trees obstructed the simple sky, no building or mountain; no hair blew in his face. He saw only sky, which made him feel simultaneously very big and very small, like one of the stars, like an eye. Each time he awoke, he could tell by the moon's place how long he had slept, and how unevenly.

No one moment was the dawn, but ten thousand blending

moments, each one a dawn. The sun edging up did not begin the morning; it was somehow always at its centre.

Noticing the foreign ways of fencing, terracing, and ricking, he walked two days. Within sight of the building that had been erected centuries ago specially for examinations, he threw away his village clothes, which were not proper clothing but wrappings and rags, and donned a black silk robe. He walked through the doorposts – fresh red posters on left and right: TO BEGIN THE YEAR, TELL ABOUT THE GREATNESS OF CHINA. MAY ALL THE EARTH'S PEOPLE DRINK WINE. And above the door: COME AND GO IN PEACE, which is a common blessing. So this was the Dragon's Gate, and he was a carp ready to run the falls.

He entered a courtyard, where scholars quietly conversed, not a one of them loud and scolding like the villagers. As he wandered among them, he heard them talk about what happened in books as if it were real. They were a different race from the splay-fingered village men, whose most imaginative talk was about the Gold Mountain. The scholars sprang riddles on one another. One would describe a situation or a relationship and the others, by calculating geomancy, rhymes, metaphors, puns, and radicals and other sections of words, guessed which ideograph it made. They clapped hands and laughed when somebody hit on the answer. Explaining to the ones who didn't get it, they opened their left palms and drew invisible calligraphy on them with the long, tapering index fingers of their right hands.

The camaraderie ended when an official stood at an inner door and called them out of the courtyard one by one. At mid-afternoon, he shouted the name BaBa had invented for himself on the occasion of taking the tests. (His baby name was like Shy Cutie, which would not do here.) It was the first time he heard his adult name said aloud by someone else. If another scholar had answered to that name, one or the other would have renamed himself on the spot, in case the name did not have enough power for two people. An official led BaBa to a cell, where he asked him to undress. The official looked over his naked body for notes written on the skin, combed through his long hair for hidden papers, cut open the seams and hems of his clothes. 'I'll bring your dinner at six,' he said, and took away BaBa's bedroll and everything in it.

BaBa sat on the cot, sat at the table. He would have enjoyed the luxury of having a window, though he did not need daylight or moonlight to study by. With hands folded behind his back, he paced, brushing the floor with the balls of his feet, and sang his memorizations. A jailer brought food, returned for the utensils, gave him back his bedroll, and locked him up 'until time for the first test', he said. He left a teapot, around which BaBa held his hands and caught the rich heat that arose. He decided to stay awake all night. The tea lasted a short while. Fireflies in a jar would have given an appearance of warmth. Back in the village he had read by their light. Steam must have been issuing from his mouth and nose, but he could not see it. Huddling in a blanket, his knees against his chest, he perched on the straight-backed chair, but the blanket turned into a nest for sleeping, and he had to discard it. Muttering the texts, he gave voice and breath to word after word. His attention was a flame; when he saw it turn into a firefly, shrinking, going out, he almost fell off the chair with alarm; for a moment or longer he had fallen asleep. He tried propping himself up by the elbows. His eyes closed, and shapes and colours began turning into dreams. He tried holding his eyelids open with his fingers, but in the dark they might as well have been closed. He understood the blue-eyed Buddha-who-cut-off-his-eyelids. He stood on the chair and stretched – and felt a hook or a ring in a beam directly overhead. So there it was; of course, the poets said it would be there. He looped the end of his pigtail into the ring and tied it tight. Then he sat in his chair to study some more. When he dozed, his own hair jerked his head back up. Hours later, when the pull on his scalp no longer kept him alert, he opened the table drawer, where he found an awl. Like the poets whose blood had been wiped off it, he jabbed the awl into his thigh, held it there, and studied on. At the worst dark of the night, he needed neither ring nor awl. 'Aiya!' Out of the disembodying dark came screams of men already driven mad, footsteps, scufflings, someone yelling, 'Ah Ma. Ah Ma.' The poets say that men have used the ring to hang themselves.

At last an official unlocked the cell to give him breakfast. He searched him again before escorting him to a testing room, where a panel of scholars sat at a long table. BaBa stood with his face to the wall and his hands clasped behind him. In this position he recited by heart from the Three Character Classics, the Five Classics (*The Book of Changes, The Book of History, The Book of Poetry, The Book of Propriety, The Spring and Autumn Annals*), and the Thirteen Classics by Confucius's disciples; the examiners also threw in some five-word poems. He had been afraid that nothing would come out of his mouth, but once the first words, many of which he had kept ready on his tongue, broke forth, the rest came tumbling out, like water, like grain. The judges wrote numbers beside his new name. When he returned to the cell, he felt lighter. On the second evening he reached the last word of the last book. He fell asleep that night without having to study for the first time in years.

On the third morning an official returned his Four Valuable Things. He set brushes, ink, inkslab, and paper on the table horizontally and vertically, aligned the papers' edges parallel to the table's edges. He sat with spine straight and ground the ink blacker and blacker. The blacker his ink, the more patient the man – the Genie of the Ink, who is no bigger than a fly, will land in it. A proctor entered and handed BaBa the topics to write about, and locked the door on his way out. His hand hollow as if fingers curled around a walnut, an actual walnut when he was a child, BaBa held the pen perpendicular, ready. So he was to write alone in a cell instead of among candidates sitting together in a hall. Poets warned about fake walls and blinds behind which established scholars hid and made fun of the candidates – the old men taking the test for the twentieth time and the young men tapping their feet and scratching as they conned words. The ceilings and walls of the cell seemed opaque enough. He concentrated on remembering the text. Knowledge fell into place, moved from head, from heart, down his arm and out the fingers to converge at the tip of the brush. At a downward pull, he made the first mark in the upper left side of the first word. The heel of his hand steady on the table, he drew the strong deliberate stem, then with a shake he quickened a branch. His fingers lifted on the thin strokes, pulling the brush up for tapering, and pressed down for the heavier, thicker lines, a flick the hook at the bottom. He worked for three days, building each word from top to bottom, left to right, water strokes, dots for flames, tailing gondolas for the boat words, never going back for repairs. He wrote in many styles including The Beauty Adorns Her Hair with Blossoms and The Maid Apes Her Mistress. The seven-hundred-word essays were geometries that demonstrated his knowledge of philosophy and, because this was modern times, of international politics. He dared one poem in the grass style and, with a new brush, one humorous poem that darted down the page like swifts in a clear sky.

He waited for three days to hear his rank among the scholars, who talked about winning and losing. They were at leisure. It was too late to study any more and too early to begin studying for the next try three years hence. Failing wasn't such a shame. Kai Li-shih hid in the gambling houses but became a poet nevertheless. Tu Fu, the Earthly Poet, sang about how he failed his third, fifth, and sixth tries, and about failing on his fortieth birthday. He had even failed a special test arranged in his honour. And he had come from eleven generations of scholars. (BaBa was the only one as far back as the family knew. We were a family of eighty pole fighters and no scholars.) Though the ignorant villagers would tease and mock, there was an honourable tradition of failing the exams. The emperors gave special honorary degrees for perseverance to eighty- and ninety-year-olds who had tried their whole lives. Ah, but winning, a scholar would become one of the philosophers who rules China; everyone would hear of him, everyone would want to befriend him. All things good come to the mandarin scholar. His ancestors would receive titles and degrees. (His descendants would not get anything, and so save the government expenses and trouble.)

BaBa did not win the top honours; he would have had an easier life then and not come to the Gold Mountain. He did not 'fly' to Canton or Peiping. He must have been a Learned Scholar or a Righteous Worthy; he won the job of village teacher. Our family painted the rooftree red and trimmed the windows with green and gold.

His new name brought him enough luck, and so he kept it; the name he has now is that name: Think Virtue, my father's name. I hesitate to tell it; I don't want him traced and deported. Even MaMa rarely calls him by name and not this one but other vocatives, like So-and-so's Father. Friends call him Uncle or

31

Brother or Teacher. Anyway, a translation, Think Virtue, is nothing like this name; the English words are like fiction, that is, their sounds are dissimilar from the Chinese sounds. Nobody would call anyone else by a translation, Think Virtue his written name anyway. He is still disguised. Think Virtue – *think* is an ideograph combining the radicals for *field* and *heart*, and *virtue* also has the root *heart* in it; his name looks like two valentines and is not as cerebral as it appears in English.

So he had once had three free days. He spent them talking to the other scholars, making friends, singing, touring the capital. Counting the days spent walking, you had seven free days.

My maternal grandparents or 'outside grandmother' and 'outside grandfather' – one of the words in *maternal grandparents* the same as in *foreigner* or *barbarian* – these 'outsiders' tracked BaBa down by following the invisible red string that ties his ankle to MaMa's. Year by year the string grew shorter.

The outside grandparents had four daughters, and so one of this grandmother's habits whenever she heard of an interesting boy or young man was to count him. Using the poor people's divining method, she took a pinchful of rice, said his name, and counted the grains to see if she had picked an odd or even number, carefully dropping each speck back into the rice box. Odd meant Yes, this boy was her daughter's true husband; even meant No, wrong boy; *four* sounds like *die*. In addition to counting rice, she confirmed the results by paying an expensive blind fortuneteller to touch a list of young men's names, and he picked out her future son-in-law. He also used the yarrow sticks and the tortoise shell and told the wedding date.

Then these outsiders sent spies to find out if their prospective son-in-law was deformed or leprous or mad or poor or ugly. His family sent counterspies. Some families bribed the neighbours to bruit it about how good looking, intelligent, rich, and good humoured their son or daughter was. But BaBa's and MaMa's families did not have to lie; he and she were exceptionally smart, the proof being their literacy. The outside grandfather, like the real one, was an unusual man in that he valued girls; he taught all his daughters how to read and write. The families had about the same amounts of money, earned by the generations going-out-on-the-road to the Gold Mountain.

On her third to the last evening at home, MaMa dressed in white. A lucky old woman, who had a good woman's long life, helped her wash her hair, though this being modern days she only sprinkled water on her head. Dressed in white, MaMa sat behind her bedcurtains to sing-and-weep. 'Come and hear the bride cry,' the village women invited one another. 'Hurry. Hurry. The bride's started singing-and-crying.' 'Listen. Listen. The bride's singing. The bride's weeping.' They sat around the bed to listen as if they were at the opera. The girl children sat too; they would learn the old and new songs. The women called out ideas: 'Cry about the years your mother held you prisoner'. 'And you're ransomed at last.' 'Scold your mother for not finding you your husband sooner.'

'Give me a rifle to shoot my mother down,' MaMa wailed. 'Mother, you've kept me working at your house. You've hidden me from my husband and family. Mother, I'm leaving you now. I'm aiming my rifle at your stomach and shooting you down.'

'Oh-h-h,' exclaimed the women. 'She's the best crying bride I've ever heard.' The drummers banged. The bride's mother stood against the wall and smiled proudly.

'Cry for widows and orphans,' the guests suggested. 'Cry for boys and men drafted into armies.' 'And leaving for the Gold Mountain.' She cried-and-sang about the three times her father left for the Gold Mountain and how he brought back two step-mothers. 'They fried dumplings for their own babies and spattered oil on my feet,' she sang. 'And my bridegroom will go too out-on-the-road and send me photographs of an old man.'

'Sing for a husband for the spinsters.' 'Sing for a husband for my older sister,' said pretty younger sisters who could not jump over the old maids.

'Pull a barrel on top of you, and cry over how heavy a man is.' The women cackled at that one.

'Cry for going hungry.'

'The men don't make enough money for spending all those years away.'

'Scold them for enjoying the barbarian lands more than home.' 'Scold unfaithful men.' 'Make up a song for scolding a man when he comes back.'

'My husband will pick a plum,' she sang. 'He'll pick a plum blossom as I become a prune.'

The women punctuated her long complaints with clangs of pot lids for cymbals. The rhymes made them laugh. MaMa wailed, her eyes wet, and sang as she laughed and cried, mourned, joked, praised, found the appropriate old songs and invented new songs in melismata of singing and keening. She sang for three evenings. The length of her laments that ended in sobs and laughter was wonderful to hear.

The bridegroom's family sent three thousand wedding cakes, two thousand of the expensive bought kind and one thousand of the homemade cheap kind. They sent either one thousand pigs or one pig and the price of a thousand pigs. The outside grandparents parcelled the cakes and hunks of crackly orange-skin pork among their friends and relatives, gave some each evening to the women who came to hear the crying-and-singing, and also sent it by messengers throughout the village.

On the morning of the fourth day, MaMa dressed in her black wedding coat with the embroidered flowers and birds. ('I'm going to order wedding coats from Hong Kong for you,' she says. 'No. No, thanks,' we say.) Layers of veiling hung from her head-dress; no one could see her face. Men carried the bridal palanquin through the streets, where a band of dancers and beggars, 'the flowery ones', who cannot be turned away on a wedding day, followed. 'She rides like a queen above the men,' said the wedding guests. 'The men are kidnapping her,' they also said. Her palanquin was called a 'bridge', She would go no more to her parents' house except as a visitor; the visit a woman makes to her parents is a metaphor for rarity.

In the middle of the courtyard of her new home, she sat on a round wicker tray. Another lucky old woman lifted the veil in back and combed her hair, but actually only touched it with a comb, her hair being already dressed. The wedding guests gasped, wanting to reach out and stop the comb; they had also been uneasy at the hairwashing and at hearing the bad words, *death, army, rifle,* and at seeing the woman riding above the men. There was a suspense, a shock to see the bride dressed in funeral white, to see her feet and butt touch the winnower, which touches food, and to watch the burning of the paper horses like a funeral. The wedding guests held still, waited, then exhaled, laughed, and shouted.

Then the bride went inside the house to meet the groom. Being a very clever bride and having been coached by the married women, when the wedding guests pulled aside the bedcurtains and she saw him for the first time – sitting in his bed 'like a Buddha statue', she said; that is, 'like a *fut*' – she leapt up on the bed and sat facing him so closely that there was no room for her to kowtow. She quickly served him the tea; the kowtowing-to-the-husband part of the ceremony was skipped.

You were sitting there on your bed when out of nowhere jumped this veiled woman. Your family had reminded you, 'Be sure to make her bow her head,' but she was already pouring tea while the wedding guests threw popcorn, which fell like a warm snowfall, covering the quilt, landing on her headdress, and catching in your long sleeves. In the kitchen more corn popped like distant gunfire.

Bride and groom arose from the cloud of popcorn and went to the family hall, where Grandfather and Grandmother sat in the two best chairs. The new couple kneeled at their feet and served them tea while they said lucky words about long life and many children and much money. The mother-in-law gave the daughter-in-law jewellery. The bride's sisters served dry tea to the women in the groom's family; dry tea is a cupful of cookie crumbs.

Finally at the feast, the groom and his brothers walked from table to table to drink an entire glass of whisky at each toast. The bride and her sisters walked to each table to pour and drink tea; the wedding guests loaded her tray with red money. Serving with both hands, she displayed her arms, covered from wrists to elbows with gold and jade bracelets, the right arm showing his family's gifts, the left arm her family's. Many of the bracelets were chains of American quarter-eagle gold pieces. Catenaries of gold necklaces strung with gold coins, jade hearts, and gold words adorned her neck. She also wore a gold ring in the shape of two clasping hands that Grandfather had brought from the Gold Mountain.

After the guests left, the bride and groom went to their room, which was fluffy with popcorn, and he saw her face for the first time.

*

BaBa made a living by being the village teacher. Every day at sunrise, he called the roll in a name chant, which was a sort of hexameter, each student's name filling half a line. Staggering the lessons, he began the older boys copying their textbook and told the six- and seven-year-olds, 'Repeat after me.' He read Lesson One to them many times, the children chorusing line by line. They copied it while he read a more advanced lesson with an older group.

At nine a.m. everyone went home for breakfast, which was recess. There was no need for other rest; reading and writing are rest, mere sitting. When all the boys were copying at once, BaBa walked up and down between tables, corrected a brush hold, switched a pen from left hand to right hand, straightened a paper and a spine. He kept a rod tucked under his arm. All seemed to go well the first few days, the students obedient enough, though when sweeping out the schoolhouse he found piles of chewed sunflower seeds in corners.

In the evening, after marking the copybooks, which were almost all poor, he began working on a project he had thought up to give his students an advantage in their education. Instead of having them buy handwriting patterns printed in Canton, he would make one for each boy, using that boy's own special words, including his father's name, which some shy or backward villagers did not tell their children. He ruled sturdy pieces of paper into squares and filled each square with a word that was the epitome of a particular kind of stroke or radical. The students would insert these master sheets into the transparent sleeves of their tracing booklets and follow the lines of their teacher's excellent handwriting. He would finish two or three patterns an evening until every student had one.

Worries, like roosters crowing in the dark, woke BaBa hours before he needed to go to school. He stared at the ceiling, listened, listed things to do, waited until his father and brothers, silent like thieves, stealing an extra hour from the night, got up and walked to the fields, and the women went to the well to catch the first water of dawn, the Glory of the Well, good for the skin. Before sunrise, he walked to the schoolhouse; the closer he came, the louder the birds, whose wakening sounded like children's voices. To his horror, children's voices, their laughter, and the scrape and thud of furniture came from the schoolhouse. A small boy at the door sprang up as he recognized his teacher. The boy ran inside, where scurrying, talking – a door slammed – scuttling stopped completely upon BaBa's entrance. The students were supposed to be studying during the hour before the teacher's arrival, their loud studious voices to accompany the farmers' walk to the fields. The whole village must have heard the chaos. He did not know which boys to punish; they were now chanting the last lines of their various lessons.

When he explained things in the common language, the students should have marvelled that they had a teacher who knew the meanings of the texts and not just the rote. Today he would explain some of the 'parallelisms' – how the directions, the elements, the humours the architecture of emperors' palaces and commoners' houses, the weather, the trees, the members of families, the hours of the day, the centuries, the dynasties of China, the winds, all have their correspondences one to another. For example, pre-dawn is the time for the unborn child and of bulbs in the earth. Mid-winter, midnight, and old age are times of sleep and death and harvest in the barns. The students ought to know that at that very moment, they were at mid-morning in spring, youth, a growing time. It was a year of Approach, when a good man is inexhaustible in his will to learn and teach. He recited the poem that had won first place at the Imperial Examinations: ' "Escaping the fire, the second grandfather ran with the pig in his arms, and the fifth son carried the sheep." The numbers, the relatives, the animals all have important meanings,' he said. 'The winner explained that he was describing an actual fire at his house.'

Eyes blinked and glazed. Heads nodded and jerked. Boys flipped their pigtails over the tops of their heads and unbraided the ends; they hid their sleeping eyes behind the hair. At any moment, they would awaken and go into uproar again. BaBa retreated. 'Read aloud after me,' he said, quitting explanations. Sometimes the boys shouted out the end of a line. He liked them for doing that, though it was just an outburst against tedium. When their voices dwindled, he looked at the clock; there was half an hour to fill. 'Read aloud by yourselves,' he said. Without his leading them, they straggled and faltered; the smartest

37

boy heard himself solo, and stopped. So he diverted them to chanting the multiplication tables until breakfast. Once he placed the rod across the shoulders of a boy who snored aloud. The rod transmitted a sense of his corporeity, the skin, the muscles, the two wing bones.

BaBa could not eat breakfast, and both his mother and my mother said, 'You have to eat. You can't use your brain all day without food.' He paced, then had to go to school again.

'Writing,' he taught, 'isn't painting. Get enough ink on the brush to complete a stroke in one movement. Don't go back to fill in. No backward painting. If you don't have enough ink, use the dry brush technique, a very advanced method.' He handed out the one-of-a-kind patterns he had made. 'What do we do with the patterns we spent money on?' the students asked. While the younger students one by one stood beside his desk and read aloud, out of the corners of his eyes he saw a writer splotch his paper, another took dab after dab to form one stroke; another outlined a word and coloured it in; another dribbled ink in the wide part of a word, then spread it out. Heavy hands moving from right to left smeared columns of writing.

At mid-afternoon, he told the students that they had been working so hard, he would treat them: he'd give them the first line of a couplet, and they could finish it almost any way they pleased. He read many examples in order to inspire them. But boredom drained their eyes. The word *poetry* had hit them like a mallet stunning cattle. As he recited, two boys were whispering; he needed to reprimand them, knock their heads together right now, but a scolding would interrupt the poem. He pressed onward, his face stiff, eyes glowering, ruining the mood of the poem, his lips mouthing the words. 'Now I'll give you a first line that establishes the season and place,' he said. 'You find the second line. You can write about an animal, a tree, a feeling, a colour, a political rank, a condition of the soil, whatever. You can write about a boat; there are many different kinds.'

'Go ahead. Start now,' he said when the boys continued to stare.

'What do you want us to do?' asked a boy who had been sighing and yawning throughout the assignment.

'Could you explain that again?' asked another boy, exasperated, rolling his eyes at the teacher's ineptness.

He had fallen into talking about the parallels they hadn't understood earlier, but it was too late; dropping a lesson once started spoils a teacher's authority.

'I don't get it.' 'We don't understand you.' 'You don't explain clearly.'

'Take a guess,' he suggested. 'Taking a guess is the same as making up a story.'

'That doesn't make sense.' 'We don't understand.' 'You're making things up because you don't know the answers.'

A flash of lightning broke red across the room. He grit his teeth. He wanted to kill. 'Finish the couplet,' he said.

'What's that?'

A blood vessel must have broken in his temple, and the red lightning was the blood spurted across the eyes.

'Could you repeat the assignment?' said someone else, whom he ignored.

'Could you repeat your half of the poem?' someone asked.

Controlling his face, he repeated the start of the couplet, and what poetry had been in the line was a mortification in his mouth.

'Explain,' said the students.

The boys spoke in the brute vulgate, and he saw that he had made a bad mistake translating literature into the common speech. The students had lost respect for him; if he were so smart, he would not speak like them. Scorn curled their lips and lifted their eyebrows. 'Explain,' they demanded without standing up for recognition.

The opening line was not even a complex one, very colloquial: 'At mid-morning in late spring, when walking west—'

'What?' 'What did he say?' The students had not seen his anger, then; it had not shown on his face. They would otherwise not act so dumb. 'Explain that again.'

Their previous teacher must have spent school time drinking tea and reading novels.

'How do you write *clear* and *bright*?' At last, one of the boys was getting down to work, though he had forgotten two of the simplest and most commonly used ideographs in the language. BaBa wrote the words invisibly on his table. 'Slower,' said the boy. BaBa wrote with ink on paper. 'How do you write *wood*?' the boy asked. BaBa wrapped his hand around the boy's and wrote the tree-like word. 'See?' BaBa said. 'It looks like a tree.'

The word written by two people's hands wiggled with impatience and with not wanting to show impatience, the little hand pulling one way and the big hand another.

BaBa kept hearing furtive motion behind him. Just you wait until I give your parents your report cards, he thought. I'll show you. You'll be sorry. ('In China parents beat children for getting beaten by the teacher,' said the adults.)

He whirled and hit a boy on the arm. 'Work!' he shouted. Neither the boy whose hand he guided nor the one he hit said 'Thank you, Teacher.'

At last he decided that they had sweated enough over the couplet, which they should have closed instantly. He had meant it as a recreation, a break in the work, just for fun. The boys were forcing him to turn literature into a weapon against them.

During the tracing hour, their heavy heads lolled like cows' heads towards whatever insect of distraction alit. Some boys drew pictures of animals. The younger children squirmed from one buttock to the other, wriggling to join the girls and baby boys playing outside.

At last the day ended. The students could not possibly have reached the last sentence in unison, but altogether they closed their books at four p.m. as if they had been dismissed. Mid-sentence, mid-word, they slapped their books shut and tricked their teacher into saying, 'Well, you may go.' Then they charged out the door without bidding 'Thank you, Teacher' or 'Good afternoon, Teacher.'

Suddenly the school was quiet. A dusty peace settled. BaBa sat down at his desk. The greased paper in the windows soaked up the afternoon sun in brownish stains. Most 'desks' were only pieces of furniture the farmers could spare. A few show-offs had given their sons heirloom tables knotty with carvings. It was a small room after all, not an unwieldy size. He sprinkled water on the floor and swept it clean – gobs of sunflower seeds again in the corner. He smoothed out the paper wads and read them. He poured the dustpan of sweepings into the stove. Long strands of shredded hair snapped in the fire. As he walked about the room, everything he touched became well ordered. He would oil new paper for the windows, perhaps white paper rather than brown so the students could see better. He would bring a hammer and nails and other tools tomorrow. He would build a fence around the school and dig a garden. Then the students might not want so much to escape. Leaving the door open for light and air, he graded papers and recorded the low grades in a ledger.

His wife was watching for him in the road when he came home late. 'I thought you'd been kidnapped by bandits,' she said. 'It's dangerous to be out after dark. Where would we get the money to ransom you?' He went immediately to dinner. Perhaps the student he hit would have felt it more if he ate better. He was losing weight teaching.

He dreamed that he was teaching mathematics but the numbers did not come out right. The correct answer wavered and changed by itself into an impossible figure; digits kept switching places. The students were yelling, 'What's the answer, Teacher?' He abandoned the calculations and, rod raised, went chasing after them. They laughed when he hit them. The rod seemed to press giggles out of them. They hid under their tables. They jumped through the paper windows. 'QUIET!' he screamed. He screamed lessons, morals, stories, poems, songs, but the students kept playing and fighting. Parents and the district principal peeked in the holes in the windows and saw that he could not teach. 'Go away!' he screamed, and woke himself up.

There came to be small difference between his day life and the nightmares. The students ran amok. They stole vegetables from the neighbouring gardens; they played war; they staged shows on top of the tables. He tried locking the door on the late boys and got some satisfaction from their shadows bobbing and passing like puppets at the windows, but they worried him when they disappeared. Where did they go? The school looked like a crazy house, like a Sung Dynasty painting of a classrooom showing kids putting boxes over one another's heads, drawing cartoons of their teacher, lying on their backs and spinning chairs and tables with their feet.

As the year went on, BaBa made a habit of staying at school during breakfast so that he would not have to wrench himself away from home twice in one morning. He used the rest period to read his own books before he forgot how. Someone had to enjoy reading in this school. The students ruined his eating; they

ruined his sleep. They spoiled the songs of birds. And they were
taking his books and calligraphy from him too – no time now
for his own reading, no time to practise his own writing. Teaching
was destroying his literacy. He was spending his brains picking out flaws and poring over them. School was the very opposite of reading and writing. The books that he taught had lost
their subtlety and life, puns dead from slow explanations, philosophy reduced to saws. He could not read without thinking up
test questions and paraphrases. He shrank poems to fit the brains
of peasant children, who were more bestial than animals; when
he used to plough, the water buffalo had let him prop a book
between its horns.

One day when the students were throwing paper at one
another, he walked over to a wad of it, the students watching,
picked it up, and put it inside his desk drawer. He opened a book
that had no connection whatsoever to school and read it. There
were indeed a few students who took up their own books and
read, did as he did; for a while on that one day, he taught by
example, which, according to sages, is the most powerful way
of teaching. Silently he unfurled a scroll and wrote as he pleased
while all around him the class fell apart.

A boy got up from his desk and, since the teacher did not
scold him, walked around him, pulled monkey faces, and peered
in his ear. Egged on by the others, the wild boy jostled his
teacher's elbow; his writing broke into a black smear. He stood
up, knocking over the chair, which fell with a silencing bang.
The students hushed. He seized the rod – the brush rolling down
the scroll – and hit the boy, not carefully on the back but anywhere. The boy rolled up into a ball. BaBa hit harder, but the
blows fell as if landing on a cushion. He struck almost as hard
as he could, but there was an inconclusiveness. Perhaps if the
boy had screamed louder when he hit harder, or if he could
himself feel the pain, then he would have had satisfaction. If
only the boy would properly kneel. If he could hit with all his
might. Suddenly he stopped; it felt like beating a doll. Like a
Japanese sensei, he ordered the boy to kneel with his head on
the ground just outside the open door, where everyone could see
him in shame, but when BaBa checked the doorway, the boy
had run away.

'Why do we need to write?' the students asked. 'We can pay letter writers.' 'We aren't going to starve,' they said. 'We'll go to sea and pick up the free gold on the Gold Mountain.'

During the next two years, BaBa had two babies; they closed up the circle of children who harried his day. The boy and girl did keep his wife busy though; she had them to dote on.

BaBa did not learn how hard and often students have to be hit to make them polite. He shot them with an imaginary pistol; he stabbed them with an imaginary knife. Sometimes while standing in front of the bad boys, he pointed the imaginary pistol at his own head, and blew it open; then they would see the insides of his skull and know what their hate had done. He also imagined lifting his arms and flying over their heads, out the door, and into the sky; then they would want to learn how he did it. If the Imperial Examinations had not been cancelled, he might have tried for a job away from children, become not a magistrate refereeing quarrels but a scribe or a bookkeeper. Mental work was harder than physical work, although it was not exactly the mind that teaching strained. He yearned for the fields with their quiet surprises, which he had ploughed around – the nest with eggs from which he had felt the warmth rise, the big mushroom with nibbles around its crown and the mouse dead underneath, a volunteer lily when the field had been sown to rice.

Grading papers night after night for years, BaBa became susceptible to the stories men told, which were not fabulations like the fairy tales and ghost stories told by women. The Gold Mountain Sojourners were talking about plausible events less than a century old. Heroes were sitting right there in the room and telling what creatures they met on the road, what customs the non-Chinese follow, what topsy-turvy land formations and weather determine the crops on the other side of the world, which they had seen with their own eyes. Nuggets cobbled the streets in California, the loose stones to be had for the stooping over and picking them up. Four Sojourners whom somebody had actually met in Hong Kong had returned from the Gold Mountain in 1850 with three thousand or four thousand American gold dollars each. These four men verified that gold rocks knobbed the rivers; the very dirt was atwinkle with gold dust. In their hunger the men forgot that the gold streets had not been there when they'd gone to look for themselves.

One night of a full moon, BaBa neglected to grade papers, and joined the talking men and listening women. His oldest brother, Dai Bak, who had already travelled to Cuba and back, told how fish the size of long squash fell with the rain. 'In Cuba the sky rains fish – live, edible fish. Fish *this* big fell on the roofs and sidewalks. Their tails and fins were flipping. Thick grey fish, little orange and yellow ones, all different species of fish. I caught a rainbow fish in my frying pan. We had to shovel them off the roofs before the sun rotted them.'

'Isn't Havana a seaport?' BaBa asked. 'Isn't Cuba an island? Couldn't it have happened that a tornado sucked the seas up into the air, and water fell back down like rain on the land, fish and seaweed and all?'

'No. We were inland, and it wasn't salt water but fresh water sprinkling in raindrops. In fact, they were freshwater trout that fell. And it wasn't storming. I saw fish fall. It rains fish in Cuba.' Everyone believed Dai Bak, since he was older than BaBa.

Most of the men had already been to the Gold Mountain and did not ask as at the beginning of going-out-on-the-road, 'Does it rain, then, on the other side of the world?'

'I saw plains covered with cattle from horizon to horizon,' said Grandfather. 'The cowboys herd thousands of head of cattle, not one cowboy leading one cow on a rope like here.'

'On the Gold Mountain, a man eats enouugh meat at one meal to feed a family for a month,' said Great Grandfather. 'Yes, slabs of meat.' The hungrier the family got, the bigger the stories, the more real the meat and the gold.

Grandfather also said, 'The Gold Mountain is lonely. You could get sick and almost die, and nobody come to visit. When you're well, you climb out of your basement again, and nobody has missed you.' 'Idiot,' shouted Grandmother. 'What do you know? Don't listen to the idiot. Crazy man. Only an idiot would bring up a bad luck story like that tonight.' They acted as if he hadn't said it.

Great Grandfather said, 'In Hawai'i the papayas are so big, the children scoop out the seeds and carve faces and light candles inside the shell. The candles grow on trees. You can make black ink from the nuts of that same tree.'

'Don't sign contracts,' he said. 'Go as free working men. Not "coolies".' He undid his shirt and showed a white scar that was almost lost in his wrinkles. 'We're men, not boy apprentices.'

'America – a peaceful country, a free country.' America. The Gold Mountain. The Beautiful Nation.

The night grew late. The men talking story, lighting chains of cigarettes, and drinking wine, did not need to sleep in order to have dreams. 'Let me show you. Let me show you. My turn. My turn.' Even the ones who had only explored the world as far as Canton and Hong Kong had stories. Second Uncle, Ngee Bak, dressed in his Western suit, grabbed an old man's cane and strutted straight through the house. 'My name is John Bully-boy,' he said, imitating a foreign walk and talk, stiff-legged and arrogant, big nostrils in the air, cane swishing about and hitting chinamen and dogs. He did not swerve for shit in his path. Those playing blindmen bumped into the English demon and knocked him over. The women scolded, 'Do we have to remind you that you have to work in the morning? You're making so much noise, you're waking the babies.' But the men talked on, and the women went to bed self-righteous and angry; *they* would rise early to feed the chickens and the children; *they* were not childish like men. But the women couldn't sleep for the rumbling laughter, and returned, not to be left out. Grandmother brought out the gold that Great Great Grandfather, Great Grandfather, Grandfather, and the uncle had earned. Hardly diluted by alloys, it gave off red glints in the lantern light. The family took turns hefting the gold, which was heavier than it looked; its density was a miracle in the hand. A chain lowering into the palm coiled and folded on its links like a gold snake. Grandmother boiled gold and they drank the water for strength. Gold blood ran in their veins. How could they not go to the Gold Mountain again, which belonged to them, which they had invented and discovered?

Suddenly a knocking pounded through the house. Someone with a powerful hand was at the front gate in the middle of the night. Talk stopped. Everyone reached for a weapon – a cleaver, a hammer, a scythe. They blew out lights and listened for breathing and footsteps. A lookout shouted down from the coign door. 'It's Kau Goong.' Great Uncle.

'Kau Goong's come home.' They threw open doors. The

children were up now too. 'Huh!' In strode Kau Goong, Grand-mother's brother, an incarnation of a story hero, returning during a night of stories, a six-foot-tall white gorilla with long hair and white eyebrows that pointed upward like an owl's, his mouth jutting like an ape's, saying 'Huh!' 'Huh! Here I am,' he roared. 'I've come back.' He threw down his bags. 'Help yourselves! Ho!' His sister's relatives scrambled for the gifts. Nobody asked where he had won these prizes. He threw off his coat and unbuckled pistols and silver knives. While the family emptied the bags, he cleaned his guns, twirled the cylinders, blew and sighted through the bullet chambers and bores. In better times, he had walked unarmed up to rich people and taken their money. He was the biggest man in the known world, and there was no law.

'It just so happened,' said Ah Po, 'that when you were on your journey, pirates boarded a passenger boat going upriver and one going downriver, and sacked them both. I'm glad you're safe.' Ransoms had been collected and paid.

'Dangerous times,' said Kau Goong. He shook his head. 'Sixty dollars for an old lady.' 'Yes, sixty dollars for an old lady.' This was a family saying, meaning nobody was safe from kidnappers.

The family divided up used shoes, a coat, a blanket, and some lunches. 'These old shoes hardly replace all the loot the bandits took from us,' said Ah Po. 'You'll have to look harder for those raiders. The last time they came here, I peeked from my hiding place up on the roof, and at that very moment, the full moon shone on a bandit's face. It was a Mah from Duck Doo. Let's raid their village and take our stuff back. Revenge.'

Too few boats were plying the rivers. Kau Goong had boarded them as far as the ocean and also far inland, and had found no money, jewels, or silks. 'Is this all?' said Ah Po.

'We need to go-out-on-the-road again,' Kau Goong roared. 'We need to go to the Gold Mountain.' And since the Chinese word for 'need' and 'want' and 'will' is one and the same word, he was also saying, 'We want to go-out-on-the-road again. We will go to the Gold Mountain.'

'Every man who leaves must reach the Gold Mountain, and every man must come home to Han Mountain,' said Grand-mother and Mother, unable to stop the emigration, and hoping that saying something would make it so. The men reassured them that, of course, they were Sojourners only, that they meant to come back, not settle in America with new wives. 'Didn't I return last time? And the time before that?' they said; 'I'm a Gold Mountain Sojourner, only a tourist,' and kept other possibilities secret from women.

'One last time out-on-the-road,' said the oldest men.

No infant cried out, no fireball flashed a warning, no careless eater dropped a dish or a chopstick, no sick neighbour knocked asking for medicine, no deer or rooster called in the moonlight, no cloud passed over the full moon. Crickets continued chirping. Nothing unusual happened; all remained in continuance. So, omens favourable, one of the grandfathers said, 'Write a list of the men going-out-on-the-road.'

BaBa set down the date, which was in 1924, and listed: Grandfather, Second Grandfather, Third Grandfather, Fourth Grandfather, Great Uncle, First Uncle, Second Uncle, and Third Uncle. After Third Uncle's name, he wrote his own name. He wanted to taste the rain fish; he wanted to pocket some gold. He wanted to say good-bye to the students. 'You'll have to find a new teacher; I'm going to the Gold Mountain.' He would quit school in the middle of a lesson.

'I'll get a legal visa,' he said. Words of anguish came up from Ah Po, 'But you're only a boy.'

The travellers teased him. 'Hoo! So he thinks he can walk about the West posing as a scholar.' 'He'll saunter up to the Immigration Demon and say, "I'm an academician. Hand over my visa."' 'They'll clap him in jail for lying.' 'How are you going to prove that you're a scholar? Open up your skull and show them your brains?' 'Just because he's skinny and too weak for physical labour, he thinks the white demons will say he's obviously a scholar. But they can't tell a teacher's body from a labourer's body.'

'I have a diploma.'

'Huh. He thinks they make laws to search out scholars to teach them and rule them. Listen, stupid, nobody gets to be classified "Scholar". You can't speak English, you're illiterate, no scholar, no visa. "Coolie". Simple test.'

A kinder uncle reminded him of a father's advice to his son.

47

' "Son, books can't be turned into food when you're hungry, nor into clothes when you're cold." '

At the request of the women, he wrote lists of things to bring back from the Gold Mountain: Dunhill lighters, Rolex wristwatches, Seth Thomas clocks, Parker pens, Singer sewing machines, glass window panes, davenports, highboys, pianos.

'You'll make a lot of money,' said MaMa. 'You'll come home rich. You'll fly. You'll show them.'

The next day the families unburied their documents – visas, passports, re-entry permits, American birth certificates, American citizenship papers – and distributed them. BaBa and Sahm Bak, Third Uncle, beginners, let it out that they were interested in purchasing papers and that they were willing to be adopted by Gold Mountain Sojourners who were legal citizens of the United States of America. These Americans had declared the birth of a new son for every year they had been visiting in China and thereby made 'slots' for many 'paper sons'. When a Sojourner retired from going-out-on-the-road or died, he made another slot. Somebody took his place. The last owner of papers taught their buyer the details about the house, the farm, the neighbourhood, the family that were nominally his now. A Test Book accompanied the papers; the Sojourners who had travelled on that set of papers had recorded the questions the Immigration Demons had asked, and how they had answered. The men preparing to go wandered in the fields and among the mud huts and great houses of the village, chanting these facts to a beat, rhymed them, quizzed one another. They ate sturgeon for mental prowess. They paid big fees to memory experts, and it was like in the old days when the Jesuit priest Matteo Ricci taught how to study for the Imperial Examinations, which were no more. BaBa read Test Books to their new owners, who repeated the words to memorize another man's life, a consistent life, an American life.

BaBa would go with two sets of papers: bought ones and his own, which were legal and should get him into the Gold Mountain according to American law. But his own papers were untried, whereas the fake set had accompanied its owners back and forth many times. These papers had a surname which was the same as our own last name – unusual luck: he would be able to keep the family name. He would carry his diplomas, and if they did not work, he would produce the fake papers.

Our family calculated money for passage. They mortgaged a field and also borrowed fifteen hundred dollars from the neighbour in the front house and another fifteen hundred dollars from the neighbour in the back house. (This three thousand dollars must have been in Chinese money.) They promised high interest, and it was also understood that our family, including the descendants, even after the monetary repayment of the debt, would show gratitude to those families, wherever their descendants, for ever.

Husbands and wives exchanged stories to frighten one another. The men told about a husband who smeared his cheating wife with honey and tied her naked on an ant hill. The women told how there was once a queen, who, jealous of the king's next wife, had this other woman's arms and legs cut off and her eyes, tongue, and ears cut out. She shoved her through the hole of the outhouse, then showed her to the king, who looked down and said, 'What's that?' 'It's the human pig,' said the queen. The wives, of course, agreed with the American antimiscegenation laws; the men would have to come home, and also they would have to be faithful, preferably celibate.

The villagers unfolded their maps of the known world, which differed: turtles and elephants supported the continents, which were islands on their backs; in other cartographies, the continents were mountains with China the middle mountain, Han Mountain or Tang Mountain or the Wah Republic, a Gold Mountain to its west on some maps and to the east on others. Yet the explorers who had plotted routes to avoid sea monsters and those who had gone in the directions the yarrow fell had found gold as surely as the ones with more scientific worlds. They had met one another as planned in Paris or Johannesburg or San Francisco.

'Bali,' said a very great grandfather, pointing at the fabulous island where the holy monkeys live. He had seen the monkeys dance. Hou Yin the Monkey God lives on Bali. A generation of great grandfathers had gone there and brought back wives. Others had remained and turned into monkeys.

'Not me,' said First Uncle, Dai Bak. 'No big cities in Bali. The money is in the big cities now. I'm going to San Francisco.'

'Chicago,' said Second Uncle, Ngee Bak. 'Right in the middle of North America.'

'Canada,' said Third Uncle, Sahm Bak. 'I hear it's easier to get into Canada.'

'I'm going as a worker if I can't go as a teacher,' BaBa said. His brothers laughed at him. Those frail hands lifting sledgehammers?

'Don't go,' said Ah Po. 'You're never coming back.' And then she wept, having spoken his life.

The band of Gold Mountain travellers walked to the ocean. Almost a troop themselves they were not challenged by bandits, rebels, government or warlord armies, or by demons, to whom China belonged now. At the waterfront, the oldest men dickered in demon language for ships, 'How much? Dollars? No, too much.' BaBa was glad that he was the youngest and had go-betweens.

BaBa never told us about sailing on a ship. He did not say whether he went as a carpenter or crewman or passenger from Canton or Macao or Hong Kong. Did masts and riggings, sails, smokestacks, and bridges block the sky, and at night did the ship's lights wash out the stars? Or could he stand on the deck and again see the sky without anything in the way? He would have had suitcases full of dried food. He would have brought seeds of every kind of vegetable.

The ship docked in Cuba, where the surf foamed like the petticoats of the dancing ladies. This part of the journey was legal. For money, BaBa rolled cigarettes and cigars ('Mexican cigarettes') and worked in the sugarcane fields. He did not see any rain of fish, but promises would be kept on the Gold Mountain mainland.

I tell everyone he made a legal trip from Cuba to New York. But there were fathers who had to hide inside crates to travel to Florida or New Orleans. Or they went in barrels and boxes all the way up the coast to New York harbour. BaBa may have been in charge of addressing those crates, marking them 'Fragile' in Chinese and English and Spanish. Yes, he may have helped another father who was inside a box.

I think this is the journey you don't tell me:

The father's friends nailed him inside a crate with no conspicuous air holes. Light leaked through the slats that he himself had fitted together, and the bright streaks jumped and winked as the friends hammered the lid shut above his head. Then he felt himself being lifted as in a palanquin and carried to a darker place. Nothing happened for hours so that he began to lose his bearings – whether or not he was in a deep part of the ship where horns and anchor chains could not be heard, whether or not there had already been a pulling away from land, a plunging into the ocean, and this was steady speed. The father sat against a corner and stretched each limb the diagonal of the box, which was a yard by a yard by a yard. He had padded the bottom with his bedding and clothes. He had stuffed dried food, a jar of water, and a chamber pot in a bag. The box contained everything. He felt caught.

Various futures raced through his mind: walking the plank, drowning, growing old in gaol, being thrown overboard in chains, flogged to tell where others were hiding, hung by the neck, returned to China – all things that happened to caught chinamen.

Suddenly – a disturbance – a giant's heart came to life; the ship shook and throbbed. A pulse had started up, and his box vibrated with it. He thought he could hear men running and calling. He must be near the engine room or a deck, near people.

The father's thoughts reached out as if stretching in four directions – skyward, seaward, back towards land, and forward to the new country. Oh, he did yearn for the open sea. The nerves in his chest and legs jumped with impatience. In the future he had to walk on deck the entire voyage, sleep on it, eat there.

He ought to have brought a knife to cut holes in the wood, or at least to carve more lines into the grain. He wanted to look out and see if his box had dropped overboard and was floating atop water, a transparency that ought not to be able to bear weight; he could have been immersed and this wooden air bubble hanging at a middle depth, or falling through the whale waters. People said that a Dragon King ruled an underwater city in the Yellow River; what larger oceanic unknown – tortoises twenty feet across, open-mouthed fish like the marine monster that swallowed the sutras – swam alongside or beneath him. What eels, sharks, jellies, rays glided a board's-width away? He heard the gruff voices of waterlizards calling for the night rain. He must not be afraid; it was sea turtles and water lizards that had formed a bridge for King Mu of Chou.

Because of fear, he did not eat nor did he feel hungry. His bowels felt loose and bladder full, but he squeezed shut ass and sphincter against using the chamber pot. He slept and woke and slept again, and time seemed long and for ever. Rocking and dozing, he felt the ocean's variety – the peaked waves that must have looked like pines; the rolling waves, round like shrubs, the occasional icy mountain; and for stretches, lulling grasslands.

He heard voices, his family talking about gems, gold, cobbles, food. They were describing meat, just as they had his last evenings home. 'They eat it raw.' 'All you can eat.' The voices must have been the sounds of the ocean given sense by his memory. They were discussing a new world. 'Skyscrapers tall as mountains.' He would fly an aerplane above the skyscrapers tall as mountains. 'They know how to do things there; they're very good at organization and machinery. They have machines that can do anything.' 'They'll invent robots to do all the work, even answer the door.' 'All the people are fat.' 'They're honest. If they say they'll do something, they do it. A handshake is enough.' 'They arrive for appointments at the very moment they say they will.' 'They wrap everything – food, flowers, clothes. You can use the paper over again. Free paper bags.' 'And westward, there are wild horses. You can eat them or ride them.' It alarmed him when the strange talk did not cease at his concentration. He was awake, not dozing, and heard mouth noises, sighs, swallows, the clicking and clucking of tongues. There were also seas when the waves clinked like gold coins, and the father's palm remembered the peculiar heaviness of gold. 'Americans are careless; you can get rich picking over what they drop.' 'Americans are forgetful from one day to the next.' 'They play games, sports; grown men play ball like children.' 'All you have to do is stay alert; play a little less than they do, use your memory, and you'll become a millionaire. 'They have swimming pools, elevators, lawns, vacuum cleaners, books with hard covers, X-rays.' The villagers had to make up words for the wonders. 'Something new happens every day, not the same boring farming.'

The sea invented words too. He heard a new language, which

might have been English, the water's many tongues speaking and speaking. Though he could not make out words, the whispers sounded personal, intimate, talking him over, sometimes disapproving, sometimes in praise of his bravery.

'It's me. It's me.' A solid voice. Concrete words. 'I'm opening the box.' It was the smuggler, who squeaked the nails out and lifted the lid. He helped the father climb out of the box with firm and generous hands. 'You're safe to come out and walk,' he said. The size of the room outside the box seemed immense and the man enormous. He brought fresh food from the dining room and fresh water and he talked to the father.

Suddenly they heard a march of footsteps, the leather heels of white demons. Coming steadily towards them. The two men gave each other a look, parted, and ran between the hallways of cargo, ducked behind crates. The door clanked open, shut, and the father heard the footsteps nearing. He made out the sounds of two people pacing, as if searching for a stowaway. Crouched like a rabbit, he felt his heart thud against his own thigh. He heard talking and fervently wished to know whether they were discussing stowaways. He looked for other places to dart, but the crates, lashed with rope, towered above him in straight stacks. He was in a wedge with an opening like a cracked door. The cargo room was small after all, a mere closet, and he could not step from aisle to aisle without being seen; his footsteps would echo on the metal floor. If only there were portholes to jump through or tarpaulins to hide under.

The white demons' voices continued. He heard them speak their whispery language whose sentences went up at the end as if always questioning, sibilant questions, quiet, quiet voices. The demons had but to walk this far and see into the wedge. His friend, the smuggler, could say, 'I came to check the ropes,' or 'The captain ordered me to take inventory.' Or 'I'm looking for stowaways, and I found one,' and deliver him up. But there were no explanations for him, a stowaway chinaman. He would not be able to talk convincingly; he would have to fight. He hardly breathed, became aware of inadequate shallow breaths through his nose.

Then, so close to his face he could reach out and touch it, he saw a white trouser leg turn this way and that. He had never seen anything so white, the crease so sharp. A shark's tooth. A silver blade. He would not get out of this by his own actions but by luck.

Then, blessedness, the trouser leg turned once more and walked away.

He had not been caught. The demons had not looked down. After a time of quiet, the two hiders called to each other and came out hysterical with relief. Oh, they had the luck of rich men. The trousers had practically brushed his face.

'It's time to go back in your box,' said the smuggler. A moment before, the father had thought it would be a joy to be back in, but as the lid shut on him again, reluctance almost overwhelmed him. He did not visit outside the box again. He rode on, coming to claim the Gold Mountain, his own country.

The smuggler came occasionally and knocked a code on the wood, and the stowaway father signalled back. Thus he knew that he had not been forgotten, that he had been visited. This exchange of greetings kept him from falling into the trance that overtakes animals about to die.

At last the smuggler let him out; the ship had docked at a pier in New York. He motioned the father up hatches, across empty decks, around corners to an unguarded gangway. He would not have to swim past patrol boats in the dark. 'Come. Come. Hurry,' the smuggler guided him. He staggered along on cramped legs; the new air dizzied him. As they were saying goodbye, the smuggler said, 'Look,' and pointed into the harbour. The father was thrilled enough to see sky and skyscrapers. 'There.' A grey and green giantess stood on the grey water; her clothes, though seeming to swirl, were stiff in the wind and the moving sea. She was a statue, and she carried fire and a book. 'Is she a goddess of theirs?' the father asked. 'No,' said the smuggler, 'they don't have goddesses. She's a symbol of an idea.' He was glad to hear that the Americans saw the idea of Liberty so real that they made a statue of it.

The father walked off the ship and on to the Gold Mountain. He disciplined his legs to step confidently, as if they belonged where they walked. He felt the concrete through his shoes. The noise and size of New York did not confuse him; he followed a map that his kinsmen had drawn so clearly that each landmark to Chinatown seemed to be waiting to welcome him. He went to the Extending Virtue Club, where people from his own village gave him a bed in a basement; it could have been a grocery shelf or an ironing table or the floor under a store counter. To lie stretched out on any part of the Gold Mountain was a pleasure to him.

Of course, my father could not have come that way. He came a legal way, something like this:

Arriving in San Francisco Bay, the legal father was detained for an indefinite time at the Immigration Station on Angel Island, almost within swimming distance of San Francisco. In a wooden house, a white demon physically examined him, poked him in the ass and genitals, looked in his mouth, pulled his eyelids with a hook. This was not the way a father ought to have been greeted. A cough tickled his chest and throat, but he held it down. The doctor demon pointed to a door, which he entered to find men and boys crowded together from floor to ceiling in bunkbeds and on benches; they stood against the walls and at the windows. These must be the hundred China Men who could enter America, he thought. But the quota was one hundred a year, not one hundred per day, and here were packed more than one hundred, nearer two hundred or three. A few people made room for him to set down his suitcases. 'A newcomer. Another newcomer,' they called out. A welcome party made its way to him. 'I'm the president of the Self-Governing Association,' one of them was telling him in a dialect almost like his. 'The most important rule we have here is that we guard one another's chances for immigration.' He also asked for dues; the father gave a few dimes towards buying newspapers and phonograph records, an invention that he had never heard before. 'Now you're eligible to vote,' said the president, who then said that he had won his office by having been on the island the longest, three and a half years. The legal father's heart sank, and rose again; must be something wrong with this man, not a good man, a criminal to be jailed for so long. 'Do you you want to spend money on a rubber ball? Vote Yes or No.' The legal father voted No. How odd it would be to say to these men, 'Play ball. Go ahead. Play with it,' as if they were boys and could play. Even the boys wouldn't play. Who can be that lighthearted? He wasn't really going to stay here for more than a day or two, was he? He made his way across the room. Some of the men were gambling, others exercising, cutting one another's hair, staring at their feet or folded hands or the floor. He saw two men handcuffed to each other. Readers chanted San Francisco newspapers, *Young China* and *Chinese World*. The legal father, who was skilful and lucky, joined a game and won forty silver dollars, and gave away one for the rubber ball. He learned who was being deported and who was serving a year's sentence before deportation.

A bell went off like a ship's alarm, but it was a dinner bell. The father followed the others to a dining hall. About ten women were coming out. They were the first women he had seen since China, and they already belonged to husbands. He did not know that he had come to a country with no women. The husbands and wives talked quickly as the guards pushed them past one another. The father saw the man ahead of him hold hands with a woman for a moment and – he saw it – pass her a note. She dropped it. She knelt and, fixing her shoe with one hand, snatched the piece of paper with the other. A big white matron grabbed her arm and took the paper. Though these people were all strangers, the father joined the men who surrounded the matron. They wrested the paper from her and tore it up. The legal father ate some of the shreds. That was the last time the men's and women's mealtimes overlapped. There seemed to be no other immediate consequences; perhaps denial of entry would be the punishment.

The China Men who worked in the kitchen brought food cooked and served in buckets. 'Poison,' the prisoners grumbled. 'A couple of years ago,' said the president of the Self-Governing Association, 'the demons tried to starve us to death. They were taking the food money for themselves. If it weren't for us rioting, you newcomers wouldn't be eating so much today. We faced bayonets for this food.' The legal father wasn't sure he would've wanted any more of the slop they were eating.

The men spent the long days rehearsing what they would say to the Immigration Demon. The forgetful men fingered their risky notes. Those who came back after being examined told what questions they had been asked. 'I had to describe all the streets in my village.' 'They'll ask, "Do you have any money?" and "Do you have a job?"' 'They've been asking those questions all this week,' the cooks and janitors confirmed. 'What's the right answer?' asked the legal fathers. 'Well, last week they liked "No job" because it proves you were an aristocrat. And they liked "No money" because you showed a willingness to work. But this week, they like "Yes job" and "Yes money" because you wouldn't be taking jobs away from white workers.' The men groaned, 'Some help.' The demons did not treat people of any other race the way they did Chinese. The few Japanese left in a day or two. It was because their emperor was strong.

Footsteps walked across the ceiling, and bedsprings squeaked above their heads. So there were more of them locked on the second floor. 'The women are up there,' the father was told. Diabolical, inauspicious beginning – to be trodden over by women. 'Living under women's legs,' said the superstitious old-fashioned men from the backward villages. 'Climbed over by women.' It was bad luck even to walk under women's pants on clotheslines. No doubt the demons had deliberately planned this humiliation. The legal father decided that for a start in the new country, he would rid himself of Chinese superstitions; this curse would not count.

He read the walls, which were covered with poems. Those who could write protested this gaoling, this wooden house (*wood* rhyming with *house*), the unfair laws, the emperor too weak to help them. They wrote about the fog and being lonely and afraid. The poets had come to a part of the world not made for honour, where 'a hero cannot use his bravery'. One poet was ready to ride his horse to do mighty American deeds but instead here he sat corraled, 'this wooden house my coffin'. The poets must have stayed long to carve the words so well. The demons were not going to free him, a scholar, then. Some were not poems exactly but statements. 'This island is not angelic.' 'It's not true about the gold.' One man blamed 'the Mexican Exclusion Laws' for his imprisonment. The writers were anonymous; no official demon could trace them and penalize them. Some signed surname and village, but they were still disguised; there were many of that name from that village, many men named Lee from Toi

Sahn, many a Hong of Sun Woi, and many a Three District Man and Four District No Such Man. There were dates of long stays.

Night fell quickly; at about four o'clock the fog poured down the San Francisco hillsides, covered the bay, and clouded the windows. Soon the city was gone, held fast by black sea and sky. The fog horns mourned. San Francisco might have been a figment of Gold Mountain dreams.

The legal father heard cries and thumps from someone locked in a separate shed. Words came out of the fog, the wind whipping a voice around the Island. 'Let me land. Let me out. Let me land. I want to come home.'

In the middle of one night when he was the only man awake, the legal father took out his Four Valuable Things, and using spit and maybe tears to mix the ink, he wrote a poem on the wall, just a few words to observe his stay. He wrote about wanting freedom. He did not sign his name; he would find himself a new American name when he landed. If the US government found out his thoughts on freedom, it might not let him land. The next morning the readers sang the new poem for the others to hear. 'Who wrote this wonderful poem during the night?' they asked, but the father modestly did not say.

For one another's entertainment, the men rehearsed and staged skits, puppet shows, and heroic parts of operas. They juggled fruit, bottles, and the new rubber ball. The father, who was travelling with the adventures of Yüeh Fei, the Patriot, in six volumes, read aloud the part where Yüeh Fei's mother carved on his back four words: FIRST – PROTECT MY NATION. He held up for all to see the illustrations of warriors in battle. He also carried the poems of Li Po, the best poet, the Heavenly Poet, the Great White Light, Venus. The father sang about a sentry stopping Li Po from entering a city. Li Po was drunk as usual and riding a mule. He refused to give his name to the sentry, but wrote a daring poem that he was a man from whose mouth the emperor had wiped the drool; the emperor's favourite wife had held his inkslab. The impressed sentry granted him entrance. This poem heartened the men; they laughed and clapped at Li Po's cleverness and the sentry's recognition of him and poetry.

'What is a poem exactly?' asked an illiterate man, a Gold

Mountain Sojourner who had spent twenty years in America and was on his way back to his family. 'Let me give it a try,' he said. 'A short poem: "On the Gold Mountain, I met black men black like coal." Is that a poem?' The literate men were delighted. 'Marvellous,' they said. 'Of course, it's a poem.' 'A simile. A simile. Yes, a poem.' The legal father liked it so much, he remembered it for ever.

The legal father learned many people's thoughts because he wrote their letters. They told their wives and mothers how wonderful they found the Gold Mountain. 'The first place I came to was The Island of Immortals,' they told him to write. 'The foreigners clapped at our civilized magnificence when we walked off the ship in our brocades. A fine welcome. They call us "Celestials".' They were eating well; soon they would be sending money. Yes, a magical country. They were happy, not at all frightened. The Beautiful Nation was glorious, exactly the way they had heard it would be. 'I'll be seeing you in no time.' 'Today we ate duck with buns and plum sauce,' which was true on days when the China Men in San Francisco sent gifts.

Every day at intervals men were called out one by one. The legal father kept himself looking presentable. He wore his Western suit and shined shoes, constantly ready.

One morning the barracks awoke to find a man had hanged himself. He had done it from a railing. At first he looked as if he had been tortured, his legs cut off. He had tied his legs bent at the knees like an actor or beggar playing a man with no legs, and hung himself by pushing over his chair. His body had elongated from hanging all night. The men looked through his papers and found Xs across them. When new arrivals looked for beds, nobody told them that a dead, hung man had slept in that one.

Also, the rumour went, a woman upstairs had killed herself by sharpening a chopstick and shoving it through her ear. Her husband had sent for her, and she did not understand why he did not come to take her home.

At last came the legal father's turn to be interrogated. He combed his hair again. He said his good-byes. Inside the interrogation room were several white demons in formal wear; the legal father gauged by the width of lapels and ties that his own suit was not quite stylish. Standing beside the table was a Chinese-looking soldier in American uniform and a demon soldier in the same uniform. This Chinese American was the interpreter. The legal father sat opposite the interrogators, who asked his name, his village, where he was born, his birth date – easy questions.

'Can you read and write?' the white demon asked in English and the Chinese American asked in Cantonese.

'Yes,' said the legal father.

But the secretary demon was already writing No since he obviously couldn't, needing a translator.

'When did you cut off your pigtail?' asked the translator.

'In 1911,' said the legal father. It was a safe answer, the year he would have picked anyway, not too early before the Republic nor too late, not too revolutionary nor too reactionary. Most people had cut their hair in 1911. He might have cut it for fashion as much as for revolution.

'Do you have relatives who are American citizens?'

The janitor, a China Man, who just then entered the room with dustpan and broom, nodded.

'Yes.'

'Who?'

'My grandfather is an American. My father is an American. So I'm an American, also my three older brothers and three uncles – all Americans.'

Then came the trap questions about how many pigs did they own in 1919, whether the pig house was made out of bricks or straw, how many steps on the back stoop, how far to the outhouse, how to get to the market from the farm, what were the addresses of the places his grandfather and father and brothers and uncles had lived in America. The interrogators liked asking questions with numbers for answers. Numbers seemed true to them. 'Quick. How many windows do you have in your house?' 'How many times did your grandfather return to the United States?' 'Twice.' 'Twice?' 'Yes, twice. He was here once and returned twice. He was here three times altogether. He spent half his life in America and half in China.' They looked into his eyes for lies. Even the Chinese American looked into his eyes, and they repeated his answers, as if doubting them. He squelched an urge to change the answers, elaborate on them. 'Do you have any money?' 'Yes.' 'How much?' He wondered if they would charge him higher fees the more money he reported. He decided to tell the truth; lying added traps. Whether or not he spoke the truth didn't matter anyway; demons were capricious. It was up to luck now.

They matched his answers to the ones his relatives and fellow villagers gave. He watched the hands with yellow hair on their backs turn the copies of his grandfather's and father's papers.

They told him to go back to the gaol, where he waited for more weeks. The next time he was called to be examined – *searched* the Chinese word – they asked again, 'What American relatives do you have?'

'My grandfather and father,' he said again, 'and also my three brothers and three uncles.'

'Your grandfather's papers are illegal,' the Chinese American translated. 'And your father is also an illegal alien.' One by one the demons outlawed his relatives and ancestors, including a Gold Rush grandfather, who had paid a bag of gold dust to an American Citizenship Judge for papers. 'There are no such things as Citizenship Judges,' said the Immigration Demon and put an X across the paper that had been in the family for seventy-five years. He moved on to ask more trap questions, the directions the neighbours' houses faced and the number of water buffaloes in 1920, and sent him back to the barracks.

He waited again. He was examined again, and since he had an accurate memory, he told them the same number of pigs as the last two times, the same number of water buffaloes (one), the same year of cutting his queue, and at last they said, 'You may enter the United States of America.' He had passed the American examination; he had won America. He was not sure on what basis they let him in – his diploma, his American lineage (which may have turned out to be good after all), his ability to withstand gaoling, his honesty, or the skill of his deceits.

This legal father then worked his way across the continent to New York, the centre of America.

Ed, Woodrow, Roosevelt, and Worldster held their bowls to their mouths and shovelled as fast as they could, chewing crackly pork and pressed duck in one bite, gulping while jabbing from the centre dishes without choosiness. They raced as if food were scarce and one of them would be left the runt pig. Woodrow picked up the soup tureen and drank directly from it. 'Uh. Uh,' the others protested, but didn't stop gulping to say 'You're cheating.'

Worldster threw down his bowl and chopsticks, spit the bones 'p-foo' out on the table, knocked back his shot of whisky, jumped up – his orange crate hit the floor with a bang – and shouted, 'I won. I won.'

But Woodrow, the soup drinker, ran out the door. 'Last one to leave the table loses,' he said.

'You're still chewing and swallowing,' Worldster yelled.

'Okay,' said Ed. 'Okay, I lose.' His friends cheered him as he leaned back and sipped his whisky. 'That was a four-and-a-half-minute dinner,' he said, looking at his new gold watch. 'It's a record.' They gave their record a cheer.

The last one to finish eating did the dishes. While the others returned to work in the front of the laundry, Ed set a kettle to boil, unfolded his newspaper, lit a Lucky Strike, the brand he had chosen, and poured another glass of whisky and a cup of coffee. Reading while drinking and smoking was one of the great pure joys of existence. He read that a Gold Mountain Sojourner, upon returning to his village, had gotten bilked by relatives, most of whom he had never met before. They had flocked to him. They tricked him with an intricate scheme for investing in a bogus Hong Kong housing project for refugees. Another Sojourner put his life savings into a bank that the entire village had set up just to get his money. The Sojourners were quoted as saying they were coming back to America.

Ed scraped the dishes on to the tablecloth, which was layers of newspapers. Then he rolled up the top layer; the table was instantly clean and already covered for the next meal. He sudsed the dishes with laundry soap and put them in a drainer. From the whistling tea kettle, he poured boiling water on them; the water was so hot, the dishes dried before his eyes. It was a method he remembered the slaves in China using. Dishwashing just took common sense; women had made such a to-do about it. The Gold Mountain was indeed free: no manners, no traditions, no wives.

When he joined his partners doing the ironing, his favourite part of laundry work, they were planning 'the weekend'.

'I want to go tea dancing,' said Worldster, 'and take driving lessons.' He had a thick moustache and tried to look like Clark Gable.

'Let's see the Statue of Liberty at night,' said Woodrow, who vowed that he would make a million bucks by 1935.

'I want to go on a date,' said Roosevelt, who was looking for a medical school that gave night classes. 'A weekend date with a Rockette,' he said in English.

'I know where *City Lights* is playing,' said Ed. 'Also *Little Miss Marker*. You know, someday, when the people from the future see the movies, they'll think people today walked and moved like Charlie Chaplin.' Oh, it was wonderful; for a dime the ushers let you stay all day through the intermissions, and the shows ran again and again. 'Every Saturday night is a party in this country.' Customers were picking up the big bundles – cash for the weekend.

Ed placed shirt after shirt on the stack that was growing beside his ironing board. Friends were fairer than brothers; there was an equality. When Tu Fu left his village, friends cared for him; 'We swore brotherhood for eternity,' he wrote. How good life was. Ed was young, and he was in New York with three new true friends who sang at their work.

They were singing the Rainy Alley Poet, who lived in Paris and followed black hair in the rain: ' "I will follow that gleam though stumbling in the haze, the twilight like a bubble of rose rising in the wine glass, and let my nostalgic eyes become ensnared in memory dark as her hair." '

'Aiya,' breathed Woodrow. 'True love. True life. The free pursuit of happiness.'

'Aiya. That's me,' said Roosevelt, ' "ensnared in memory dark as her hair", except it should be blonde hair. "Ensnared in memory yellow as her hair!" '

They sang Wang Tu Ching, a Sojourner, who had done all the wonderful things that a young man ought to do in Paris – having affairs, getting French girls pregnant. ' "Oh, this endless journey home. I am Chinese, and must not expect happiness but tears and sacrifice. Farewell, Latin Quarter, chestnut trees, bookstalls along the Seine." ' ' "Latin Quarter, chestnut trees",' Ed repeated.

' "I'm madly in love with Europe," ' they sang, ' "where I

played my reed flute on an empty stomach." ' This was a song by Ai Ch'ing, a fellow Kwangtung man.

They sang an old poet, too, Yüan Mei, who had advocated educating women and written from a woman's point of view: ' "For years I've been imagining a boat/Shooting over the waves as fast as any bird/But never taking the traveller away from friends/Always carrying the traveller back to his home." '

'Oh, that's beautiful,' said Roosevelt. He rested under the fan and smoked a cigarette with tears in his eyes. 'That's how I feel.' The men were thinking not about one another but of life-long friends.

'And listen to this one,' said Ed. 'The first wife welcomes her man home: "If it were not for Second Wife, you would not come home. She is your plum blossom." '

'Oh, oh,' moaned the lonesome men. 'Welcomed home by two wives.'

They worked very late at night, and after a while did not sing or talk. The two fans whirred, blowing the calendars, the monthly calendars swinging on the walls, and the pages of the daily calendars riffling. Ed's legs ached. At about eleven o'clock, he spoke the bitter verses of 'The Laundry Song', by Wen I-to of Chicago:

A piece, two pieces, three pieces –
Wash them clean,
Four pieces, five pieces, six –
Iron them smooth.

No, they were not going to be welcomed home by wives; they would stay here working for ever. He thumped his iron on the accents.

Years pass and I let drop but one homesick tear.
A laundry lamp burns at midnight.
The laundry business is low, you say,
Washing out blood that stinks like brass –
Only a Chinaman can debase himself so.
But who else wants to do it? Do you want it?
Ask for the Chinaman. Ask the Chinaman.

The other men were so tired, they only grunted in agreement.

At midnight they switched off the lights in the windows, turned the Open sign around to Closed, and pulled down the shades. They worked without interruptions from customers, then made the ironing tables into beds.

Under his desk lamp, Ed did the accounts on his abacus and wrote down the profits in ledgers. Woodrow, who had bought a Kodak with a part of his million, took a picture of him. 'You can send this to your wife and tell her you study a lot,' he said. When Ed finished the bookkeeping, the others were asleep. In the quiet of the night, he practised his calligraphy by writing down modern poems for his friends to paste on the walls over their ironing tables. He wrote a letter to his wife, and went to bed.

On Saturday Ed and Woodrow went to Fifth Avenue to shop for clothes. With his work pants, Ed wore his best dress shirt, a silk tie, grey silk socks, good leather shoes with pointed toes, and a straw hat. At a very good store, he paid two hundred dollars cash for a blue and grey pinstripe suit, the most expensive suit he could find. In the three-way mirror, he looked like Fred Astaire. He wore the suit out of the store. Woodrow took a picture of him dancing down the New York Public Library steps next to one of the lions. 'I don't see why you have to spend all this money on clothes,' said Woodrow, whose entire wardrobe came from the unclaimed laundry. He was the one who had written the sign in English: WE WILL NOT BE RESPONSIBLE FOR CLOTHES UNCLAIMED AFTER 30 DAYS. He shot his cuffs and said, 'You must admit I look pretty swanky in these secondhand outfits.' The two of them strolled Fifth Avenue and caught sight of themselves in windows and hubcaps. They looked all the same Americans.

Suddenly a band of white demons came up from behind them. One picked off Ed's straw hat and kicked its lid through. Before Ed and Woodrow could decide what to do for the shame on China Men, they saw the whites stomp on other whites' hats. 'It must be a custom,' said Ed.

That afternoon, the partners trimmed one another's hair with their barber's shears and electric hair clippers. They copied Ed's professional haircut, parted in the middle and the two sides lifted just so in 'pompadours'. Then all four gentlemen went to a tearoom. Ed regretted having to check his grey felt hat at the door. It looked good with his new suit. Girls liked the way he cocked his head and looked at them sideways with his hat brim tilted at a smart angle. The hatcheck girl also sold them strips of tickets for ten cents apiece. The hostess escorted them to a table, where they ordered cookies, open-faced raw cucumber sandwiches, strawberry parfaits, and tea. They nibbled carefully at their sandwiches, chewed with their mouths shut, sipped tea, and dabbed their lips even though they had not slobbered or made crumbs. They looked around at the couples to decide which dancing girls they were going to ask. 'Look at the legs on that one,' said Roosevelt. 'She must be a Rockette.'

'The main difference between them and us Tang People,' Woodrow observed, 'is the shape of their nostrils, which are oval instead of small, neat, and round like ours.'

They were saying those things in Chinese, so weren't being rude. They were sophisticated New York gentlemen, and knew more about American manners than white people. 'When I was a waiter,' said Worldster, 'there were hick tourists who tipped us after every course. Every time we came to the table they tipped us.' Since the music took so long stopping, he went over to a couple, tapped the white man on the shoulder, and cut in. 'What's your name, sweetheart?' he said like in the movies.

The others waited until the orchestra stopped, then stood and walked out on to the dance floor. 'Dance with me?' Ed asked, holding out his tickets. 'Sure,' the blonde dancing girl of his choice said, smiling, taking several tickets, which was a compliment; he would get to dance with her a lot. He smiled back and said, 'Sure.' The music did not start up right away. 'You like come my table after you dance with me?' he invited. 'Of course,' she said. 'You speak English very well,' she said. 'Thank you,' he said. 'You be very beautiful. Pretty. You be pretty. I like you.' 'How nice,' she said. 'Thank you. You're very handsome. You're good looking. Do you understand *handsome*?' 'Sure. Of course. How nice. Thank you.' A fox-trot started, and he put out his hand; she put her hand in it, and he led her, his feet in their new leather shoes, glissading across the waxed wood floor. He saw himself and her in the mirrors, and they looked like the movies. He guided her a little closer with the intimate

66

hand at her waist. He looked down at the gold eyebrows and curving lashes and her blue eyes. He pulled their two clasped hands closer so that her gold hair brushed his hand. Her hair was fine and soft, not like hair at all. He dared a dip, and her wonderful hair rippled near the floor and swung back against his other hand. When the music stopped, she said, 'You're a very good dancer.' 'And handsome too?' he asked. She laughed with her beautiful lipsticked mouth.

The others had also brought their blondes over to the table under the potted palm, and they ate the sandwiches, drank tea, and smoked cigarettes. 'Is he really a Chinese prince?' Worldster's girl asked. 'What's "prince"?' asked Ed. 'A king's son,' she said. 'A king's son,' said Worldster in Chinese. 'Oh, yes,' said Ed, 'in China, we all be prince with so much money. Too much money. But. Now we all the same Americans.'

They danced until they had no more tickets. And they danced with as many different blondes as they pleased. And Ed was so handsome that some danced with him for free, vied with one another to dance with him. He became bold enough to ask the friendliest blonde, one who had been studying his eyes, his high cheekbones, and neat nose, who had made him unbutton his sleeve and hold his tan arm against her pink arm, 'You like come home with me? Please?'

'No, honey,' she said. 'No.'

Not one of the four of them told any blonde that they were married and were fathers. 'See you next week,' they said, learning new ways to say good-bye. 'See ya.' 'So long.'

On Sunday they rode the ferry boat to Coney Island. Woodrow asked a blonde to take pictures of the four friends with their arms on the railing and their black hair flying in the wind. At the beach, a bathing beauty photographed them in their bathing suits, nobody wearing a jockstrap, which might not yet have come into fashion. Ed had bought a beach robe, 'which is different from a bedroom robe', he explained. He sent many pictures to his wife, including one of himself sitting on the sand with his arms around his knees and his sweat shirt tied around his neck; he was smiling and looking out to sea.

On another weekend, Worldster, who had taken flying lessons, rented an aeroplane and invited each of his friends up into the sky. (*Friends* in Chinese connotes play, good times, and youth.) 'We're men of the Twentieth Century,' he lectured as Ed marvelled at the speed and height. 'We're modern men, and have to learn to make use of the new machines.' He explained how to move the plane right and left and up and down, then said, 'You try it,' and let go of the controls. Ed flew over rivers, trees, and houses, raced cars, and made the plane go back up when it fell into air pockets. They circled the airport and waggled their wings at Roosevelt and Woodrow down there.

Ed sent his wife pictures of himself in the cockpit; he wore a white scarf flying behind him, goggles, and a leather skullcap with flaps over the ears. He also sent several shots of the plane in the air, an insect against the white sky.

Woodrow bought a car, and Roosevelt a motorcycle. Each of the four friends stood by the car for his picture. They also took pictures of one another leaning into curves on the motorcycle. Ed did not pass the driver's test but drove anyway. 'You can drive without a licence here,' he wrote to people in China. 'It's a free country.'

In the spring, Ed sent his wife a picture of the four partners with their arms around one another's shoulders, laughing next to a Keep Off the Grass sign. He was wearing another two-hundred-dollar suit, a navy blue one, and a shirt with French cuffs, which closed with gold cuff links. For a winter picture, he sat on a rock in Central Park in his new grey greatcoat and jaunty hat and leather gloves lined with rabbit fur.

In his quiet time at night, he mounted the photographs in a fine leather album. With his first spending money, he had bought a postcard of the Statue of Liberty, the album, picture mounts, white ink, and a pen with a steel nib. He pasted that postcard in his expensive album, then added the other pictures.

Ed's wife wrote often and sometimes sent lichee, which she had picked from the three trees that Ed's father had planted and the twenty trees that Ed's brother had planted. When would he return to plant lichee trees?

Then she wrote that their two children had died. What should she do? 'I think you ought to come back right now,' she said.

He did much worrying, and hit upon a plan. He would not end his American life but show her how to live one. 'Here's what you have to do if I'm to bring you to America,' he wrote, though there was a law against her. 'I will bring you to America on one condition, and that is, you get a Western education. I'll send you money, which you must only spend on school, not on food or clothes or jewellery or relatives. Leave the village. Go to Hong Kong or Canton and enrol in a Western scientific school. A science school. Get a degree. Send it to me as evidence you are educated, and I'll send you a ship ticket. And don't go to a school for classical literature. Go to a scientific school run by white people. And when you get your degree, I'll send for you to come here to the United States.' He would figure out later how to accomplish that.

When next she wrote, she had enrolled in medical school; she was writing him from there. As years passed and sometimes she became discouraged with how long her education was taking and how difficult the work, he wrote encouragement: 'If you don't get that degree, I'll not send for you. We will never see each other again.' He did not want an ignorant villager for his American wife.

So much time went by, he saved another two hundred dollars, which he spent on a grey suit and a Countess Mara tie.

At last she mailed him her diploma. He spent another few years saving passage money, and fifteen years after they had last seen one another, he sent for her. Applying for her, he risked having his citizenship again scrutinized. She would enter legally and gracefully, no question of asking a lady to ride the sea in a box or to swim to an unwatched shore.

At dinner one evening, he announced to his partners, 'I've sent for my wife, who will be here in January.' They were so surprised that they stopped their eating race.

'How did you save enough money?' Worldster asked.

'I guess you'll be moving to your own apartment,' said Roosevelt.

'Why do you want to do that?' asked Woodrow.

After writing letters for fifteen years, Ed and his wife ended their correspondence. They were near each other, she on Ellis Island, where there was no mail, and he on Manhattan. When he saw her on the ferry, she was standing surrounded by bundles and bags, no child tugging her coat and no baby in her arms. He recognized her, though she was older. Her hair was slicked against her head with a bun in back, a proper married-lady hair-do. In spite of the law against her, she was landing, her papers in order. Her immigration verified the strength of his citizenship.

'Here you are,' he said. 'You've come.'

'You look like a foreigner,' she said. 'I can barely recognize you.'

'Was it a rough journey?' he asked.

'It was terrible,' she exclaimed. 'The Japanese were right behind me. When I tried to board the ship from Canton to Hong Kong, the man acted as if my papers were wrong and asked for a seventy-five-dollar bribe. So I ran to another gangplank and found out seventy-five dollars wasn't policy at all; this man wanted a hundred dollars. I had to run back to the first entrance. Then I paid another hundred to get off the ship. It was the last ship out of Canton before the Japanese took the harbour. And I was so seasick, I vomited the whole way across the Atlantic. And what a questioning I got on the Island. They asked me what year you had cut your queue, and a workman shook his head, hawked and spat. It was a signal. So I said, "I don't know." On my way to be locked up again, I said to that workman, "That was a delicious bun you gave me. Thank you. I hope you bring me another if you have more." Get it? It was a code I made up, meaning, "Thank you for giving me the right answer. Please give me more help." Oh, I was so scared. If it weren't for him I might not be here.'

'Don't worry any more,' said Ed. 'That's over now. Don't worry any more.' Her big eyes had lines around them. 'That's all over now,' he said.

'I had to build roads,' she said. 'Since your father is too crazy to work, and you were away, I had to pay the labour tax for two men. Your father followed me and wept on the road when I left.'

'Never mind now,' he said. 'That's all over now.'

They rode the subway to the room he had rented in preparation for her coming. He taught her the name of the subway stop for the laundry. 'Easu Bu-odd-way Su-ta-son,' she repeated. 'That's good,' he said. 'Remember that, and you can't get lost.'

She unpacked jars of seeds. 'But we aren't farmers any more,' he said. 'I'll plant in tin cans and put them out here on the fire escape,' she said. 'You'll see how many vegetables we can grow in cans.'

She showed him a piece of cloth. 'Do you recognize this?' she asked. 'The Japanese were right behind me, and I had time to take just one keepsake – the trimming on the bed canopy.' She had ripped it off and shoved it in her purse. She unfolded it. 'This is the only thing we have left from China,' she said. 'The heirloom.' A red phoenix and a red dragon played across the strip of linen; the Chinese words down one end and English words across the top said, 'Good morning.' She had cross-stitched it herself.

'You could write English even then,' he teased her, 'and getting ready to come here.' 'I didn't know what it said,' she demurred, 'I only copied it from a needlework book.'

He took her shopping and bought her a black crêpe dress with a bodice of white lace ruffles and buttons of rhinestone and silver. 'You look very pretty,' he told her. They bought a black coat with a fur collar and a little black-eyed animal head over her shoulder, high heels, silk stockings, black kid gloves, and a picture hat with a wide, wide brim and silk fluttery ribbon. They strolled in their finery along Fifth Avenue. 'I washed all these windows,' he told her. 'When I first came here, I borrowed a squeegee and rags and a bucket, and walked up and down this street. I went inside each store and asked if they wanted the windows washed. The white foreigners aren't so hard to get along with; they nod to mean Yes and shake their heads to mean No, the same as anybody.' New York glittered and shined with glass. He had liked pulling the water off the panes and leaving brief rainbows. While working, he had looked over the displays of all the wonderful clothes to own and wear. He had made the money to pool for starting the laundry. 'In the spring,' he promised her, 'we'll buy you white cotton gloves.'

'On the first day of autumn,' he told her, 'New Yorkers stomp on one another's straw hats. I wear my grey felt one as soon as summer's over. I save the straw for spring. I'm not extravagant. You ought to put your earrings in the safe deposit box at the bank. Pierced ears look a little primitive in this country.' He also told her to buy makeup at a drugstore. 'American people don't like oily faces. So you ought to use some powder. It's the custom. Also buy some rouge. These foreigners dislike yellow skin.'

She also bought a long black rat of hair to roll her own hair over for an upswept hairdo. At a beauty parlour, she had her wavy hair cut and curled tighter with a marcel. She washed, ironed, and wrapped her silk pants and dresses and never wore them again.

He took her to see the Statue of Liberty. They climbed the ladder, she in high heels, up the arm to the torch, then the stairs to the crown. 'Now we're inside her chin. This part must be the nose.' From the windows of the crown, he showed her his city.

They also went to the top of the Empire State Building, took the second elevator to the very top, the top of the world. Ed loved the way he could look up at the uncluttered sky. They put money in the telescopes and looked for the laundry and their apartment. 'So I have been on the tallest building in the world,' she said. 'I have seen everything. Wonderful. Wonderful. Amazing. Amazing.'

'Yes,' he said. 'Everything's possible on the Gold Mountain. I've danced with blondes.' 'No, really?' she said. 'You didn't. You're making that up, aren't you? You danced with demonesses? I don't believe it.'

Her favourite place to go was the free aquarium, 'the fish house', where all manner of creatures swam. Walking between the lighted tanks, she asked, 'When do you think we'll go back to China? Do you think we'll go back to China?' 'Shh,' he said. 'Shh.' The electric eels glowed in their dark tank, and the talking fish made noises. 'There are bigger fish in China,' she said.

They went to the movies and saw *Young Tom Edison* with Mickey Rooney. They both liked the scene where the mother took Eh-Da-Son into the barn, but only pretended to thrash him; she faked the slaps and crying and scolding to fool the strict father, the father 'the severe parent', according to Confucius, and the mother 'the kind parent'. ('My bones, my flesh, father and mother,' said Tu Fu.) After the movie, Ed explained to his wife that this cunning, resourceful, successful inventor, Edison, was who he had named himself after. 'I see,' she said. 'Eh-Da-Son. Son as in *sage* or *immortal* or *saint*.'

They also saw a movie where a big man bridged two mountain peaks with his prone body. He held on to one cliff of a chasm with his fingers and the other with his toes. Hundreds of little people walked across on him.

The four partners no longer had to race to get out of doing the dishes. Ed's wife shopped and cooked. She bought a tiered food carrier, filled each pot with a different accompaniment to rice, and carried it and a pot of soup through the subway to the laundry. The first day she did this, she got off at the wrong stop in the underground city. She went from white ghost to white ghost shouting over the trains, which sounded like the Japanese bombing, 'Easu Bu-odd-way Su-ta-son?' And a conductor said, 'Of course. East Broadway Station. Go that way.'

'He understood me,' she proudly told the men. 'I can speak English very well.' She set the table with her homemade meal so they didn't get to buy restaurant take-out food any more. And they did not race but had manners. 'Tell me how you started this laundry,' she said. Woodrow described their Grand Opening. 'Our friends sent stands of flowers tied in wide red ribbons, on which your husband wrote good words in gold ink. We exploded firecrackers out on the sidewalk, right out there on Mott Street. And then the customers came.' 'Working for ourselves, we can close whenever we please and go do as we like,' Ed said.

The partners did not tell her that they hardly ever celebrated holidays. They had learned that holidays do not appear with the seasons; the country does not turn festive just because a rubric day appears on the calendar. The cooking women, the shopping and slicing and kneading and chopping women brought the holidays. The men let holidays pass. If they did not go to the bother of keeping it, a holiday was another free day. It was that free a country. They could neglect attending the big public celebrations such as those at the benevolent associations and New Year's eve at Times Square, and no one minded. Neglecting the planting and harvest days made no difference in New York. No neighbours looked askance. And there were no godly repercussions. They had no graves to decorate for the memorial days of Clarity and Brightness. They did arrange cotton snow, reindeer, a stable scene, and a Santa Claus in the laundry window at Christmas. 'We don't want them to break our window or not bring their laundry,' Ed explained. His wife brought back the holidays. She made the holidays appear again.

Her arrival ended Ed's independent life. She stopped him from reading while eating. She'd learned at the school of Western medicine, she said, that doing those two actions at once divides the available blood between brain and stomach; one should concentrate. She kept telling Ed to cut down on his smoking. She polished his World's Fair copper souvenir ashtray clean. She cut new covers from brown wrapping paper and shirt cardboards for his books, and resewed the bindings. He inked the new covers with the titles, authors, and volume numbers.

When the partners took the couple to a restaurant, the men wiped their chopsticks and bowls with napkins. 'That doesn't really clean them, you know,' she said. 'All you're doing is wiping the germs around. Germs are little animals invisible to the naked eye.' 'That must be a superstition from your village, a village superstition,' said Worldster. 'You ought to give up village superstitions in America.' The next day she brought her microscope to the laundry and showed them the germs under their fingernails and on their tongues and in the water.

At one of their dinners, Worldster handed papers to Woodrow and Roosevelt, and the three of them started discussing business.

'What is this?' said Ed.

'Deeds for the business,' said Worldster, 'contracts for the partnership.'

'Where's mine?' said Ed. 'What contracts? Why contracts all of a sudden?'

'Where's his?' asked his wife.

'You weren't at the meeting,' said Worldster.

'Since when did we have to have contracts?' Ed asked. 'We had a spoken partnership. We shook hands. We gave one another our word.'

'We wrote it down too,' said Worldster. 'I guess you have the status of an employee.'

'I don't see why you didn't show up for the meeting,' said Roosevelt.

'This is all perfectly legal,' said Woodrow. 'Look – registered with the demon courts.' It was in English. There wasn't anything Ed could do. They had ganged up on him and swindled him out of his share of the laundry. 'You were always reading when we were working,' somebody said.

'What are we going to do?' said his wife, the lines around her eyes and mouth deepening.

'Don't worry,' he said. 'I've been planning for us to go to California anyway.'

So the two of them took a train across the United States, stopping in Chicago to visit some relatives – they saw more of the United States than they had ever seen of China – and went to live in California, which some say is the real Gold Mountain anyway.

The ghostmate

Many times it has happened that a young man walks along a mountain road far from home. He may have passed the Imperial Examinations ('entered the toad palace on the moon') or failed. If he failed, he would be singing a song, 'What Does the Scholar Do with His Bagful of Books After Failing?' Or he may not have been a student at all but a farmer at market overnight – or an artisan, whose wife will be pleased with the good money he made on pots or rugs or shoes. Or he carries a satisfying batch of cotton or silk on his back and is heading into town. On the nooning day, sun and leaves dapple his face with shadows and golden coins. The fine road opens before him coming around turns and over rises. Grass and water above and below him, he glimpses the road ahead threading the mountains. Some of the one hundred kinds of birds that fly the sky and nest the earth let him see them, and even the phoenix seems to hover near. A music accompanies him. Released for this day from his past and future, the young traveller feels his freedom. His walk is loose. He cocks his head; the music is real. He laughs at its cacophony, which blasts any worries out of his head. He sings melodies that wind like ribbons into the vistas. His conducting hands lift notes out of the air, stroke them, and let them go. Long streams drop down mountains. Beyond mountains, still higher mountains rise until the peaks fade from human sight. He is climbing a dragon's spine. Green-black trees twist overhead, taller than distant mountains. The man is the size of the far trees.

Suddenly it starts to rain. The naked drought-dwarfs with the one eye on top of their heads run for cover. Thunder and lightning close out the day. The trees howl, bend to earth, and snap back as if giants were stepping on them in their run downhill. The grass flattens against the ground. The wind, though it's only the wind, whips up a sense of danger in him, and the young man hurries along, hoping for a shrine to use as a shelter. When he begins to despair of finding any such signs of other people having come this way, a big house appears in the woods, and simultaneously the smell of a strong flower fills his head. Lightning reveals him knocking at the unfamiliar emblems on the outer gate; thick passion flower vines like elephant trunks twist around the carved and lacquered pillars.

The storm dies for a moment as if listening to his knocks. The forms and colours of the clouds change rapidly. A gold, silver, and pink mist covers the house.

An old servant answers, and dogs charge out, barking at him. Sometimes, though, the beautiful lady lives there alone and comes to the gate herself. She is the most beautiful women he has ever seen. She must have come from the West Lake region, land of the most beautiful women in the world. (Kwangtung women are the second most beautiful.) 'Enter, stranger,' she says, and later he remembers that the cheerless wind again quieted, the guard dogs subsided, and he heard her voice. In the garden, lumps of peacocks squat on the branches of swaying, laden trees. He follows her on a long path to the inner door; he walks under a horizontal scroll of mountains and sea. The red paper surely means a good house; a spirit woman or a fox would not have it, would she? Walking on through the cool rooms, he follows her retreating back. She is wearing a light-coloured dress, her hair a black tail alive down the middle. She turns one corner after another until he wonders if he can find his way out alone. She finally enters a small room and faces him. 'Change your wet clothes,' she says in a voice that sings. 'I'll return with more food.' On a stool by the fire he finds clothing and slippers, which fit him. A tureen of hot soup sits on a table, and one bowl has already been poured. The tea steeps. How luck am I, he thinks; a stranger is owed no more than a drink of water.

'Please eat with me.' Her voice startles him because he did not hear her return to the room. She is dressed in the old style. (No matter what year this is, China is old enough for there to have been an old style.) She wears the combs with the long prongs. Her eyebrows are moth's wings joined at the centre, and her eyes are like bronze bells with brights and deeps.

Holding her right sleeve with her left hand, she uncovers the complex dishes – duck in sheets, embryonic chicks in soup and in cakes, minces, and stuffings. Steam rises as if a mirage of food floated on the table. The meal lasts for a long while. He sucks bones thoroughly of marrow. He pushes an almond sliver over all the taste buds in his mouth, the ones along the upper gums, the lower gums, the ones under his tongue, and the corners of his cheeks. Then he bolts meat and rice. He gorges; he indulges his appetite. Food seems to reappear, the bowls bottomless. She pours tea and gives him the tiny cup with her own hands. He accepts it carefully so that his fingers do not oafishly touch hers. He feeds like an aristocrat.

If he knows ceramics and manners, he picks up a piece of tableware and says, 'How beautiful.' 'Yes, hold it up to the light and see the glow,' she says. The orange of the firelight suffuses the porcelain. He hears a deer cry outside. She ignores it. She is looking into his face, and her mouth forms a delightful O. She touches his wrist. 'Tell me a story about your life,' she says. As he talks, feeding her admiration, he understands that he is a special man. Up to now he was only filling his work-habituated hands with the clay from the least fertile part of his land; he made utensils, but she calls him an artist. If he is a failed student, he has his poems to sing to her, and she comforts him so that he is almost glad he lost at the exams. If he won, then what triumph – a position in government service and a beautiful woman – the beginning of a run of victories.

If he is a cobbler, she asks him to sew a pair of shoes for her, challenging him to do it before the storm abates. From the suede she brings him, he cuts pieces as symmetrical as butterflies. Until now he frugally used scraps from the winter coats. After finishing the seams, he nimbly works flowers into the tops and sides. He kneels before her chair, where she sits enthroned, and she steps into the shoes. Her tiny feet in each of his palms, he has the impression that he is holding a fairy dancing on his hands. 'I can give you your wishes,' she is saying. 'I can give you time to study, money to buy gold thread and rare glazes.' He laughs, 'Spoken like a woman who never has to work. I wish never to have to work at all.' What a strange woman. If he were a farmer, would she give him a shovel or a bag of manure as a present?

A farmer whose wife and babies are waiting for him would

mean to stay only until the rain stops, only until the end of the slow night. He would memorize each moment and the scrolls and the furniture and the food: his wife would enjoy hearing about this lucky night.

His wife is waiting at home, cooking roots and bark for the children, the adopted daughter or son, the widower uncle, the old folks with no teeth. She is a brave cooking wife. She has never had a romantic dinner for two. He'll have to ask her if she can manage without sweating so, and he doesn't like the calluses on her hands and feet either.

The young husband should have hinted for some leftovers to bring home to his dying grandparents and hungry parents and toilsome wife. When he found out there was going to be free food, he could have sent the rich woman's servant to fetch his family. Instead he feeds like a zoo animal, a pet.

Towards the end of the meal, he asks, 'Do you live here alone?'

'I'm a widow,' she says, and he feels all the erotic things the words *young widow* arouse in men.

As if she expected just him and no other, his hostess brings him the very fruits, the very poem, the very game he likes best. 'I'll leave when the storm flags,' he says. 'I'll leave after the winning point.' The storm heightens. She wins a game, and he wins a game; they have to play again. She tells him the long, long story of how she came to be a young widow. Tears magnify her eyes and brim on the lids, the prisms breaking and melting, wetting the pink cheekbones, the white cheeks, the corners of her mouth. When she talks, the words give her mouth such shapes that he cannot cease watching it. His wife's tears were no more interesting than his own tears; her nose turned red when she cried. One more fascination, and yet one more holds him. Through the windows, there gleams weather fit for travel, but he stays. He becomes drowsy. He will see his wife the next day, for lunch at the latest.

For breakfast the beautiful widow feeds him more foods he has never eaten before, shows him more things he has only known in stories. When he asks if he can pack a few leftovers for his wife, she looks at him gravely, and says, 'Let me give you a better present. You must take a lasting gift from me. Tell me about your work, and I can show you how to improve it and make lots of money.' She says 'lots of money' as if she were a girl imitating adult talk, guessing at his grown-up concerns. She seems to have come from a world where the inhabitants do not use money. She brings glazes in textures, blues, and greens the potter has not been able to mix, mounds of white lamb's wool to the weaver, paper with deer and willow and mountain watermarks to the poet, rolls of leather and cloth, threads like skeins of rainbows to the cobbler and tailor. To try the new substances, his hands begin their familiar work. They move smoothly now, not encountering bumps or tangles, knots, or nodes. The slips run exactly. Then, of course, he has to wait for the kiln to fire, the ink to dry, the glue to set. The embroidery artist has begun stitching the first of the one hundred birds, that is, two hundred birds, a pair of each kind, composed about a tree. Then, time to go to bed again, too late to travel. He should have observed the custom of refusing gifts.

The morning light shows his work to him; he sees in what he has done the possibility of the lightest, smallest shoe, the true poem, the embroidery or painting of the phoenix. He may fathom at this moment how many more pieces he has to make before the masterpiece. He bows to the years he must remain at his work. Each piece draws him on to the next one. Days go by. Nights.

And it is not only the work that holds him but the woman. If he is a tailor, her sews for her; the clothes are her size, and he does not mind that she cannot sew or cook, or that she sometimes laughs inappropriately. With clean tools and rich materials to choose from, he does the most elegant work of his life. He has a new life, a new quotidian. He does not forget the old life, but he remembers it like a bedtime story heard as a child. The beautiful lady pleases him easily; she disappears for a part of each day so that he can work. The student writes his poem about her and looks forward to her listening to it. The potter dedicates his vases to her. He used to make them for his wife, but that was not the same. At first he is very happy. The beautiful lady gives him enough to eat, robes, music from nowhere. 'Love me,' she says. 'I love you,' she says. 'Do you love me?' Like a salt plum, she makes his mouth water. He and his wife never talked about loving each other. Now whenever he conjures up thoughts about his family, he sees their black and white portraits. 'I love you,' she says, and he loves this stranger more than mother and father.

But one day there seems a surplus of pots, shoes, scrolls. The embroidery artist has finished his two hundredth bird. When he has completed this much, doesn't he usually go to market?

The beautiful lady, braceleted up to her elbows like a bride, draws her eyebrows and the line connecting them with special care. She feeds him and charms him.

'Tell me you've been happy here,' she says. 'Tell me you are happy.'

'I have been happy here. I have never been happier than here with you. Why are you crying? Why are you looking like that?'

'Stay with me today.'

'I'll be gone for just a few hours.' Or 'I'll be back in just a few days.'

'I love this scroll. Let me have it. Don't sell it.' 'And these shoes.' She says, 'I love this cup, its lines, its design, its handle. Let me keep it,' pulling things out of his pack.

'But I've already given you the best pieces. These are for market.'

'But you don't need to go to market any more,' she says.

He says, 'I don't need to study any more. I'm ready to take the examination again.'

'It's harvest time,' he says. Or 'Time for the planting.'

She puts on the same dress she wore when he first saw her. She brings festive food as for Sweethearts' Day, but when he finishes eating, he takes up his pack. 'I have to find out,' says the student, 'if I can beat this year's crop of scholars.' Suddenly he yearns for air that does not smell feverish with gardenias. She kneels at his feet and begs him to stay. Perhaps it is now that the deer cries. She stands, opens her robe, opens it like wings, and wraps him inside, enclosing him against her naked body, reminding him how unwifely her breasts and thighs are, how helplessly her body works as his touches it. Unable to remain joined, connected, he breaks from her, and leaves.

On the road, breathing dizzies him. The sky looks as big as it is. He has been seeing window-framed pieces of it for too long. Its immensity dazzles him – blue without end.

His appearance startles the townspeople, who run, pretending they are late for something important, not looking back. Dogs slink from him. He could leave his bundles on the street and no thief would touch them because of the phosphorescence that would rub off like contagious death. Children point at him, and the mothers hit them and rush them away. Confusedly, he arranges his wares on the ground in wait for shoppers. The vendors on either side of him and the letter writers across the way dismantle their tables and awnings; not discussing it, they leave quickly. Even with no competition, he cannot lure any customers. He picks up his goods and stumbles to a better location.

This young man must have had a good family and a loyal village because as he wanders like a ghost, a villager from his former life grabs him. 'Brother Brother,' calls the fellow villager, and the sounds of 'Brother Brother' are like a rooster's crow in the morning. 'What's wrong? What's happened to you? Where have you been all this time? We've missed you. Aiya! Look at you. You're so thin. Have you been ill? Why, I can feel your bones. What black bags under your eyes, and why do you let your hair hang like this? Here, let me braid it for you. You shouldn't be travelling when you're sick. Let me see you home.' The villager puts his arms around the young man. The familiar is so comforting that he sobs.

His friend guides him along the mountain road towards the home village. They are like two bugs in the landscape. The nearby oaks are gnarling and the far pines standing straight. The trees hold grey antlers high, already budded with leaves. Midway home, the young man stops. He seems to hear something, and though he stares straight ahead, the whites under his irises show. Marionette strings pull him into the tall grass. He remembers a beautiful lady he met in a previous incarnation or a dream last night.

The closer he comes to where the house had been, the more the home village becomes the dream. 'Look,' says his friend. 'A grave.'

Where a front door stood is the marker for a noblewoman's grave. The rain and wind have not quite rubbed the dates and the strange emblems off. She has been dead for years, centuries.

Fear burns along the young man's spine, and he runs from the lonely spot where no paths meander, no house looms, no peacocks or dogs stalk among the lilac trees. His friend dashes after him, not to be left by himself at the grave.

The young man walks home with his fellow villager. Sun, air, wind chase away his memory of nightingales singing and night-blooming cereus. The young husband returns to his family. The hero's home has its own magic.

Fancy lovers never last.

The great grandfather of the Sandalwood Mountains

About a year ago, I mailed fifty dollars to China to a cousin who is black, they say, and not strictly a cousin. 'You don't have to send anything,' my mother said several times. 'It's entirely up to you,' which, of course, it wasn't; we'd already been asked. Like his father before him, my maternal grandfather had brought a third wife back from his third trip West, Bali or Hawai'i or South America or Africa. They had one black boy child, who is MaMa's half-brother. He grew up and got married and now has a son, the cousin to whom I sent the fifty dollars. He had written saying that a bicycle costs fifty dollars, and that it would change his life to own one. 'I'll make sure in my letter,' said MaMa, 'to specify that it was you who sent it.' 'It doesn't matter,' I said. 'You don't have to do that.' I don't want anybody attached to me for ever with gratitude.

A few weeks later, a letter came from my black 'uncle', the bicycle cousin's father. 'Why did you send him money and me nothing?' he wrote. 'I'm the father. I deserve the money. If you don't send me my money, I'm going to kill him.' Even though they are black Chinese Red Communists living on the other side of the world, and even though they are poor, I do not believe he meant that. He must have only threatened to use his son as a hostage because he thinks us so entirely foreign we would be susceptible to such a threat; he was appealing to us Americans in a language we'd understand. 'Furthermore,' he said, 'you have disrupted the economy and technology of the commune. Send fifty dollars in reparations.' We don't feel an obligation to send him anything.

But in case he means what he said and Communists are as wild as the stories about them, I won't tell the name of our village. I don't want anybody arresting my uncle for extortion or confiscating the bicycle. The Chinese American newspapers list names of tourists from the United States and Hong Kong who disappear visiting China.

I am glad to see that the black grandmother ended up with a son and a grandson who are articulate. When she came to China she 'jabbered like a monkey', but no one answered her. 'Who knows what she was saying anyway?' She fell mute.

Many men on my mother's side of the family, even today, even the young men in countries where polygamy has been outlawed, have two wives, two houses, two families. The men in the past had three wives. The first wife, of course, was the important one; the others were 'for love'.

At a party in Honolulu, I met a dancer just returned from China, where she studied for six months. (Her aunt in China danced the Dark Haired Girl's part in *The White Haired Girl*.) She visited her ancestral village, Chung Sahn, where Sun Yat Sen was born, where the ancestors of most Chinese Americans in Hawai'i came from. She said that all the people were housed and fed. Her uncle's house had been divided into apartments, and he lived in one of them. 'Were very many killed during the Revolution – I mean, Liberation?' I asked. She said No. 'Nobody in my family,' she said. I said, 'Most of the men in our family were killed. The relatives write letters asking for money and bicycles.' She said, 'There are remote parts of the country where people are still ignorant, greedy, and lazy.'

A physicist wrote me a letter about his trip to China; he visited his ancestral village, which, it so happens, is also my ancestral village. He had been born there, but emigrated to America as a child. After lecturing at Beijing University, he was given a Volkswagen. Dressed like one of the people and speaking both Mandarin and Cantonese, he travelled about freely. When he arrived at the village, he saw houses from his childhood; the ones that had belonged to families that had sent men to the United States had been decorated with expensive tiles. He met a woman whom he recognized from his childhood as an aunt and went home with her. An automobile and some electrical kitchen appliances were rusting in the yard, stuff brought back from the Gold Mountain; there was no gasoline or electricity in the village. A young man was sitting idle by the door; he was some kind of a cousin. 'Stay for dinner,' the aunt invited the physicist, but the young man said rudely, 'He's too busy to have dinner.' The physicist ate at the communal dining room; the commune people also showed him around. Though the land in this area was more fertile than in most other parts of China, he found the farmers less eager to meet production quotas. In the middle of the work day, young men sat talking about how someday soon they would move to the Gold Mountain, where their ancestors, American pioneers, had gone for hundreds of years. The physicist felt that indeed there was something different about the people in our village.

I'd like to go to China if I can get a visa and – more difficult – permission from my family, who are afraid that applying for a visa would call attention to us: the relatives in China would get in trouble for having American capitalist connections, and we Americans would be put in relocation camps during the next witch hunt for Communists. Should I be able to convince my family about the goodwill of normalization, it's not the Great Wall I want to see but my ancestral village. I want to talk to Cantonese, who have always been revolutionaries, nonconformists, people with fabulous imaginations, people who invented the Gold Mountain. I want to discern what it is that makes people go West and turn into Americans. I want to compare China, a country I made up, with what country is really out there.

I have gone east, that is, west, as far as Hawai'i, where I have stood alongside the highway at the edge of the sugarcane and listened for the voices of the great grandfathers. But the cane is merely green in the sunlight; the tassels waving in the wind make no blurry fuzzy outlines that I can construe as a message from them. The dirt and sun are red and not aglitter with gold motes like in California. Red and green do not readily blend, nothing lurking in the overlaps to bend the eyes. The winds blowing in the long leaves do not whisper words I hear. Yet the rows and fields, organized like conveyor belts, hide murdered and raped bodies; this is a dumping ground. Old Filipino men die in abandoned sheds. Mushrooms and marijuana grow amidst the cane, irrigated by the arches of vaulting water. People with friends on the mainland steal long-distance calls on the field telephones.

Driving along O'ahu's windward side, where sugarcane grew in my great grandfather's day, I like looking out at the ocean and seeing the pointed island offshore, not much bigger than a couple of houses, nothing else out in that ocean to catch the eye – Mokoli'i Island, but nobody calls it that. I had a shock when I heard it's also named Chinaman's Hat. I had only encountered that slurred-together word in taunts when walking past racists. (They would be the ones loafing on a fence, and they said the chinaman was sitting on a fence '. . . trying to make a dollar out of fifty cents'.) But Hawai'i people call us Paké, which is their way of pronouncing Bak-ah, Uncle. They even call Chinese women Paké.

When driving south, clockwise, there is an interesting optical illusion. At a certain point in the road, the sky is covered with Chinaman's Hat, which bulges huge, near. The closer you drive towards what seems like a mountain, the farther it shrinks away until there it is, quite far off, an island, a brim and crown on the water.

At first, I did not say Chinaman's Hat; I didn't call the island anything. 'You see the island that looks like a Chinaman's hat?' locals ask, and visitors know right away which one they mean.

I swam out to Chinaman's Hat. We walked partway in low tide, then put on face masks. Once you open your eyes in the water, you become a flying creature. Schools of fish – zebra fish, rainbow fish, red fish – curve with the currents, swim alongside and away; balloon fish puff out their porcupine quills. How unlike a dead fish a live fish is. We swam through spangles of silver-white fish, their scales like sequins. Sometimes we entered cold spots, deserts, darkness under clouds, where the sand churned like grey fog, and sometimes we entered golden chambers. There are summer forests and winter forests down there. Sea cucumbers, holothurians, rocked side to side. A sea turtle glided by and that big shell is no encumbrance in the water. We saw no sharks, though they spawn in that area, and pilot fish swam ahead in front of our faces. The shores behind and ahead kept me unafraid.

Approaching Chinaman's Hat, we flew around and between a group of tall black stones like Stonehenge underwater, and through there, came up on to the land, where we rested with arms out holding on to the island. We walked among the palm trees and bushes that we had seen from the other shore. Large white birds were nesting on the ground under these bushes. We hurried to the unseen side of the island. Even such a tiny island has its windward and leeward. On the ocean side, we found a miniature pirate's cove with a finger of ocean for its river, a beach of fine yellow sand, a blowhole, brown and lavender cowry shells, not broken, black live crabs side-stepping and red dead crabs drying in the red sun, a lava rock shelf with tide pools as warm as baths and each one with its ecology. A brown fish with a face like a cartoon cow's mugged at me. A white globule quivered, swelled, flipped over or inside out, stretched and turned like a human being getting out of bed, opened and opened; two arms and two legs flexed, and feathery wings, webbing the arms and the legs to the body, unfolded and flared; its thighs tapered to a graceful tail, and its ankles had tiny wings on them – like Mercury; its back was muscled like a comic book superhero's – blue and silver metallic leotards outlined with black racing stripes. It's a spaceman, I thought. A tiny spaceman in a spacesuit. Scooping these critters into another tide pool, I got into theirs, and lying in it, saw nothing but sky and black rock, the ocean occasionally flicking cold spit.

At sunset we built a campfire and sat around it inside a cleft in the hillside. We cooked and ate the fish we caught. We were climbing along a ledge down to the shore, holding on to the face of the island in the twilight, when a howling like wolves, like singing, came rising out of the island. 'Birds,' somebody said. 'The wind,' said someone else. But the air was still, and the high, clear sound wound through the trees. It continued until we departed. It was, I know, the island, the voice of the island singing, the sirens Odysseus heard.

The Navy continues to bomb Kaho'olawe and the Army blasts the green skin off the red mountains of O'ahu. But the land sings. We heard something.

It's a tribute to the pioneers to have a living island named after their work hat.

I have heard the land sing. I have seen the bright blue streaks of spirits whisking through the air. I again search for my American ancestors by listening in the cane.

Ocean people are different from land people. The ocean never stops saying and asking into ears, which don't sleep like eyes. Those who live by the sea examine the driftwood and glass balls that float from foreign ships. They let scores of invisible imps loose out of found bottles. In a scoop of salt water, they revive the dead blobs that have been beached in storms and tides: fins, whiskers, and gills unfold; mouths, eyes, and colours bloom and spread. Sometimes ocean people are given to understand the newness and oldness of the world; then all morning they try to keep that boundless joy like a little sun inside their chests. The ocean also makes its people know immensity.

They wonder what continents contain the ocean on its other side, what people live there. Hong Kong off the coast tugged like a moon at the Cantonese; curiosity had a land mass to fasten upon, and beyond Hong Kong, Taiwan, step by step a leading out. Cantonese travel, and they gamble.

But China has a long round coastline, and the northern people enclosed Peiping, only one hundred miles from the sea, with walls and made roads westward across the loess. The Gulf of Chihli has arms, and beyond, Korea, and beyond that, Japan. So the ocean and hunger and some other urge made Cantonese people explorers and Americans.

Bak Goong, Great Grandfather, came to Hawai'i at the invitation of the Royal Hawaiian Agricultural Society. Their agent, who had been born in our district and spoke like us, came straight into the village and talked about how he got to be a recruiter. Even today the family trusts any insurance, encyclopedia, or gadget salesman who talks like us, our language a music that charms away common sense. The family knew the growing habits of cane; a stand grew in the courtyard. Convoys used to relay lichee and sugarcane from Canton to the Imperial palace. A few times a year, on a holiday or a birthday, Grandmother cut a stalk and divided it into small chunks, one for each person. The sweet taste affected Bak Goong. The recruiter told his fellow villagers, Chinese were the first sugarmakers in Hawai'i; they brought the first millstones and vats in 1802. 'Right now,' said the agent, 'we're offering free passage, free food, free clothing, and housing. In fact, we're advancing you six dollars. Here. See. I have six dollars right here. Here, Grandma. We'll let Po Po hold it; she can return it to me if she wants to. Couldn't you use six dollars before you've even begun to work? You repay it with just six weeks' work. After six weeks, clear profit. Figure it out. You're joining us at a lucky time. The pay just went up again. You're getting an instant raise. We need every kind of labour. You inexperienced kids can be house servants for two dollars a month. Now, once you secure this fine job, you'll want to protect it, right? You're thinking, What if I get to the Sandalwood Mountains, and they fire me? Well, listen to this. We can't fire you. We protect you against firing. We can't fire you because you sign this three-year contract, and for more protection, this five-year contract.' 'Mm,' said the family. 'Of course, there'll be some hardships, but that's life, isn't it? You'll be travelling with a shipload of fellow Chinese, with whom you'll be sharing free housing. You'll have people to discuss things with. We're giving you a dormitory just like going to college. And did you know that the Sandalwood Mountains are very close to the Gold Mountain? You get free passage as far as the Sandalwood Mountains, where you can stay as long as you want, and you invest a little of your profits in passage to California. You'll get there before the Gold Rush is over. Why, in Hawai'i, you're already halfway there. Figure: You start with nothing. You already have six dollars' advance. Three years from today, home with riches.'

Impressed by the agent's homely dialect, his suit, his title, and his philosophic bent, Bak Goong muttered what Confucius taught on the occasion of breaking a promise to his captors, ' "Heaven doesn't hear an oath which is forced on one," ' and made his X.

He told his family that he would be back in three years. Travelling alone he watched armies march or straggle by, close calls, he on a cliff, an army in the ravine; he behind a waterfall, an army drinking at the river; he flattened like a shadow on the earth, an army silhouetted against the moon. He spied British demons with big noses and guns. He was walking on dangerous and sick land. In the north, the Yellow River had reversed its course overnight; it reared up, coiled in the air, and slapped down backwards to run the other way, south instead of north. It troughed new watercourses and flooded four provinces before settling on its route. Winds collided. The Yangtze also flooded. Eels hung from ceilings, and red worms curled inside wells and jars. Migrating from lakes of drowned crops and trees, farmers came to fields of dust where drought cracked the ground, the land was burned, and there were no fishing boats on the rivers. New monsters were appearing on the earth, barbarians everywhere; the British demons opened the seaports to opium and soldiers. A crazy Cantonese (whose name is pronounced like our own last name but isn't the same at all), either fooling the Jesus demons or deranged by Christian education, taught that Mary had given two virgin births, Jesus and himself. With a sister and two brothers, Jesus Christ's Younger Brother led sixteen provinces and the Taiping, the army of the Great Peace, the Long Hairs, in revolt against the emperor and his British and French armies. The Shao Lin, an order of fighting monks, famous for their battles against the Manchus, were emerging again. The Manchus had burned the Shao Lin Temple, but their five Founding Fathers had escaped by hiding under a bridge (Pagoda and Bridge their symbols), then trained successors, who were the teachers of the monks fighting for the Great Peace. The Miao tribes and the Nien were also uprising, as were the Moslems of Yunan. The magnetic poles of the world had switched; gravity itself had come loose. China was changing again, as it does every thirty years in small cycles and every hundred years in large cycles.

Bak Goong recognized a century-size upheaval; he shook his head and walked away, turned his back and walked away. He arrived in Canton without being conscripted, and signed on a schooner as a crewman to make extra money while travelling. He would jump ship in Hawai'i if he wasn't allowed to quit there.

The Chinese who had sailed before him had painted a sea bird on the side of the ship, which protected it from storms. His first free moment he lowered himself on a rope and painted eyes on the bow. He tied poles and lines to the rails and caught fish.

The ocean was a bowl with horizon all around. Lucky to be a crewman.

He met all manner of men, broad faced and sharp faced Han Men, tall dark ones, white ones, little ones like the Japanese. One group spoke the language so queerly that he laughed out loud. He imitated their *thl* sound blown out of the mouth with big, airy cheeks and spit. 'One, two, three, *four*.' Sputtering and spitting as he shouted out the *four*, which has that *thl*, he called out the rhythm for lifting and hauling. 'Do you come from near our village?' a man from the *thl* village asked. 'Yes, I also come from the *Four* Districts,' said Bak Goong. He mimicked men with staccato consonants and a lone northerner who spoke a soft dialect like English, and he would have talked to the Englishmen too except that he could not hear their sliding, slippery little voices out of the fronts of their pursed mouths. 'Their asses must be as tight as their mouths,' he said out loud right in front of them.

The Chinese passengers were locked belowdeck though they were not planning to escape. Their fresh air was the whiff and stir when crewmen exchanged the food buckets for the vomit and shit buckets. Some men brought their pigs, which slept under the bottom bunks. The beds looked like stacks of coffins in a death house. 'Here we are,' said Bak Goong, who had to sleep in this hold too, 'emigrating with our pigs our only family.'

He gave advice to the boys who were away from their mothers for the first time. 'You'll be a rich man in three years,' he said. 'Three years is for ever for a kid, but for a man in his thirties like me, the years pass too quickly. Don't you notice how one year passes faster than the last? The first year abroad will be the worst; then we'll wish that time would slow up for our lives to last longer.' (He talked about time as going from up to down, last week being the 'upper week' and next week the 'lower week', time a sort of ladder that one descends.)

'Be quiet, Dog Vomit,' somebody hollered. 'Shut up and let me sleep.'

'Don't say "vomit",' somebody else groaned.

'Try laughing,' said Bak Goong. 'I'll bet you can't laugh and vomit at the same time.' *Laugh* is another word that has the *thl* combination in that queer dialect. 'And as for the dark,' he advised the children, 'it makes the room feel larger, doesn't it?'

'Tobacco shit stops the seasickness,' said an opium smoker, who passed his pipe.

'No, no, shit cures colds, not seasickness.'

'Let's try it for seasickness.'

'Your mother's cunt. You make this room smoky, and I'll throw up all over you.'

The berths, come to think of it, were also stacked like beds in an opium house. 'Is opium bitter?' asked Bak Goong. 'It's not addicting if you just try it once, right?' The tempted men had a discussion on exactly which pipe – the twelfth? the hundredth? – addicted, and how often – once a week? five times a day? once a month? – an addict smoked. 'It takes two years of smoking three times a day to learn the opium habit,' an addict said confidently.

So Bak Goong gave a tobacco shit man some money and smoked. The silver and wooden water pipes gurgled like rivers; the bowl pipes drew airily. Bak Goong leaned against the wall, and the meaning of life and time and what he was doing on this ship all became clear to him; even his vomity feeling fell into its place in the scheme of the universe. His thoughts branched and flowed and branched again and connected like rivers, veins, roads, ships' lanes. New ideas sparked, and he caught his breath when he saw their connections to old ideas. Circles wheeled by, whirled concentrically, and stilled into a simple light. The bald heads of monks, who sit in circles, bowed towards the centre like a hand, a lotus flower, or wood sorrel closing. The world's people arranged themselves in parades, palaces, windows, roads, stadiums, attempting to form this bond. These men in the hold were trying to circumnavigate the world. Men build bridges and streets when there is already an amazing gold electric ring connecting every living being as surely as if we held hands, flippers and paws, feelers and wings. Though he was leaving his good wife and his village, they were connected to him by a gold net or a light; it shimmered when the people and other creatures moved about. Even the demons abovedeck let out a glow. Bak Goong thought he understood the Tao, which is everywhere and in everything, even in our excrement, which is why opium is shit. It seemed that he would have to bring his mind hard to bear in order to discriminate between sleeping and waking, work and play, yours and mine. Wars are laughable; how could a human being remember which side he was on? Fear gives us red to brighten the world, and meanings are for decoration. 'Is this true?' he asked, and answered, 'Yes.' Everything was true. He was Lao Tse's great thinker, who can embrace opposing thoughts at the same moment. He loved the strangers around him as much as he loved his family. He closed his eyes and saw islands in the sea or planets in space or lakes he could dive into or observe. Suffering, happiness, hurt children were similar dots. He felt wise. But after enjoying his wisdom for a while, he noticed that there had been all along a weight or a rock at the bottom of his well-being, the familiar nag of tasks to do. The opium must be wearing off soon; was there a last question he wanted to ask it? 'How am I going to withstand pain, plain physical hurt?' An accidental cut could make him say, 'I can't bear it.' He dug his nails into his arm. How could he take lonely inevitable death? What about death with pain, pain unto death? That his body felt content now did not mean that it had learned a sufficient lesson in the habit of well-being. An urge to touch the ground with bare feet came over him, not to have floorboards or shoes between him and earth. What if his body had to undergo deliberate torture, for example? 'Don't hurt,' he answered himself, or opium, the reminder, answered him. 'Don't give pain. Don't take pain.' The ring of light was disbanding, slivers of it returning to the various separate bodies of flesh and bone. How not to take pain? How to have no pain?' 'Be able,' he said. 'Be capable.' Capable. Opium was merely a rest from constant pain. He said aloud, repeating, 'Be capable,' to remember this answer for use later when these unwordable feelings were gone. 'I am a capable man. An able man,' he said, and did feel a touch of dreariness at this mundane answer. He wrapped himself in his quilt and patted his money belt to feel his sugarcane contract crackle. 'No pain. Don't give pain. Don't take pain.' He did not smoke opium again on the journey because he did not want to become an addict or to spend money.

After three months at sea, Bak Goong smelled in the wind a sweetness like a goddess visiting. Whenever the hatches and doors opened in the right combinations, the men below also smelled it. 'It's sandalwood,' Bak Goong said, looking for land on the horizon. The smell of boxes and chests of drawers, statues, castanets and fans, incenses and powders must have inspired him to come here. Chinese had followed that essence to India, where sandalwood grew in phoenix-shaped roots in the caves of lions, and to Persia, where it congealed in the Eastern Ocean as a cicada. And now they followed sandalwood to its home here.

One day Bak Goong opened the hatches for the men below, who stumbled through the passageways and up ladders to the top deck, where they blinked in the sunlight. A demon from shore counted and recounted the China Men. There were three or four fewer live ones than when they began the journey. The demon strung a tab about each neck. Bak Goong climbed down to the longboat, past the weeds that had grown like skirts on the ship's sides.

On shore among crates, burlap bags, barrels, haystacks, they waited for their bosses, some of whom were China Men. The men with no papers signed anything that was handed them; most made a cross like the ideograph *ten*; 'The Word Ten', they called their signatures. A pair of horses, which delighted Bak Goong, pulled a wagon to the dock, but only a few workers rode to those fields close enough to Honolulu to be reached by roads. Bak Goong's group was to walk, led by a demon boss on a horse. He bade good-byes to friends he had made on the ship. Walking after rolling on the sea confused his legs, but with his seabag across his back, he edged quickly to the front of the group. He buffered himself in case the demon used his whip on the men.

They walked out of the town and up a mountain road so narrow that the demon dismounted and led his horse. The trail led upward among banana trees. Bak Goong ate bananas to his heart's content, throwing away the peels instead of scraping their insides and eating the fibres; there were that many bananas, hands of them, overripe fruit rotting on the ground. He ate fruit and nuts he had never seen before. And mangoes like in China. He wished he could give his wife some. With a handful of rice a day, he could live here without working. Five-petalled flowers spun from the trees, pink stars, white stars, yellow stars, striped red and white stars. At one beautiful spot, white trumpet flowers hung above his head like hats. He walked on ground royally carpeted with jacaranda. When the sun became hot, a tall rain fell and made two rainbows across the sky, the colours of the top one in the opposite order of the bottom one. 'Aiya,' said the men. 'Beautiful. Beautiful.' 'Is that a good omen or a bad omen?' 'How does it happen?' 'It has to be a good omen.' The rainbows moved ahead of them. Before they became too wet, the rain stopped; the sun and breeze dried them. Bak Goong memorized all this to tell his wife.

He sucked in deep breaths of the Sandalwood Mountain air, and let it out in a song, which reached up to the rims of volcanoes and down to the edge of the water. His song lifted and fell with the air, which seemed to breathe warmly through his body and through the rocks. The clouds and frigate birds made the currents visible, and the leaves were loud. If he did not walk heavy seated and heavy thighed like a warrior, he would float away, snuggle into the wind, and let it slide him down to the ocean, let it make a kite, a frigate bird, a butterfly of him. He would dive head first off the mountain, glide into the airstreams thick with smells, and curve into the ocean. From this mountaintop, ocean before him and behind him, he saw the size of the island. He sang like the heroes in stories about wanderers and exiles, poets and monks and monkeys, and princes and kings out for walks. His arias unfurled and rose in wide, wide arcs.

The men passed a hutment of grass shacks with long yellow thatch weathered and fine, rippling and ruffling in the breeze like the hair of blonde ladies. Roofs had fallen, and the frames showed like bones. The doorways were empty. They did not see brown people come and go.

They descended another side of the mountain and walked along the sea all day, and at last came to the place where they were to work. They had arrived in the middle of the workday, and were to start at once. There was no farm, no sugarcane ready to tend. It was their job to hack a farm out of the wilderness, which they were to level from the ocean to the mountain. To do this, Bak Goong was given a machete, a saw, an axe, and a pickaxe. The green that had looked like grass at a distance was a tangle of trees so thick that they shut out sunlight. Leaves grew only on their tops and bent backs. They were not tall trees, branch having wrestled branch into a knot that gnarled for miles. It may have been one tree that had replanted itself tighter and tighter. A criminal dropped into the midst of the webwork would be imprisoned for ever. Beginning anywhere, Bak Goong chopped into the edge of this strange forest. He could not take hold of the branches because of the thorns on them. Dust shook down. Coughing, alarmed at how quickly he grew hot, tired, and thirsty in the intervals between the water-and-tea man's rounds, he shook a silver ball from the flat glass bottle he carried in his pocket and swallowed it for thirst. He gave pills to the boys working on either side of him. Though he chopped, hacked and sawed with all his might, the knot of trees did not seem smaller. Black birds with flashes of white wings flew easily straight through the maze.

After work, though he could get sick and die from mixing cold water with hot sweat – open pores draw in the cold – he ran with the others into the ocean, and let it wash him. In the water rushing away from him, he held on to his body and mind with effort. The horizon seemed to be up in the air. He would have gone to sleep right there on the beach, but the ones who had arrived earlier had established an eating system. 'Eh, China Man, come eat,' the China Men invited. They had already organized the food, decided who would cook and on what terms. 'Eh, China Man, come eat,' Bak Goong imitated their English. So he got to sit down to a good dinner on plank tables. They passed around candy before dinner; it was a regular welcome party. The few Hawaiian workers passed around salt. Chinese take a bit of sugar to remind them in times of bitter struggle of the sweetness of life, and Hawaiians take a few grains of salt on the tongue because it tastes like the sea, like the earth, like human sweat and tears. Some fishermen and surfers and a demon traveller also ate with them, as did the other great grandfather, Bak Sook Goong, who was not yet related. (They would have called one another Bak and Sook in any case – Uncles.) These strangers ate like a family, drank from the same soup tureen, ate from the same plates of accompaniments to the rice. They did not gobble directly from the centre dishes to the mouth but first touched the meat or vegetable to the rice. Bak Goong was lucky to have fallen among the civilized in the wild Sandalwood Mountains. He ate chunks of coconut wet in its milk and the fruit they had gathered on the way that morning. The hot tea on the hot day cooled him.

In the talk-story time after dinner, young men gave advice to young men. There were no old men in the Sandalwood Mountains. 'Mind your own business, and work like an ox.' 'Don't gamble.' 'Keep your machete sharp, and hold it like so when you smell a demon near you.' 'Wrap your queue around your head or tuck it inside your shirt.' 'If you have the opium habit, you can ask for your wages by the week.' Bak Goong congratulated himself on what a good ear he had; he could understand much of what these unusual men were saying. He had travelled to the middle of the ocean and was getting along with the people he found. He spoke to the most foreign, barbarous-looking China Men. When a storyteller lost him with apocopations, he wondered whether a puff of opium would help him understand language more clearly, but 'No,' he said politely, 'I'd not be able to repay you.' The men who had come earlier also said that the plantation had a rule that they not talk at work, but this rule was so absurd, he thought he must have misheard tones.

He lay down out in the open. The sights of the day unreeled behind his eyelids – the ocean jumping with silver daggers, fronds shredding in wind, twin rainbows, spinning flowers, the grey mass of the maze tree like all the roads of many lives. How was he to marvel adequately, voiceless? He needed to cast his voice out to catch ideas. I wasn't born to be silent like a monk, he thought, then promptly said. 'If I knew I had to take a vow of silence,' he added, 'I would have shaved off my hair and become a monk. Apparently we've taken a vow of chastity too. Nothing but roosters in this flock.'

The next morning at five a.m., he was again standing before the fist of trees. The dimness of shapes gave the coming day many possibilities until the sun delineated the bleached trees, the mountains, and another day of toil. He worked for that day and the next and the next without saying anything, but got angry, chopping as if cutting arms and legs. He withstood the hours; he did the work well, but the rule of silence wrought him up whenever a demon rode by. He wanted to talk about how he sawed tree trunks and the interlocked branches held the trees upright. He suddenly had all kinds of things to say. He wanted to tell the men who worked beside him about the rewards to look forward to, for example, chewing cane for breakfast; the fibres would clean their teeth like a toothbrush. 'You go out on the road to find adventure,' he wanted to say, 'and what do you find but another farm where the same things happen day after day. Work. Work. Work. Eat. Eat. Eat. Shit and piss. Sleep. Work. Work.' He axed a limb at each word. 'Actually, I like being bored,' he would have said. 'Nothing bad is happening, no useless excitement.' He wanted to discuss mutes and kings who rip out tongues by the roots.

And one day – he could not help it – he sang about the black mountains reddening and how mighty was the sun that shone on him in this enchanted forest and on his family in China. The sweep of the ocean was so wide, he watched the sun rise and set in it. In the heat of noon, he wished he could shoot out the sun, like Prince I, who dropped nine suns with his bow and arrows. The demons paid his singing no mind. They must have thought he was singing a traditional song when he was really commenting and planning.

'I've solved the talking,' he said to his fellow workers. 'If that demon whips me, I'll catch the whip and yank him off his horse, crack his head like a coconut. In an emergency a human being can do miracles – fly, swim, lift mountains, throw them. Oh, a man is capable of great feats of speed and strength.'

There was a bang or crack next to his ear. The demon was recoiling his whip. 'Shut up, Paké.' He heard distinct syllables out of the white demon's moving mouth. 'Shut up. Go work. Chinaman, go work. You stay go work. Shut up.' He caught every word, which surprised him so much, he forgot to grab the whip. He laboured on, muttering, 'Shut up. Shut up, you.' He found a cut on his shoulder.

The men tried burning instead of cutting the trees. They set fires in the red heat of the sun. Bak Goong felt the fire was the same as his anger; his anger was this size and this red. But only the dead branches and leaves burned. Cutting the burned trees, the men became sooted black. To make them work faster, the demons had a trick of telling the slowest man that he was sick and had to take the day off without pay.

On their own time, after five p.m., the workers built two huts for bunkhouses, each with wooden beds laid head to foot one above another like the shelves on ships. They arranged gourds and vines, buckets, and hats on the verandas, which they kept adding to the huts. Bak Goong wove a hammock, and it was as comfortable as his mother's lap.

At the very end of the day, the men exchanged remedies. They scraped one another's backs with spoons to get rid of rheumatism and arthritis. For heat sickness they scraped necks with the edge of a coin cooled in water, the square hole in the middle of the coin giving a good grip. They slapped the insides of one another's elbows and knees, where tiredness collects. They soaked cuts and sores, and rubbed bruises with tobacco and whisky. Some exercised, and Bak Goong learned some kung fu movements and also some ways of breathing that would strengthen his body and sharpen his brain. They nursed runaways who had escaped from other work camps. Bak Goong showed his scarring shoulder and said, 'I will talk again. Listen for me.' Boys put rocks under their pillows to stop crying at night. Several people not from the same village believed in 'passing fear over fire', which means lifting one who has been badly frightened and passing him over a fire. Some 'passed rice over hearts' and some 'over heads'. Everybody thought that his way of doings things was the way all Chinese were supposed to do them.

Bak Goong worried that he had overlooked a trick clause in his contract and that he would not be paid at all; this was some kind of a slave labour camp. But pay day came. When the demon handed him his money Bak Goong counted it in front of him in Chinese and in business ('pidgin') English. He came out short. 'Too little,' he complained, holding up his fingers. 'Too little bit money. Are you trying to catch a pig?' he asked, which means to cheat, to take advantage of a greedy person.

The paymaster demon said, 'Shut up, you. You shut up,' clapping a hand over his own mouth several times. Bak Goong had been fined for talking. And sick men had been docked for every day they had been lying lazy in bed. Those who had not recovered from crossing the ocean got an accounting of how much they owed for food and lodging plus passage. The strong workers had money subtracted for broken tools.

The men cursed as they reckoned their pay. 'Dead man.'

'Rotten corpse afloat.' 'Corpse on the roadside.' 'Hunchback with a turtle on his back,' that is 'Cuckold.' 'Your mother's ass.' 'Your mother's cunt.' 'They take my piss and shit away from me to feed their fields. Take my shit.' 'Eat my shit and piss. Drink piss white monster. Eat shit.' Bak Goong turned his ass at the pig catcher demon's face. He was finding out that the dollar a week wasn't the minimum wage but the maximum to strive for, that hoeing paid less than other jobs. The China Man accountant told them their wages were reduced until the plantation made a bigger profit. If Bak Goong did not give any dinner parties did not drink or smoke or gamble he would bring home maybe a hundred dollars after three years. The big talk about a thousand dollars must have been about men who came home old to die after scrimping for thirty years and more.

One day, like a knight rescuing a princess, Bak Goong broke clear through the thicket. The demons bought bullocks; they had longer horns than water buffaloes. He yoked them to stumps, which they yanked out. But the Hawaiians quit rather than help pull the boulders out of the earth. The remaining workers ploughed around groups of big rocks in the middle of the fields. They were the first human beings to dig into this part of the island and see the meat and bones of the red earth. After rain the mud ran like blood. The maze tree and woodrose sprouted behind the ploughs.

A team of six men including Bak Goong was sent to a plantation farther up the coast where cane already stood like a green army; the tassels were called 'arrows'. On the same day as he cleared land, he cut cane twice as tall as a man. The cane and rice growers were trying out the seasons. The workers stripped the long leaves like shucking corn. Dust shook loose, and they breathed it even through their kerchiefs. They cut the stalks close to the ground. The new men tasted the cane in which the sap was running warm. They cut the tips beneath the top three nodes for seed cane. There were seeds in the arrows, but it was faster to plant the nodes. The men seemed small and few wading among the sticky mounds.

The wagoners, who had a good job, drove the cane to the sugar mill on a route along the sea. It was crushed into molasses and boiled into sugar, for which the world was developing an insatiable hunger as for opium.

Bak Goong and his team brought the seed cane and a few bottles of rum back. The land was ready to be sown. They bagged the slips in squares of cloth tied over their shoulders. Flinging the seed cane into ditches, Bak Goong wanted to sing like a farmer in an opera. When his bag was empty, he stepped into the furrow and turned the seed cane so the nodes were to the sides, nodes on either side of the stick like an animal's eyes. He filled the trenches and patted the pregnant earth.

The work changed from watering season to hoeing season. He weeded the ivy that wrapped and would choke the young cane, the ratoons. The vines pulled like rubber. Using a short hoe, he knelt to uproot them, and carried the weeds to the fires at the ends of the rows else they take root where they fell. He worked even in the rain lest he lose money. Then there was a stripping season when he peeled the plants so they would use their strength to make sugar instead of leaves.

The next harvest, the men invented a burning season when they set the cane on fire to burn off the outer leaves instead of stripping by hand. They chose a dry and moderately windy day. Like a savage, Bak Goong ran with brands, torching the cane along the border. During the night watches, fires like furry red beasts lurked and occasionally roared into the black sky, showing it endless, nothing illuminated but smoke as high as the flames climbed. In the day the smoke curled like white snakes in the directions of the winds. Demons in white suits walked gingerly inspecting the char. Then there was clearing and planting, the hoeing, and harvest, and the planting season again.

The cough that had begun when he cut trees and stripped leaves worsened because of breathing the hot sweet smoke and because of the hoeing in the rains. On the hottest days, the coughing made his nose bleed. He stuffed rags in his nostrils and kept working. The blood clotted in the back of his throat, and he spit out gouts. He hawked and spat to entertain the men and to disgust the demons. His cough did come in handy. When the demons howled to work faster, faster, he coughed in reply. The deep, long, loud coughs, barking and wheezing, were almost as satisfying as shouting. He let out scolds disguised as coughs. When the demon beat his horse and dust rose from its brown flanks, he coughed from his very depths. All Chinese words conveniently a syllable each, he said, 'Get – that – horse – dust –

away – from – me – you – dead – white – demon. Don't – stare – at – me – with – those – glass – eyes. I – can't – take – this – life.' He felt better after having his say. He did not even mind the despair, which dispelled upon his speaking it. The suicides who walked into the ocean or jumped off the mountains were not his kindred.

At night the very thought of dust tickled his lungs. In order to sleep, he imagined his lungs warming and becoming two red diamonds.

If the moisture and soil had been natural to cane, the men would not have had to work so hard coaxing it, leading water to it. The weather and soil were just good enough for cane to require constant nursing and effort. There was a scarcity of animals on the island too, and of labourers.

Whenever Bak Goong looked up from the work, the mountains were there above him. They rose, sheer green walls without slope like great stage curtains that could part or rise, and then he would see behind them what really runs the world, whether the gods' faces are kind or evil. The beings on either side of the curtains would have a look at one another – surprise – before they shut again. Perhaps the gods did fly this far from China and landed on this island for a rest in mid-ocean. Perhaps China Men attracted them. On a grey day, the mountains looked like Chinese mountains. But usually they were stark, bright green curtains. After a rainstorm, waterfalls dropped like silver scrolls down each fold. Bak Goong said, 'Aiya!' in wonder. He counted over twenty waterfalls before his eyes.

For recreation, because he was a farmer and as antidote for the sameness of the cane, he planted a garden near the huts. Planting as if in his old village, which was like this island in weather and red dirt, he even grew flowers, for which there was no edible use whatsoever. 'It's a regular park with coppices and flowers,' he said. He ticked off in a chant the cuttings, seeds, and bulbs he had brought across the ocean – pomelo, kumquat, which is 'golden luck', tangerines, citron also known as five fingers and Buddha's hand, ginger, bitter melon and other kinds of melon, squashes, peas, beans, narcissus, orchids, and chrysanthemums. To see how his plants had grown and changed overnight gave him eagerness, a reason, and curiosity for getting out of bed in the morning. The transplants another gardener had given him would be standing up. Tomatoes the size of pinheads would have appeared in the centres of the yellow flowers. His orange tree would have grown a pair of balls. He took his morning piss in his garden. He garnered and ate thinnings for breakfast. 'Harvest,' he said with one skinny luffa in his hand. For free, he found mushrooms, full-blown white domes and orange puffs in the grass and fluted wooden ears in the trees. He let at least one of each kind of plant go to seed and collected their generations. Harvest gave him a happy sense of order. 'Li Shih Min,' he informed the others, 'established such order in his kingdom that criminals came out of gaol for harvests and returned for the winter executions.'

On their 'day offu', the China Men went into Honolulu to spend their pay. They could ride cane and mill wagons as far as they had built roads, and they walked until there was another road, where they could catch another wagon for a few cents more. A family could eat for a week on that fare. They dressed for town in their black silk suits and yellow straw boaters with the black band and forked streamers; their braids hung between the swallowtails. 'I'm going to town,' Bak Goong sang and sang *town* as if Honolulu were his own village. A family man, he walked the entire way and reached town by noon. He went directly to the general store, where he bought a money order for his wife and dictated a letter about how well and lighthearted he was in this Sandalwood paradise. The leftover money was his to keep or spend on careful gambling (more for the companionship than the money), a restaurant meal with a shot of whisky, and a yearly picture taken at the photo studio. Unlike Bak Sook Goong, the other great grandfather, he did not spend money on Sandalwood Mountain women. He wandered about on the wooden sidewalks creaking underfoot and sat in the stores. 'Come in and sit awhile,' the store owners said as if inviting him into their own houses in China, and he was a real uncle or brother.

Most of the men were young enough to have their entire lives changed on a day off. A farmer could come to town, change his name, and become a merchant. Bak Goong met men who had forgotten the names of their Chinese family or the name and location of their Chinese village. They kept shaking their heads when he named village after village. They had lost a last piece of paper or a letter with the address on it. The gambling men played with fate for a new life. They bought chances. It was no work at all to throw the dice, flip a card, or pick a word in the pigeon lottery. In one Sunday, a lucky man could buy a farm or take a ship home or to California, stand up from the gambling table and walk to the harbour. Or he could sign his years away, mortgage his labour and future, not go home yet, ever. Two poor men gamble and one becomes a rich man. The other becomes a flea-man. A day in town was full of possibilities.

The other great grandfather, Bak Sook Goong, did not spend much of his time off with the men. One day off, when following a stream, he heard the voices and laughter of women, and from behind bushes, saw them in a pool at the foot of a waterfall. Some naked women were bathing. Nude women sitting on the rocks were weaving flowers and leaves into crowns for their drying hair. They were singing, and laughed at the ends of lines, so he knew it had to be a lascivious song. And one of them was look-ing at him, into his eyes. Instead of covering herself, she held his gaze and washed herself here and there. Then she said some-thing, and the women tugged him out of hiding. They made him bathe with them. 'But this is just like stories,' he told them, though they did not understand everything he said. 'Let me sing you one.' He stood garlanded and sang to them about a prince on horseback who came upon naked sisters bathing and singing. 'Sun and water double and touch, double and touch,' he sang. 'Wash up here – and here – and wash down there.' He did the movements as he sang, and the beautiful women understood and laughed. The end of that song was that the prince had burst out laughing, and the sisters covered themselves and vanished, but these women asked him to have a picnic with them.

'Come eat, Brother,' they said in English. 'Sit, Brother. You stay eat. Stay eat, Brother.' As he ate with them serving him, he was reminded that this was the right way for a man to live, and how much he missed his family, which was a family of women, two wives and many daughters, also many slaves. He turned to the woman who had looked so boldly at him. 'I come live with you?' he asked. 'Let me come live with you.'

'Yes,' she said. 'You come live with me.' He became the god-father of many Hawaiian children. 'Paké godfather,' they called him.

When the China Men asked Bak Sook Goong how his family was doing, they continued to mean the one in China, and he answered that way too. After work and on days off, he went to his Hawaiian village.

Bak Goong, meanwhile, helped build a dragon for the many New Years to come. He collected metal and glass shards, sea-shells, and wood shavings, which he glued and sewed into scales. Once a month, he brought his dragon section to town and added it to the tail, which grew very layered and long. When the clothes he had brought from China and the new clothes he had bought here turned into rags, he worked them into the dragon. The island dragon was more splendid than any village dragon he had left behind. None of the men had seen a longer dragon in China. 'This is the longest dragon in the world,' they said. Only the men who regularly practised kung fu were dragon dancers. They argued about which postures and moves were the correct kung fu. They had been taught by different teachers in contradicting traditions. On New Year's the dragon in its fierce dance undu-lated like the Pacific Ocean, coiled and twisted, leapt and stepped nimbly among the firecrackers. Bak Goong had his picture taken inside the dragon, not in motion but stretched out straight, the dancers' feet in white socks aligned in front of the wooden sidewalks.

Bak Goong spoke kindly and happily at the beginning of the New Year, saying only good things. But some aggravation would make him swear, and no year was perfect.

Once he saw five humpback whales on their New Year's birth-ing journey pass like spouting islands, backs like wet rocks, alive with moss and lichen. A wind blew leaves across the beach.

In 1856 every great grandfather on every island gave some of his money to throw a Grand Ball for the Sandalwood Mountain king and queen's wedding. Neither Bak Goong nor Bak Sook Goong went to it, but they were represented by wealthy China Men. 'He practises quadrilles alone in front of a mirror in his room at night,' the plain men gossiped. The ball was held at the courthouse. Four white demons, named with Chinese names and dressed in mandarin gowns, acted as hosts. The queen danced the opening quadrille with a real China Man, the king with a demoness. Six whole sheep and one hundred and fifty chickens were eaten. The China Men's Ball was the most elegant ever held in Hawai'i. The newspapers praised the China Men for their dancing and generosity; a ball was not above their comprehension. Great grandmothers were to understand that their husbands did not spend $3,700 on a Grand Ball to dance with the blonde Jesus demonesses or the princesses of the wild people but to prove their civility.

When Bak Goong needed to get off this rock of an island, he sat at an edge of the ocean where he often watched the sun pop out on his left and later drop back in on his right. One moonless night the winds blowing from Kona met the winds blowing trade, and the air was still; the fronds hung silent. Two people were standing in the black water halfway between him and the horizon, halfway between the sky and earth. A yellow light shown from them; their random movements repeated in series, a dance. They revolved in the only brightness, and stopped, hands and feet held like Balinese temple dancers. Time moved at their rate of motion. It was either two people or one Hindoo with four arms. He heard music draw out into one long note. The waves going in and out for ever was the same as no motion at all. The ocean remains the same basic water. Flesh does not evolve into the necessary iron. He yearned for the sun to blast out of the ocean. He sat for hours in the exact centre of eternity.

Then it all started up again; the couple on the water stirred. A fisherman and woman suddenly came out of the sea and walked towards him. 'Want to see our catch?' He could barely answer for staring at their ordinary faces. Between the time the Hindoo danced and these two stood beside him, he had seen streaming up to him rows of shining people; they had had wings flapping light and bare feet and hands glowing. It had been bright as day.

'You like fish, Brother?' 'You like fish, Uncle?' said the human voices coming from flesh and blood bodies. The light was contained in lanterns the man and-woman were carrying and also came from the rising moon. The two figures were only an elderly Hawaiian couple he had met before; they had been nightfishing. They handed him a fish, 'Eh, you like fish?' and walked away along the beach.

Later when he heard people say they had seen the torches of the dead warriors who walk across the water, he would say, 'You saw the Hawaiians nightfishing or checking their lobster traps.' But when someone said, 'Those are Hawaiians nightfishing,' Bak Goong, a fanciful, fabulous man, said, 'It may be dead Hawaiian warriors walking.' If a human being crossed the path of the walkers, he could die on the spot, but Bak Goong said that he knew for a fact that this was not true. He mustn't sit so long looking at the ocean, he resolved. The opium must have had a permanent effect; he would not take any more. He asked the tobacco shit men, 'How can you tell it hasn't changed you once and for all? Could everything have become permanently exaggerated?' Now that he was in a new land, who could tell what normal was?

Among the cane weeds, he found a new, free opiate: a mushroom with a speckled brown cap that turned purple when picked. It tasted of earth and must, but he did not see much new vision; perhaps he had seen all there was to see. He did not eat it again. Nor did he chew the wood whose Hawaiian name sounded like *ka fa*, 'fake flower' in Cantonese. So he had smoked opium, eaten mushroom and gambled, but he would not become an opium addict or mushroom addict or gambler. He was a talk addict.

On another day off, he got lost while exploring and came upon abandoned huts he had not seen before. The doors and windows gaped. Some huts only had a hole for crawling in and out of. The stones, however, had not tumbled down but sat stacked one on top of another in god shapes or human shapes – he did not know what they meant. There were no rocks wrapped in fresh ti leaves. In case it had been measles or smallpox that had emptied the village, he did not go inside any house.

Suddenly out of the air and lifting the hair on the back of his neck like the wind lifting the grass on the roofs came a howling that was high and long. It's a bird, he reasoned. It's crying in flight. That's why the notes come now here, now there. It's wild dogs on the hillside. But it grew louder and in it he heard sobs, the lamentations of old men and children, thousands of souls

111

wailing in separate voices. He could not make out the quivering words, or it was a language he did not know. 'Ghosts,' his wife would have said. I'm imagining this, he thought. It's really wild dogs. Or wolves. They sounded hungry. He felt like weeping in sympathy; sorrow filled his chest, but he kept the tears back not to blind himself as he ran out of the village.

A woman standing by the last hut called to him. 'This way. This way,' she said. 'You hear?' he asked. 'Yes,' she said, but the noise stopped. She stood under plumeria, the star flower, the deadman's flower that grows in graveyards. The hut behind her had been mended, the earth around it swept. She touched his arms; he felt a tiredness come from her and weight his arm. His face nodded towards hers, his head heavy and helpless. Though no icy breath came from her mouth, his chicken skin was proof of the supernatural nearby, and he left quickly, rudely. When he looked back, she had gone inside her hut.

He entered town in an unfamiliar place with the sun setting and no wagons in sight. A police demon stopped him, but English phrases had flown out of his mind. The police demon was about to arrest him, runaway chinamen a menace now, but just then Bak Goong saw a young countryman across the street, someone who could help him. 'Sook-ah,' he called out. 'Sook-ah,' that is, 'Hey, Father's Younger Brother.' 'Sook-ah.'

'Sugar?' said the police demon. 'Sugar plantation? You better hurry. The wagon is leaving soon.' He pointed with his nightstick to a street that jumped into recognition. Bak Goong returned on the last wagon.

Old men laugh with tears in their eyes every time they hear or tell the 'sugar' story. Another way it goes is like this: A China Man enters a grocery store, where he wants to buy some sugar for New Year's Day. But at the counter he can't think of the word. Luckily, a young man walks past the door. 'Sook-ah,' the older man calls, and the grocer demon gets him a bag of sugar, a good omen for the New Year.

On days off, it was safest to stay on the plantation. There was entertainment to be had without spending money. It was a recreation to sleep like winter gods. Peddlers came bringing medicines and toiletries; they talked story and talked stink about people on the other plantations. The pesky missionary Jesus

112

demons also came nosing and sniffing out Hawaiians and China Men even in the remote valleys. They were like the wandering persuaders in China. Some workers walked about with them, whispering and nodding. Converts got extra days off on demon holidays. 'I'm just a pig catcher,' they said as they dressed up for church, where they ate free food, 'and you get to go inside demon houses.' Bak Goong went to Christian church once or twice, but they talked 'baptism', and he quit. He asked the converts, 'Who's the pig that got caught?' They didn't even talk like China Men any more, the salt gone from their speech. 'Thank God,' they said instead of 'Your mother's cunt.'

Jesus demonesses with pale eyebrows and gold lashes visited on a Sunday. They spoke a well-intoned Cantonese, which sounded disincarnated coming out of their white faces. They said they had lived in China and respected Chinese. They wanted to come in and talk story. Fingers in black books, they took peeks to see what to say next.

Bak Goong walked about the room to look at these strange women from various angles. No rudeness seemed to discomfit them; when any of the men did some interesting Chinese antic, they complimented him or did not notice. They handed out presents – candy, clothes, toothpaste, combs, soaps, medicines, Jesus pictures, which were grisly cards with a demon nailed to a cross, probably a warning about what happened to you if you didn't convert. In China, Bak Goong had seen pictures of soldiers eating Christians, whose meat looked like drumsticks. The briny men asked the Jesus demonesses, 'Would you administer this medicine to me?' They grinned lewdly at one another, but the demonesses did not see Chinese facial expressions. The men brushed up against their yellow hair, reached behind and touched it. They talked about what was under the long dresses; no lady would understand anyway.

A mischievousness came into the room. Bak Goong brewed tea for the ladies. 'It's the custom to drink it all,' he said, scooping sugar into the cups. The sugar made the demonesses thirstier, and they asked for more tea. The men asked for more stories so that the women stayed and stayed. The listeners did like the one about the baby being born and the childless wise men searching for him and finding him. 'Speak English,' Bak

Goong requested. If anybody talked long enough in a foreign language and he heard enough, he understood. At last the ladies got up one at a time, and everyone knew they were going to the outhouse to piss.

Later the men rolled on the flooor laughing. Bak Goong told the origin of the joke they'd played: 'The Story of Chan Moong Gut and the Gambling Wives,' he announced, and clanged his pot-lid cymbals. 'Chan invited all the rich women to his house to play cards while their husbands were at work. He lured them with prizes and pastries. He served them syrup with just a little water. The sweetness made the ladies drink tea and go to the urine bucket continually. No, no, don't laugh yet. There's more. There's more. Chan Moong Gut had wet the rim of the bucket with red paint. That night their husbands beat the ladies. "What man did you allow to paint a red ring around your ass?" the husbands hollered. They spanked their wives' asses redder. Wait till the white demonesses' husbands see their asses.' The men drew rings with lascivious fingers. 'You're going to hell,' said the demon convert China Men. 'Straight to hell, you demons.'

Bak Goong told more stories about Chan Moong Gut, Fortunate Dream Chan, a trickster who never worked but lived by his wits gambling and catching pigs. He used to put chicken shit at the bottom of the rice for the blindman. When the blindman ate past the nicely mounded top, he said, 'Oh, how wonderfully seasoned. How kind to put sauce in my rice.'

'Every morning Chan would shit on his neighbour's doorstep. The first couple of days the neighbour stepped in it when he went out. After that, he opened the door cautiously and cleaned it up, cursing all the while. Chan Moong Gut arranged that this neighbour would run into him at market. Chan was boasting what an undauntable appetite he had. 'I can eat anything,' he said, tricking the people around him into buying him food. They were wagering on how much and how fast he could eat. He was good at sleight of hand, and was hiding food in his clothes. The neighbour thought of a bet, and he set the terms himself instead of letting wily Chan do it. 'I'll bet,' said the neighbour, 'that you can't eat whatever appears on my doorstep tomorrow morning.' Chan Moong Gut took the bet. Instead of shitting on the step, however, he arranged bananas dipped in brown sugar sauce.

The neighbour could barely stand to look, but he felt gratified watching Chan hold his nose and weep as he ate shit. He was glad to give Chan the money and believed that he had caught a pig.' People with the name Chan have asked storytellers to change the trickster's name, or to forget those stories in America.

It wasn't right that Bak Goong had to save his talking until after work when stories would have made the work easier. He grew the habit of clamping his mouth shut in a line, and the sun baked that expression on him. If he opened his mouth, words might tumble forth like coral out of the surf; spit would spout like lava. He still hacked at the cane while coughing: 'Take – that – white – demon. Take – that. Fall – to – the – ground – demon. Cut you – into – pieces. Chop – off – your – legs. Die – snake. Chop you – down – stinky – demon.' His sentences shortened, angry pellets that shot out of him.

He woke one morning and felt a yang wind blow too hot through his body. He forced himself to sit up, not to be left behind among the sick, who were one-third of the workers. He rolled out of bed, stood, and fell. The healthier men were heading out into the humid day. He pulled himself up and dropped into his bunk. Asleep, again and again he seemed to jump out of bed, run sluggishly about gathering his clothes and tools, run through thick air in search of the fields, hear the demon boss in wait for him saying, 'Late. You late, Paké,' only to wake up and find that nothing had been done, no shoes put on, no breakfast eaten. He slept while the gecko lizards tsked-tsked-tsked at his sloth. He slept while a mushroom grew in a corner of the hut. His garden did not cajole him out of bed.

Each time he awoke, he was lying among the sick men, some breathing with clogged lungs like his, some doubled up holding their stomachs, cripples soaking their limbs. A few men looked bodily healthy but did not move. Somebody seemed to be piling dry leaves near the door and lighting them.

In his fever, he yearned so hard for his family that he felt he appeared in China. He reached out his arms and said, 'Wife. Wife, I'm home.' But she said, 'What are you doing here? What are you doing here without the money? Moneyless and bodiless, you better go back to the Sandalwood Mountains. Go back and pick up your money and your body. Go back where you belong. Go now.' He tried to talk to her, but his tongue was heavy and his throat blocked. He awoke certain that he had to cure himself by talking whenever he pleased.

Yin, the cool, was returning a little. Raindrops plunked loudly on the banana and ti leaves. It was what the Hawaiians called a cane-tapping rain. He chuckled with the geckos, their fingers and toes spread like little suctioning stars on the walls and ceilings, where they waited to flick at bugs. They were so sly playing dead, but through their translucent skins he saw their blue hearts beating and their organs swallowing. He shouted to make them leap to the ground. When they hid, he heard their clucking and chuckling. He had learned to recognize some of them individually. He told the sick men around him, 'You can't die because then your poor wife will miss you, your family will go hungry awaiting your pay, and your mother will be uncertain for ever what became of you. If there were only yourself, you would have the luxury of dying. Uncle and Brothers, I have diagnosed our illness. It is a congestion from not talking. What we have to do is talk and talk.

He lurched out to the rain barrel, poured water down his back and splashed it on his face. His wife would have scolded him for drinking cold water, a Sandalwood Mountain habit he was acquiring. He was carrying water to the sicker men when a demon galloped towards him, boss and horse both with cavernous nostrils wide open. Bak Goong turned towards the fields. The demon pushed sick men out the door. He pulled a boy by the hair. Bak Goong could tell he was saying, 'Aha! I caught you malingering, you fake, lazy, sneaky chinaman.' He pointed the whip towards the cane. 'Go work, Paké. No stay sick.' The demons had changed their rules again, no longer sending stragglers back to the huts. Bak Goong put his left arm around the stalks and leaned his face and body against them while his right arm swung at the feet of the cane. He neither sang nor spoke. Unhealthily, he wet handkerchiefs and plastered them on his head.

That evening, he talked an apt story to the silenced men, who had heard it already in the long ago place where there had been mothers and children: 'Old Uncles and Young Uncles, I have an appropriate story to tell. It cannot be left unsaid.' He recalled a land arranged in layers like clouds or stages, where animals, common men and women, kings and gods held adventures. 'Bak-ah, Sook-ah, a long time ago in China, there lived a king who would have given his kingdom for a son. Powerful but childless, sonless, yearning to be a father, he bought ponies of various sizes for his someday son to ride as he grew. He would trot behind his father on tours of the kingdom. Together they would shoot arrows, snare rabbits, and catch fish. Longing to hold his son to his chest, he felt envious looking at ordinary fathers. He read tea leaves and oil wicks looking for a son. But at last, when his wish was granted and his own only boy was born, the queen and the midwives hesitated to show him the new prince. "Is it a boy?" he asked. "It is a boy, isn't it?" He pushed aside the blanket and saw that on either side of the bald head, the prince had little pointed furry ears like a kitten's. "Oh, no," said the king. "Cat ears. The prince has cat ears. We order everyone present never to tell that the prince has cat ears. Keep our secret. Don't tell the people."

'So the years went by; the prince grew into noble perfection except for the kitty ears. The queen combed his long hair over them. Only in appearance were the ears strange; the prince heard as clearly as anyone else. The subjects exclaimed over his handsomeness. The king never mentioned the cat ears, and so the secret grew large inside his chest and mouth.

'One day when the boy was almost grown, the king could not hold the secret inside himself any more. He walked alone in a winter field, where he scooped out a hole. He shouted into it, "The king's son has cat ears. The king's son has cat ears." He shouted until he was empty of his secret, and satisfied, relieved, he pushed the dirt back into the hole and stamped it down.

'In the spring, grass grew in that field, and when the wind blew through it, the people heard words. The sounds swelled through the summer, enunciated until the people knew for sure what the tall grass and the wind said louder and louder: "The king's son has cat ears. The king's son has cat ears." It grew into a song. "The king's son has cat ears." The news spread throughout the land. It made the people laugh to hear it.'

The listening men thought how they would love their baby

boy even if he had cat ears; he'd be even cuter with cat ears. They would brag as they handed out red eggs to the other un-familied men, who would come to visit the baby. 'See?' the fathers would say. 'Cat ears. Bet you've never seen anything like them.' 'Eh, Father,' the other China Men would say enviously. 'A father, are you?' They'd make much of giving the baby red money.

The next day the men ploughed, working purposefully, but they dug a circle instead of straight furrows. They dug a wide hole. They threw down their tools and flopped on the ground with their faces over the edge of the hole and their legs like wheel spokes.

'Hello down there in China!' they shouted. 'Hello, Mother.' 'Hello, my heart and my liver.'

'I miss you.' 'What are you doing right now?' 'Happy birthday. Happy birthday for last year too.'

'I've been working hard for you, and I hate it.'

'Sometimes I forget my family and go to clubs. I drink all night.' 'I lost all the money again.' 'I've become an opium addict.' 'I don't even look Chinese any more.' 'I'm sorry I ate it all by myself.'

'. . . and I fell to my knees at the sight of twenty waterfalls.' 'I saw only one sandalwood tree.'

They said any kind of thing. 'Blonde demoness.' 'Polynesian demoness.'

'I'm coming home by and by.' 'I'm not coming home.' 'I'm staying here in the Sandalwood Mountains.'

'I want to be home,' Bak Goong said.

'I'm bringing her home,' said Bak Sook Goong.

They had dug an ear into the world, and were telling the earth their secrets.

'I want home,' Bak Goong yelled, pressed against the soil, and smelling the earth. 'I want my home,' the men yelled to-gether. 'I want home. Home. Home. Home. Home.'

Talked out, they buried their words, planted them. 'Like cats covering shit,' they laughed.

'That wasn't a custom,' said Bak Goong. 'We made it up. We can make up customs because we're the founding ancestors of this place.'

They made such a noise that the demons could have come charging upon them and the hole fill with the sounds of battle. But the demons hid, the China Men so riled up, who knows what they were up to?

From the day of the shout party, Bak Goong talked and sang at his work, and did not get sent to the punishment fields. In cutting season, the demons no longer accompanied the knife-wielding China Men into deep cane.

Soon the new green shoots would rise, and when in two years the cane grew gold tassels, what stories the wind would tell.

Bak Goong, the great grandfather with a good memory, kept his promises and so chose to go back to China. Bak Sook Goong also went back, though the king and queen of the Sandalwood Mountains had ruled that a China Man who married a Hawaiian would be called Hawaiian, and many another Paké godfather stayed. Bak Sook Goong brought his Sandalwood Mountain wife back with him. She would become sister of his other two wives. He would abandon none of them. So these two great grandfathers made their lives of a piece.

On mortality

As you know, any plain person you chance to meet can prove to be a powerful immortal in disguise come to test you.

Li Fu-yen told a story about Tu Tzu-chun, who lived from AD 558 to 618, during the Northern Chou and Sui dynasties. Tu's examiner was a Taoist monk, who made him rich twice, and twice Tu squandered his fortune though it took him two lifetimes to do so. The third time the Taoist gave him money, he bought a thousand li of good land, ploughed it himself, seeded it, built houses, roads, and bridges, then welcomed widows and orphans to live on it. With the leftover money, he found a husband for each spinster and a wife for every bachelor in his family, and also paid for the weddings. When he met the Taoist again, he said, 'I've used up all your money on the unfortunates I've come across.'

'You'll have to repay me by working for me,' said the Taoist monk. 'I need your help on an important difficult task.' He gave Tu three white pills. 'Swallow these,' he said, pouring him a cup of wine. 'All that you'll see and feel will be illusions. No matter what happens, don't speak; don't scream. Remember the saying "Hide your broken arms in your sleeves." '

'How easy,' said Tu as he swallowed the pills in three gulps of wine. 'Why should I scream if I know they're illusions?'

Level by level he descended into the nine hells. At first he saw oxheads, horsefaces, and the heads of generals decapitated in war. Illusions. Only illusions, harmless. He laughed at the heads. He had seen heads before. Soon fewer heads whizzed through the dark until he saw no more of them.

Suddenly his wife was being tortured. Demons were cutting her up into pieces, starting with her toes. He heard her scream; he heard her bones crack. He reminded himself that she was an illusion. *Illusion*, he thought. She was ground into bloodmeal.

Then the tortures on his own body began. Demons poured bronze down his throat and beat him with iron clubs and chains. They mortar-and-pestled and packed him into a pill.

He had to walk over mountains of knives and through fields of knives and forests of swords. He was killed, his head chopped off, rolling into other people's nightmares.

He heard gods and goddesses talking about him, 'This man is too wicked to be reborn a man. Let him be born a woman.' He saw the entrance of a black tunnel and felt tired. He would have to squeeze his head and shoulders down into that enclosure and travel a long distance. He pushed head first through the entrance, only the beginning. A god kicked him in the butt to give him a move on. (This kick is the reason many Chinese babies have a blue-grey spot on their butts or lower backs, the 'Mongolian spot'.) Sometimes stuck in the tunnel, sometimes shooting helplessly through it, he emerged again into light with many urgent things to do, many messages to deliver, but his hands were useless baby's hands, his legs wobbly baby's legs, his voice a wordless baby's cries. Years had to pass before he could regain adult powers; he howled as he began to forget the cosmos, his attention taken up with mastering how to crawl, how to stand, how to walk, how to control his bowel movements.

He discovered that he had been reborn a deaf-mute female named Tu. When she became a woman, her parents married her to a man named Lu, who at first did not mind. 'Why does she need to talk,' said Lu, 'to be a good wife? Let her set an example for women.' They had a child. But years later, Lu tired of Tu's dumbness. 'You're just being stubborn,' he said, and lifted their children by the feet. 'Talk, or I'll dash its head against the rocks.' The poor mother held her hand to her mouth. Lu swung the child, broke its head against the wall.

Tu shouted out, 'Oh! Oh!' – and he was back with the Taoist, who sadly told him that at the moment when she had said, 'Oh! Oh!' the Taoist was about to complete the last step in making the elixir for immortality. Now that Tu had broken his silence, the formula was spoiled, no immortality for the human race. 'You overcame joy and sorrow, anger, fear, and evil desire, but not love,' said the Taoist and went on his way.

On mortality again

The last deed of Maui the Trickster, the Polynesian demigod who played jokes, pushed the sky higher, roped the sun with braided pubic hair from his mother, pulled the land up out of the ocean, and brought fire to the earth, was to seek immortality for men and women by stealing it from Hina of the Night. He instructed the people, the beasts, the birds, and the elements to be silent. Hunters walked through forests and fishermen waited in this same silence. In silence the snarer caught birds alive, plucked the few red feathers, and released them; the seer read the clouds, heard spirits and did not disturb them. Children learned and worked silently. There was a chant that could hardly be discerned from silence. Maui dived into the ocean, where he found great Hina asleep. Through her vagina like a door, he entered her body. He took her heart in his arms. He had started tunnelling out feet first when a bird, at the sight of his legs wiggling out of the vagina, laughed. Hina awoke and shut herself, and Maui died.

The grandfather of the Sierra Nevada mountains

The trains used to cross the sky. The house jumped and dust shook down from the attic. Sometimes two trains ran parallel going in opposite directions; the railroad men walked on top of the leaning cars, stepped off one train on to the back of the other, and travelled the opposite way. They headed for the caboose while the train moved against their walk, or they walked towards the engine while the train moved out from under their feet. Hoboes ran alongside, caught the ladders, and swung aboard. I would have to learn to ride like that, choose my boxcar, grab a ladder at a run, and fling myself up and sideways into an open door. Elsewhere I would step smoothly off. Bad runaway boys lost their legs trying for such rides. The train craunched past – pistons stroking like elbows and knees, the coal cars dropping coal, cows looking out between the slats of the cattlecars, the boxcars almost stringing together sentences – Hydro-Cushion, Georgia Flyer, Route of the Eagle – and suddenly sunlight filled the windows again, the slough wide again and waving with tules, for which the city was once named; red-winged blackbirds and squirrels settled. We children ran to the tracks and found the nails we'd placed on them; the wheels had flattened them into knives that sparked.

Once in a while an adult said, 'Your grandfather built the railroad.' (Or 'Your grandfathers built the railroad.' Plural and singular are by context.) We children believed that it was that very railroad, those trains, those tracks running past our house; our own giant grandfather had set those very logs into the ground, poured the iron for those very spikes with the big heads and pounded them until the heads spread like that, mere nails to him. He had built the railroad so that trains would thunder over us, on a street that inclined towards us. We lived on a special spot of the earth, Stockton, the only city on the Pacific coast with three railroads – the Santa Fe, Southern Pacific, and Western Pacific. The three railroads intersecting accounted for the flocks of hoboes. The few times that the train stopped, the cows moaned all night, their hooves stumbling crowdedly and banging against the wood.

Grandfather left a railroad for his message: We had to go somewhere difficult. Ride a train. Go somewhere important. In case of danger, the train was to be ready for us.

The railroad men disconnected the rails and took the steel away. They did not come back. Our family dug up the square logs and rolled them downhill home. We collected the spikes too. We used the logs for benches, edged the yard with them, made bases for fences, embedded them in the ground for walkways. The spikes came in handy too, good for paperweights, levers, wedges, chisels. I am glad to know exactly the weight of ties and the size of nails.

Grandfather's picture hangs in the dining room next to an equally large one of Grandmother, and another one of Guan Goong, God of War and Literature. My grandparents' similarity is in the set of their mouths; they seem to have hauled with their mouths. My mouth also feels the tug and strain of weights in its corners. In the family album, Grandfather wears a greatcoat and Western shoes, but his ankles show. He hasn't shaved either. Maybe he became sloppy after the Japanese soldier bayoneted his head for not giving directions. Or he was born slow and without a sense of direction.

The photographer came to the village regularly and set up a spinet, potted trees, an ornate table stacked with hardbound books of matching size, and a backdrop with a picture of paths curving through gardens into panoramas; he lent his subjects dressy ancient mandarin clothes, Western suits, and hats. An aunt tied the fingers of the lame cousin to a book, the string leading down his sleeve; he looks like he's carrying it. The family hurried from clothes chests to mirrors without explaining to Grandfather, hiding Grandfather. In the family album are group pictures with Grandmother in the middle, the family arranged on either side of her and behind her, second wives at the ends, no Grandfather. Grandmother's earrings, bracelets, and rings are tinted jade green, everything and everybody else

126

black and white, her little feet together neatly, two knobs at the bottom of her gown. My mother, indignant that nobody had readied Grandfather, threw his greatcoat over his nightclothes, shouted, 'Wait! Wait!' and encouraged him into the sunlight. 'Hurry,' she said, and he ran, coat flapping, to be in the picture. She would have slipped him into the group and had the camera catch him like a peeping ghost, but Grandmother chased him away. 'What a waste of film,' she said. Grandfather always appears alone with white stubble on his chin. He was a thin man with big eyes that looked straight ahead. When we children talked about overcoat men, exhibitionists, we meant Grandfather, Ah Goong, who must have yanked open that greatcoat – no pants.

MaMa was the only person to listen to him, and so he followed her everywhere, and talked and talked. What he liked telling was his journeys to the Gold Mountain. He wasn't smart, yet he travelled there three times. Left to himself, he would have stayed in China to play with babies or stayed in the United States once he got there, but Grandmother forced him to leave both places. 'Make money,' she said. 'Don't stay here eating.' 'Come home,' she said.

Ah Goong sat outside her open door when MaMa worked. (In those days a man did not visit a good woman alone unless married to her.) He saw her at her loom and came running with his chair. He told her that he had found a wondrous country, really gold, and he himself had gotten two bags of it, one of which he had had made into a ring. His wife had given that ring to their son for his wedding ring. 'That ring on your finger,' he told Mother, 'proves that the Gold Mountain exists and that I went there.'

Another of his peculiarities was that he heard the crackles, bangs, gunshots that go off when the world lurches; the gears on its axis snap. Listening to a faraway New Year, he had followed the noise and come upon the blasting in the Sierras. (There is a Buddhist instruction that that which is most elusive must, of course, be the very thing to be pursued; listen to the farthest sound.) The Central Pacific hired him on sight; chinamen had a natural talent for explosions. Also there were not enough work-ingmen to do all the labour of building a new country. Some of the banging came from the war to decide whether or not black people would continue to work for nothing.

Slow as usual, Ah Goong arrived in the spring; the work had begun in January 1863. The demon that hired him pointed up and up, east above the hills of poppies. His first job was to fell a redwood, which was thick enough to divide into three or four beams. His tree's many branches spread out, each limb like a little tree. He circled the tree. How to attack it? No side looked like the side made to be cut, nor did any ground seem the place for it to fall. He axed for almost a day the side he'd decided would hit the ground. Halfway through, imitating the other lumberjacks, he struck the other side of the tree, above the cut, until he had to run away. The tree swayed and slowly dived to earth, creaking and screeching like a green animal. He was so awed, he forgot what he was supposed to yell. Hardly any branches broke; the tree sprang, bounced, pushed at the ground with its arms. The limbs did not wilt and fold; they were a small forest, which he chopped. The trunk lay like a long red torso; sap ran from its cuts like crying blind eyes. At last it stopped fighting. He set the log across sawhorses to be cured over smoke and in the sun.

He joined a team of men who did not axe one another as they took alternate hits. They blew up the stumps with gunpowder. 'It was like uprooting a tooth,' Ah Goong said. They also packed gunpowder at the roots of a whole tree. Not at the same time as the bang but before that, the tree rose from the ground. It stood, then plunged with a tearing of veins and muscles. It was big enough to carve a house into. The men measured themselves against the upturned white roots, which looked like claws, a sun with claws. A hundred men stood or sat on the trunk. They lifted a wagon on it and took a photograph. The demons also had their photograph taken.

Because these mountains were made out of gold, Ah Goong rushed over to the root hole to look for gold veins and ore. He selected the shiniest rocks to be assayed later in San Francisco. When he drank from the streams and saw a flash, he dived in like a duck; only sometimes did it turn out to be the sun or the water. The very dirt winked with specks.

He made a dollar a day salary. The lucky men gambled, but

he was not good at remembering game rules. The work so far was endurable. 'I could take it,' he said.

The days were sunny and blue, the wind exhilarating, the heights godlike. At night the stars were diamonds, crystals, silver, snow, ice. He had never seen diamonds. He had never seen snow and ice. As spring turned into summer, and he lay under that sky, he saw the order in the stars. He recognized constellations from China. There – not a cloud but the Silver River, and there, on either side of it – Altair and Vega, the Spinning Girl and the Cowboy, far, far apart. He felt his heart breaking of loneliness at so much blue-black space between star and star. The railroad he was building would not lead him to his family. He jumped out of his bedroll. 'Look! Look!' Other China Men jumped awake. An accident? An avalanche? Injun demons? 'The stars,' he said. 'The stars are here.' 'Another China Man gone out of his mind,' men grumbled. 'A sleepwalker.' 'Go to sleep, sleepwalker.' 'There. And there,' said Ah Goong, two hands pointing. 'The Spinning Girl and the Cowboy. Don't you see them?' 'Homesick China Man,' said the China Men and pulled their blankets over their heads. 'Didn't you know they were here? I could have told you they were here. Same as in China. Same moon. Why not same stars?' 'Nah. Those are American stars.'

Pretending that a little girl was listening, he told himself the story about the Spinning Girl and the Cowboy: A long time ago they had visited earth, where they met, fell in love, and married. Instead of growing used to each other, they remained enchanted their entire lifetimes and beyond. They were too happy. They wanted to be doves or two branches of the same tree. When they returned to live in the sky, they were so engrossed in each other that they neglected their work. The Queen of the Sky scratched a river between them with one stroke of her silver hairpin – the river a galaxy in width. The lovers suffered, but she did devote her time to spinning now, and he herded his cow. The King of the Sky took pity on them and ordered that once each year, they be allowed to meet. On the seventh day of the seventh month (which is not the same as 7 July), magpies form a bridge for them to cross to each other. The lovers are together for one night of the year. On their parting, the Spinner cries the heavy summer rains.

Ah Goong's discovery of the two stars gave him something to look forward to besides meals and tea breaks. Every night he located Altair and Vega and gauged how much closer they had come since the night before. During the day he watched the magpies, big black and white birds with round bodies like balls with wings; they were a welcome sight, a promise of meetings. He had found two familiars in the wilderness: magpies and stars. On the meeting day, he did not see any magpies nor hear their chattering jaybird cries. Some black and white birds flew overhead, but they may have been American crows or late magpies on their way. Some men laughed at him, but he was not the only China Man to collect water in pots, bottles, and canteens that day. The water would stay fresh for ever and cure anything. In ancient days the tutelary gods of the mountains sprinkled corpses with this water and brought them to life. That night, no women to light candles, burn incense, cook special food, Grandfather watched for the convergence and bowed. He saw the two little stars next to Vega – the couple's children. And bridging the Silver River, surely those were black flapping wings of magpies and translucent-winged angels and faeries. Towards morning, he was awakened by rain, and pulled his blankets into his tent.

The next day, the fantailed orange-beaked magpies returned. Altair and Vega were beginning their journeys apart, another year of spinning and herding. Ah Goong had to find something else to look forward to. The Spinning Girl and the Cowboy met and parted six times before the railroad was finished.

When cliffs, sheer drops under impossible overhangs, ended the road, the workers filled the ravines or built bridges over them. They climbed above the site for tunnel or bridge and lowered one another down in wicker baskets made stronger by the lucky words they had painted on four sides. Ah Goong got to be a basketman because he was thin and light. Some basketmen were fifteen-year-old boys. He rode the basket barefoot, so his boots, the kind to stomp snakes with, would not break through the bottom. The basket swung and twirled, and he saw the world sweep underneath him; it was fun in a way, a cold new feeling of doing what had never been done before. Suspended in the quiet sky, he thought all kinds of crazy thoughts, that if a man didn't want to live any more, he could just cut the ropes or, easier, tilt the basket, dip, and never have to wory again. He could spread his arms, and the air would momentarily hold him before he fell past the buzzards, hawks, and eagles, and landed impaled on the tip of a sequoia. This high and he didn't see any gods, no Cowboy, no Spinner. He knelt in the basket though he was not bumping his head against the sky. Through the wicker-work, slivers of depths darted like needles, nothing between him and air but thin rattan. Gusts of wind spun the light basket. 'Aiya,' said Ah Goong. Winds came up under the basket, bouncing it. Neighbouring baskets swung together and parted. He and the man next to him looked at each other's faces. They laughed. They might as well have gone to Malaysia to collect bird nests. Those who had done high work there said it had been worse; the birds screamed and scratched at them. Swinging near the cliff, Ah Goong stood up and grabbed it by a twig. He dug holes, then inserted gunpowder and fuses. He worked neither too fast, nor too slow, keeping even with the others. The basketmen sig-nalled one another to light the fuses. He struck match after match and dropped the burnt matches over the sides. At last his fuse caught; he waved, and the men above pulled hand over hand hauling him up, pulleys creaking. The scaffolds stood like a row of gibbets. Gallows trees along a ridge. 'Hurry, hurry,' he said. Some impatient men clambered up their ropes. Ah Goong ran up the ledge road they'd cleared and watched the explosions, which banged almost synchronously, echoes booming like war. He moved his scaffold to the next section of cliff and went down in the basket again, with bags of dirt, and set the next charge.

This time two men were blown up. One knocked out or killed by the explosion fell silently, the other screaming, his arms and legs struggling. A desire shot out of Ah Goong for an arm long enough to reach down and catch them. Much time passed as they fell like plummets. The shreds of baskets and a cowboy hat skimmed and tacked. The winds that pushed birds off course and against mountains did not carry men. Ah Goong also wished that the conscious man would fall faster and get it over with. His hands gripped the ropes, and it was difficult to let go and get on with the work. 'It can't happen twice in a row,' the bas-ketmen said the next trip down. 'Our chances are very good.

The trip after an accident is probably the safest one.' They raced to their favourite basket, tested the pulleys, oiled them, reminded the pulleymen about the signals, and entered the sky again.

Another time, Ah Goong had been lowered to the bottom of a ravine, which had to be cleared for the base of a trestle, when a man fell, and he saw his face. He had not died of shock before hitting bottom. His hands were grabbing at air. His stomach and groin must have felt the fall all the way down. At night Ah Goong woke up falling, though he slept on the ground, and heard other men call out in their sleep. No warm women tweaked their ears and hugged them. 'It was only a falling dream,' he reassured himself.

Across a valley, a chain of men working on the next mountain, men like ants changing the face of the world, fell, but it was very far away. Godlike, he watched men whose faces he could not see and whose screams he did not hear roll and bounce and slide like a handful of sprinkled gravel.

After a fall, the buzzards circled the spot and reminded the workers for days that a man was dead down there. The men threw piles of rocks and branches to cover bodies from sight.

The mountainface reshaped, they drove supports for a bridge. Since hammering was less dangerous than the blowing up, the men played a little; they rode the baskets swooping in wide arcs; they twisted the ropes and let them unwind like tops. 'Look at me,' said Ah Goong, pulled open his pants, and pissed overboards, the wind scattering the drops. 'I'm a waterfall,' he said. He had sent a part of himself hurtling. On rare windless days he watched his piss fall in a continuous stream from himself almost to the bottom of the valley.

One beautiful day, dangling in the sun above a new valley, not the desire to urinate but sexual desire clutched him so hard he bent over in the basket. He curled up, overcome by beauty and fear, which shot to his penis. He tried to rub himself calm. Suddenly he stood up tall and squirted out into space. 'I am fucking the world,' he said. The world's vagina was big, big as the sky, big as a valley. He grew a habit: whenever he was lowered in the basket, his blood rushed to his penis, and he fucked the world.

Then it was autumn, and the wind blew so fiercely, the men had to postpone the basketwork. Clouds moved in several directions at once. Men pointed at dust devils, which turned their mouths crooked. There was ceaseless motion; clothes kept moving; hair moved; sleeves puffed out. Nothing stayed still long enough for Ah Goong to figure it out. The wind sucked the breath out of his mouth and blew thoughts from his brains. The food convoys from San Francisco brought tents to replace the ones that whipped away. The baskets from China, which the men saved for high work, carried cowboy jackets, long underwear, Levi pants, boots, earmuffs, leather gloves, flannel shirts, coats. They sewed rabbit fur and deerskin into the linings. They tied the wide brims of their cowboy hats over their ears with mufflers. And still the wind made confusing howls into ears, and it was hard to think.

The days became nights when the crews tunnelled inside the mountain, which sheltered them from the wind, but also hid the light and sky. Ah Goong pickaxed the mountain, the dirt filling his nostrils through a cowboy bandanna. He shovelled the dirt into a cart and pushed it to a place that was tall enough for the mule, which hauled it the rest of the way out. He looked forward to cart duty to edge closer to the entrance. Eyes darkened, nose plugged, his windy cough worse, he was to mole a thousand feet and meet others digging from the other side. How much he'd pay now to go swinging in a basket. He might as well have gone to work in a tin mine. Coming out of the tunnel at the end of a shift, he forgot whether it was supposed to be day or night. He blew his nose fifteen times before the mucus cleared again.

The dirt was the easiest part of tunnelling. Beneath the soil, they hit granite. Ah Goong struck it with his pickaxe, and it jarred his bones, chattered his teeth. He swung his sledgehammer against it, and the impact rang in the dome of his skull. The mountain that was millions of years old was locked against them and was not to be broken into. The men teased him, 'Let's see you fuck the world now.' 'Let's see you fuck the Gold Mountain now.' But he no longer felt like it. 'A man ought to be made of tougher material than flesh,' he said. 'Skin is too soft. Our bones ought to be filled with iron.' He lifted the hammer high, careful that it not pull him backwards, and let it fall forwards of its own weight against the rock. Nothing happened to that grey wall; he had to slam with strength and will. He hit at the same spot over and over again, the same rock. Some chips and flakes broke off. The granite looked everywhere the same. It had no softer or weaker spots anywhere, the same hard grey. He learned to slide his hand up the handle, lift, slide and swing, a circular motion, hammering, hammering, hammering. He would bite like a rat through that mountain. His eyes couldn't see; his nose couldn't smell; and now his ears were filled with the noise of hammering. This rock is what is real, he thought. This rock is what real is, not clouds or mist, which make mysterious promises, and when you go through them are nothing. When the foreman measured at the end of twenty-four hours of pounding, the rock had given a foot. The hammering went on day and night. The men worked eight hours on and eight hours off. They worked on all eighteen tunnels at once. While Ah Goong slept, he could hear the sledge-hammers of other men working in the earth. The steady banging reminded him of holidays and harvests; falling asleep, he heard the women chopping mincemeat and the millstones striking.

The demons in boss suits came into the tunnel occasionally, measured with a yardstick, and shook their heads. 'Faster,' they said. 'Faster. Chinamen too slow. Too slow.' 'Tell us we're slow,' the China Men grumbled. The ones in top tiers of scaffolding let rocks drop, a hammer drop. Ropes tangled around the demons' heads and feet. The cave China Men muttered and flexed, glared out of the corners of their eyes. But usually there was no diversion – one day the same as the next, one hour no different from another – the beating against the same granite.

After tunnelling into granite for about three years, Ah Goong understood the immovability of the earth. Men change, men die, weather changes, but a mountain is the same as permanence and time. This mountain would have taken no new shape for centuries, ten thousand centuries, the world a still, still place, time unmoving. He worked in the tunnel so long, he learned to see many colours in black. When he stumbled out, he tried to talk about time. 'I felt time,' he said. 'I saw time. I saw world.' He tried again, 'I saw what's real. I saw time, and it doesn't move. If we break through the mountain, hollow it, time won't have moved anyway. You translators ought to tell the foreigners that.'

Summers came again, but after the first summer, he felt less nostalgia at the meeting of the Spinning Girl and the Cowboy. He now knew men who had been in this country for twenty years and thirty years, and the Cowboy's one year away from his lady was no time at all. His own patience was longer. The stars were meeting and would meet again next year, but he would not have seen his family. He joined the others celebrating Souls' Day, the holiday a week later, the fourteenth day of the seventh month. The supply wagons from San Francisco and Sacramento brought watermelon, meat, fish, crab, pressed duck. 'There, ghosts, there you are. Come and get it.' They displayed the feast complete for a moment before falling to, eating on the dead's behalf.

In the third year of pounding granite by hand, a demon invented dynamite. The railroad workers were to test it. They had stopped using gunpowder in the tunnels after avalanches, but the demons said that dynamite was more precise. They watched a scientist demon mix nitrate, sulphate, and glycerine, then flick the yellow oil, which exploded off his fingertips. Sitting in a meadow to watch the dynamite detonated in the open, Ah Goong saw the men in front of him leap impossibly high into the air; then he felt a shove as if from a giant's unseen hand – and he fell backward. The boom broke the mountain silence like fear breaking inside stomach and chest and groin. No one had gotten hurt; they stood up laughing and amazed, looking around at how they had fallen, the pattern of the explosion. Dynamite was much more powerful than gunpowder. Ah Goong felt a nudge, as if something kind were moving him out of harm's way. 'All of a sudden I was sitting next to you.' 'Aiya. If we had been nearer, it would have killed us.' 'If we were stiff, it would have gone through us.' 'A fist.' 'A hand.' 'We leapt like acrobats.' Next time Ah Goong flattened himself on the ground, and the explosion rolled over him.

He never got used to the blasting; a blast always surprised him. Even when he himself set the fuse and watched it burn, anticipated the explosion, the bang – *bahng* in Chinese – when it came, always startled. It cleaned the crazy words, the crackling, and bingbangs out of his brain. It was like New Year's, when every problem and thought was knocked clean out of him by firecrackers, and he could begin fresh. He couldn't worry during an explosion, which jerked every head to attention. Hills flew up in rocks and dirt. Boulders turned over and over. Sparks, fires, debris, rocks, smoke burst up, not at the same time as the boom (*bum*) but before that – the sound a separate occurrence, not useful as a signal.

The terrain changed immediately. Streams were diverted, rockscapes exposed. Ah Goong found it difficult to remember what land had looked like before an explosion. It was a good thing the dynamite was invented after the Civil War to the east was over.

The dynamite added more accidents and ways of dying, but if it were not used, the railroad would take fifty more years to finish. Nitroglycerine exploded when it was jounced on a horse or dropped. A man who fell with it in his pocket blew himself into red pieces. Sometimes it combusted merely standing. Human bodies skipped through the air like puppets and made Ah Goong laugh crazily as if the arms and legs would come together again. The smell of burned flesh remained in rocks.

In the tunnels, the men bored holes fifteen to eighteen inches deep with a power drill, stuffed them with hay and dynamite, and imbedded the fuse in sand. Once, for extra pay, Ah Goong ran back in to see why some dynamite had not gone off and hurried back out again; it was just a slow fuse. When the explosion settled, he helped carry two-hundred-, three-hundred-, five-hundred-pound boulders out of the tunnel.

As a boy he had visited a Taoist monastery where there were nine rooms, each a replica of one of the nine hells. Lifesize sculptures of men and women were spitted on turning wheels. Eerie candles under the suffering faces emphasized eyes poked out, tongues pulled, red mouths and eyes, and real hair, eyelashes, and eyebrows. Women were split apart and men dismembered. He could have reached out and touched the sufferers and the implements. He had dug and dynamited his way into one of these hells. 'Only here there are eighteen tunnels, not nine, plus all the tracks between them,' he said.

One day he came out of the tunnel to find the mountains white, the evergreens and bare trees decorated, white tree sculptures and lace bushes everywhere. The men from snow country called the icicles 'ice chopsticks'. He sat in his basket and slid down the slopes. The snow covered the gouged land, the broken trees, the tracks, the mud, the campfire ashes, the unburied dead. Streams were stilled in mid-run, the water petrified. That winter he thought it was the task of the human race to quicken the world, blast the freeze, fire it, redden it with blood. He had to change the stupid slowness of one sunrise and one sunset per day. He had to enliven the silent world with sound. 'The rock,' he tried to tell the others. 'The ice.' 'Time.'

The dynamiting loosed blizzards on the men. Ears and toes fell off. Fingers stuck to the cold silver rails. Snowblind men stumbled about with bandannas over their eyes. Ah Goong helped build wood tunnels roofing the track route. Falling ice scrabbled on the roofs. The men stayed under the snow for weeks at a time. Snowslides covered the entrances to the tunnels, which they had to dig out to enter and exit, white tunnels and black tunnels. Ah Goong looked at his gang and thought, If there is an avalanche, these are the people I'll be trapped with, and wondered which ones would share food. A party of snowbound barbarians had eaten the dead. Cannibals, thought Ah Goong, and looked around. Food was not scarce, the tea man brought whisky barrels of hot tea, and he warmed his hands and feet, held the teacup to his nose and ears. Someday, he planned, he would buy a chair with metal doors for putting hot coal inside it. The magpies did not abandon him but stayed all winter and searched the snow for food.

The men who died slowly enough to say last words said, 'Don't leave me frozen under the snow. Send my body home. Burn it and put the ashes in a tin can. Take the bone jar when you come down the mountain.' 'When you ride the first car back to China, tell my descendants to come for me.' 'Shut up,' scolded the hearty men. 'We don't want to hear about bone jars and dying.' 'You're lucky to have a body to bury, not blown to smithereens.' 'Stupid man to hurt yourself,' they bawled out the sick and wounded. How their wives would scold if they brought back deadmen's bones. 'Aiya. To be buried here, nowhere.' 'But this is somewhere,' Ah Goong promised. 'This is Gold Mountain. We're marking the land now. The track sections are numbered, and your family will know where we leave you.' But he was a crazy man, and they didn't listen to him.

Spring did come, and when the snow melted, it revealed the past year, what had happened, what they had done, where they had worked, the lost tools, the thawing bodies, some standing with tools in hand, the bright rails. 'Remember Uncle Long Winded Leong?' 'Remember Strong Back Wong?' 'Remember Lee Brother?' 'And Fong Uncle?' They lost count of the number dead; there is no record of how many died building the railroad. Or maybe it was demons doing the counting and chinamen not worth counting. Whether it was good luck or bad luck the dead were buried or cairned next to the last section they had worked on. 'May his ghost not have to toil,' they said over graves. (In China a woodcutter ghost chops eternally; people have heard chopping in the snow and in the heat.) 'Maybe his ghost will ride the train home.' The scientific demons said the transcontinental railroad would connect the West to Cathay. 'What if he rides back and forth from Sacramento to New York for ever?' 'That wouldn't be so bad. I hear the cars will be like houses on wheels.' The funerals were short. 'No time. No time,' said both China Men and demons. The railroad was as straight as they could build it, but no ghosts sat on the tracks; no strange presences haunted the tunnels. The blasts scared ghosts away.

When the Big Dipper pointed east and the China Men detonated nitroglycerine and shot off guns for the New Year, which comes with the spring, these special bangs were not as loud as the daily bangs, not as numerous as the bangs all year. Shouldn't the New Year be the loudest day of all to obliterate the noises of the old year? But to make a bang of that magnitude, they would have to blow up at least a year's supply of dynamite in one blast. They arranged strings of chain reactions in circles and long lines, banging faster and louder to culminate in a big bang. And most importantly, there were random explosions – surprise. Surprise. SURPRISE. They had no dragon, the railroad their dragon.

The demons invented games for working faster, gold coins for miles of track laid, for the heaviest rock, a grand prize for the first team to break through a tunnel. Day shifts raced against night shifts, China Men against Welshmen, China Men against Irishmen, China Men against Injuns and black demons. The fastest races were China Men against China Men, who bet on their own teams. China Men always won because of good team-work, smart thinking, and the need for the money. Also, they had the most workers to choose teams from. Whenever his team won anything, Ah Goong added to his gold stash. The Central Pacific or Union Pacific won the land on either side of the tracks it built.

One summer day, demon officials and China Man translators went from group to group and announced, 'We're raising the pay – thirty-five dollars a month. Because of your excellent work, the Central Pacific Railroad is giving you a four-dollar raise per month.' The workers who didn't know better cheered. 'What's the catch?' said the smarter men. 'You'll have the opportunity to put in more time,' said the railroad demons. 'Two more hours per shift.' Ten-hour shifts inside the tunnels. 'It's not ten hours straight,' said the demons. 'You have time off for tea and meals. Now that you have dynamite the work isn't so hard.' They had been working for three and a half years already, and the track through the Donner Summit was still not done.

The workers discussed the ten-hour shift, swearing their China Man obscenities. 'Two extra hours a day – sixty hours a month for four dollars.' 'Pig catcher demons.' 'Snakes.' 'Turtles.' 'Dead demons.' 'A human body can't work like that.' 'The demons don't believe this is a human body. This is a chinaman's body.' To bargain, they sent a delegation of English speakers, who were summarily noted as troublemakers, turned away, docked.

The China Men, then, decided to go on strike and demand forty-five dollars a month and the eight-hour shift. They risked going to gaol and the Central Pacific keeping the pay it was banking for them. Ah Goong memorized the English, 'Forty-five dollars a month – eight-hour shift.' He practised the strike slogan: 'Eight hours a day good for white man, all the same good for China Man.'

The men wrapped barley and beans in ti leaves, which came from Hawai'i via San Francisco, for celebrating the fifth day of the fifth month (not May but mid-June, the summer solstice.) Usually the way the red string is wound and knotted tells what flavours are inside – the salty barley with pickled egg, or beans and pork, or the gelatin pudding. Ah Goong folded ti leaves into a cup and packed it with food. One of the literate men slipped in a piece of paper with the strike plan, and Ah Goong tied the bundle with a special pattern of red string. The time and place for the revolution against Kublai Khan had been hidden inside autumn mooncakes. Ah Goong looked from one face to another in admiration. Of course, of course. No China Men, no railroad. They were indispensable labour. Throughout these mountains were brothers and uncles with a common idea, free men, not coolies, calling for fair working conditions. The demons were not suspicious as the China Men went gandying up and down the track delivering the bundles tied together like lines of fish. They had exchanged these gifts every year. When the summer solstice cakes came from other camps, the recipients cut them into neat slices by drawing the string through them. The orange jellies, which had a red dye stick inside soaked in lye, fell into a series of sunrises and sunsets. The aged yolks and the barley also looked like suns. The notes gave a Yes strike vote. The yellow flags to ward off the five evils – centipedes, scorpions, snakes, poisonous lizards, and toads – now flew as banners.

The strike began on Tuesday morning, 25 June 1867. The men who were working at that hour walked out of the tunnels and away from the tracks. The ones who were sleeping slept on and shaved their moustaches and wild beards. Some went fishing and hunting. The violinists tuned and played their instruments. The drummers beat theirs at the punchlines of jokes. The gamblers shuffled and played their cards and tiles. The smokers passed their pipes, and the drinkers bet for drinks by making figures with their hands. The cooks made party food. The opera singers' falsettos almost perforated the mountains. The men sang new songs about the railroad. They made up verses and shouted Ho at the good ones, and laughed at the rhymes. Oh, they were madly singing in the mountains. The storytellers told about the rise of new kings. The opium smokers when they roused themselves told their florid images. Ah Goong sifted for gold. All the while the English-speaking China Men, who were being advised by the shrewdest bargainers, were at the demons' headquarters repeating the demand: 'Eight hours a day good for white man, all the same good for China Man.' They had probably negotiated the demons down to nine-hour shifts by now.

The sounds of hammering continued along the tracks and occasionally there were blasts from the tunnels. The scabby white demons had refused to join the strike. 'Eight hours a day good for white man, all the same good for China Men,' the China Men explained to them. 'Cheap John Chinaman,' said the demons, many of whom had red hair. The China Men scowled out of the corners of their eyes.

On the second day, artist demons climbed the mountains to draw the China Men for the newspapers. The men posed barechested, their fists clenched, showing off their arms and backs. The artists sketched them as perfect young gods reclining against rocks, wise expressions on their handsome noble-nosed faces, long torsos with lean stomachs, a strong arm extended over a bent knee, long fingers holding a pipe, a rope of hair over a wide shoulder. Other artists drew faeries with antennae for eyebrows and brownies with elvish pigtails; they danced in white socks and black slippers among mushroom rings by moonlight.

Ah Goong acquired another idea that added to his reputation for craziness: The pale, thin Chinese scholars and the rich men fat like Buddhas were less beautiful, less manly than these brown muscular railroad men, of whom he was one. One of ten thousand heroes.

On the third day, in a woods – he would be looking at a deer or a rabbit or an Injun watching him before he knew what he was seeing – a demon dressed in a white suit and tall hat beckoned him. They talked privately in the wilderness. The demon said, 'I Citizenship Judge invite you to be US citizen. Only one bag gold.' Ah Goong was thrilled. What an honour. He would accept this invitation. Also what advantages, he calculated shrewdly; if he were going to be jailed for this strike, an American would have a trial. The Citizenship Judge unfurled a parchment sealed with gold and ribbon. Ah Goong bought it with one bag of gold. 'You vote,' said the Citizenship Judge. 'You talk in court, buy land, no more chinaman tax.' Ah Goong hid the paper on his person so that it would protect him from arrest and lynching. He was already a part of this new country, but now he had it in writing.

The fourth day, the strikers heard that the US Cavalry was riding single file up the tracks to shoot them. They argued whether to engage the Army with dynamite. But the troops did not come. Instead the cowardly demons blockaded the food wagons. No food. Ah Goong listened to the optimistic China Men, who said, 'Don't panic. We'll hold out for ever. We can hunt. We can last fifty days on water.' The complainers said, 'Aiya. Only saints can do that. Only magic men and monks who've practised.' The China Men refused to declare a last day for the strike.

The foresighted China Men had cured jerky, fermented wine, dried and strung orange and grapefruit peels, pickled and preserved leftovers. Ah Goong, one of the best hoarders, had set aside extra helpings from each meal. This same quandary, whether to give away food or to appear selfish, had occurred during each of the six famines he had lived through. The foodless men identified themselves. Sure enough, they were the shiftless, piggy, arrogant type who didn't worry enough. The donors scolded them and shamed them the whole while they were handing them food: 'So you lived like a grasshopper at our expense.' 'Fleaman.' 'You'll be the cause of our not holding out long enough.' 'Rich man's kid. Too good to hoard.' Ah Goong contributed some rice crusts from the bottoms of pans. He kept how much more food he owned a secret, as he kept the secret of his gold. In apology for not contributing richer food, he repeated a Mohist saying that had guided him in China: ' "The superior man does not put humaneness to the point of stupidity." ' He could hear his wife scolding him for feeding strangers. The opium men offered shit and said that it calmed the appetite.

On the fifth and sixth days, Ah Goong organized his possessions and patched his clothes and tent. He forbore repairing carts, picks, ropes, baskets. His work-habituated hands arranged rocks and twigs in designs. He asked a reader to read again his family's letters. His wife sounded like herself except for the polite phrases added professionally at the beginnings and the ends. 'Idiot,' she said, 'why are you taking so long? Are you wasting the money? Are you spending it on girls and gambling and whisky? Here's my advice to you: Be a little more frugal. Remember how it felt to go hungry. Work hard.' He had been an idle man for almost a week. 'I need a new dress to wear to weddings. I refuse to go to another banquet in the same old dress. If you weren't such a spendthrift, we could be building the new courtyard where we'll drink wine among the flowers and sit about in silk gowns all day. We'll hire peasants to till the fields. Or lease them to tenants, and buy all our food at market. We'll have clean fingernails and toenails.' Other relatives said, 'I need a gold watch. Send me the money. Your wife gambles it away and throws parties and doesn't disburse it fairly among us. You might as well come home.' It was after one of these letters that he had made a bonus investigating some dud dynamite.

Ah Goong did not spend his money on women. The strikers passed the word that a woman was travelling up the railroad and would be at his camp on the seventh and eighth day of the strike. Some said she was a demoness and some that she was a Chinese and her master a China Man. He pictured a nurse coming to bandage wounds and touch foreheads or a princess suveying her subjects; or perhaps she was a merciful Jesus demoness. But she was a pitiful woman, led on a leash around her waist, not entirely alive. Her owner sold lottery tickets for the use of her. Ah Goong did not buy one. He took out his penis under his blanket or bared it in the woods and thought about nurses and princesses. He also just looked at it, wondering what it was that it was for, what a man was for, what he had to have a penis for.

There was rumour also of an Injun woman called Woman Chief, who led a nomadic fighting tribe from the eastern plains as far as these mountains. She was so powerful that she had four wives and many horses. He never saw her though.

The strike ended on the ninth day. The Central Pacific announced that in its benevolence it was giving the workers a four-dollar raise, not the fourteen dollars they had asked for. And that the shifts in the tunnels would remain eight hours long. 'We were planning to give you the four-dollar raise all along,' the demons said to diminish the victory. So they got thirty-five dollars a month and the eight-hour shift. They would have won forty-five dollars if the thousand demon workers had joined the strike. Demons would have listened to demons. The China Men went back to work quietly. No use singing and shouting over a compromise and losing nine days' work.

There were two days that Ah Goong did cheer and throw his hat in the air, jumping up and down and screaming Yippee like

143

a cowboy. One: the day his team broke through the tunnel at last. Towards the end they did not dynamite but again used picks and sledgehammers. Through the granite, they heard answering poundings, and answers to their shouts. It was not a mountain before them any more but only a wall with people breaking through from the other side. They worked faster. Forward. Into day. They stuck their arms through the holes and shook hands with men on the other side. Ah Goong saw dirty faces as wondrous as if he were seeing Nu Wo, the creator goddess who repairs cracks in the sky with stone slabs; sometimes she peeks through and human beings see her face. The wall broke. Each team gave the other a gift of half a tunnel, dug. They stepped back and forth where the wall had been. Ah Goong ran and ran, his boots thudding to the very end of the tunnel, looked at the other side of the mountain, and ran back, clear through the entire tunnel. All the way through.

He spent the rest of his time on the railroad laying and bending and hammering the ties and rails. The second day the China Men cheered was when the engine from the West and the one from the East rolled towards one another and touched. The transcontinental railroad was finished. They Yippee'd like madmen. The white demon officials gave speeches. 'The Greatest Feat of the Nineteenth Century,' they said. 'The Greatest Feat in the History of Mankind,' they said. 'Only Americans could have done it,' they said, which is true. Even if Ah Goong had not spent half his gold on Citizenship Papers, he was an American for having built the railroad. A white demon in top hat tap-tapped on the gold spike, and pulled it back out. Then one China Man held the real spike, the steel one, and another hammered it in.

While the demons posed for photographs, the China Men dispersed. It was dangerous to stay. The Driving Out had begun. Ah Goong does not appear in railroad photographs. Scattering, some China Men followed the north star in the constellation Tortoise the Black Warrier to Canada, or they kept the constellation Phoenix ahead of them to South America or the White Tiger west or the Wolf east. Seventy lucky men rode the Union Pacific to Massachusetts for jobs at a shoe factory. Fifteen hundred went to Fou Loy Company in New Orleans and San Francisco, several hundred to plantations in Mississippi, Georgia, and Arkansas, and sugarcane plantations in Louisiana and Cuba. (From the South, they sent word that it was a custom to step off the sidewalk along with the black demons when a white demon walked by.) Seventy went to New Orleans to grade a route for a railroad, then to Pennsylvania to work in a knife factory. The Colorado State Legislature passed a resolution welcoming the railroad China Men to come build the new state. They built railroads in every part of the country – the Alabama and Chattanooga Railroad, the Houston and Texas Railroad, the Southern Pacific, the railroads in Louisiana and Boston, the Pacific Northwest, and Alaska. After the Civil War, China Men banded the nation North and South, East and West, with crisscrossing steel. They were the binding and building ancestors of this place.

Ah Goong would have liked a leisurely walk along the tracks to review his finished handiwork, or to walk east to see the rest of his new country. But instead, Driven Out, he slid down mountains, leapt across valleys and streams, crossed plains, hid sometimes with companions and often alone, and eluded bandits who would hold him up for his railroad pay and shoot him for practice as they shot Injuns and jackrabbits. Detouring and backtracking, his path wound back and forth to his railroad, a familiar silver road in the wilderness. When a train came, he hid against the shaking ground in case a demon with a shotgun was hunting from it. He picked over camps where he had once lived. He was careful to find hidden places to sleep. In China bandits did not normally kill people, the booty the main thing, but here the demons killed for fun and hate. They tied pigtails to horses and dragged chinamen. He decided that he had better head for San Francisco, where he would catch a ship to China.

Perched on hillsides, he watched many sunsets, the place it was setting, the direction he was going. There were fields of grass that he tunnelled through, hid in, rolled in, dived and swam in, suddenly jumped up laughing, suddenly stopped. He needed to find a town and human company. The spooky tumbleweeds caught in barbed wire were peering at him, waiting for him; he had to find a town. Towns grew along the tracks as they did along rivers. He sat looking at a town all day, then ducked into it at night.

At the familiar sight of a garden laid out in a Chinese scheme – vegetables in beds, white cabbages, red plants, chives, and coriander for immortality, herbs boxed with boards – he knocked on the back door. The China Man who answered gave him food, the appropriate food for the nearest holiday, talked story, exclaimed at how close their ancestral villages were to each other. They exchanged information on how many others lived how near, which towns had Chinatowns, what size, two or three stores or a block, which towns to avoid. 'Do you have a wife?' they asked one another. 'Yes. She lives in China. I have been sending money for twenty years now.' They exchanged vegetable seeds, slips, and cuttings, and Ah Goong carried letters to another town or China.

Some demons who had never seen the likes of him gave him things and touched him. He also came across lone China Men who were alarmed to have him appear, and, unwelcome, he left quickly; they must have wanted to be the only China Man of that area, the special China Man.

He met miraculous China Men who had produced families out of nowhere – a wife and children, both boys and girls. 'Uncle,' the children called him, and he wanted to stay to be the uncle of the family. The wife washed his clothes, and he went on his way when they were dry.

On a farm road, he came across an imp child playing in the dirt. It looked at him, and he looked at it. He held out a piece of sugar; he cupped a grassblade between his thumbs and whistled. He sat on the ground with his legs crossed, and the child climbed into the hollow of his arms and legs. 'I wish you were my baby,' he told it. 'My baby.' He was very satisfied sitting there under the humming sun with the baby, who was satisfied too, no squirming. 'My daughter,' he said. 'My son.' He couldn't tell whether it was a boy or a girl. He touched the baby's fat arm and cheeks, its gold hair, and looked into its blue eyes. He made a wish that it not have to carry a sledgehammer and crawl into the dark. But he would not feel sorry for it; other people must not suffer any more than he did, and he could endure anything. Its mother came walking out into the road. She had her hands above her like a salute. She walked tentatively towards them, held out her hand, smiled, spoke. He did not understand what

146

she said except 'Bye-bye.' The child waved and said, 'Bye-bye,' crawled over his legs, and toddled to her. Ah Goong continued on his way in a direction she could not point out to a posse looking for a kidnapper chinaman.

Explosions followed him. He heard screams and went on, saw flames outlining black windows and doors, and went on. He ran in the opposite direction from gunshots and the yell – *eeha awha* – the cowboys made when they herded cattle and sang their savage songs.

Good at hiding, disappearing – decades unaccounted for – he was not working in a mine when forty thousand chinamen were Driven Out of mining. He was not killed or kidnapped in the Los Angeles Massacre, though he gave money towards ransoming those whose toes and fingers, a digit per week, and ears grotesquely rotting or pickled, and scalped queues, were displayed in Chinatowns. Demons believed that the poorer a chinaman looked, the more gold he had buried somewhere, that chinamen stuck together and would always ransom one another. If he got kidnapped, Ah Goong planned, he would whip out his Citizenship Paper and show that he was an American. He was lucky not to be in Colorado when the Denver demons burned all chinamen homes and businesses, nor in Rock Springs, Wyoming, when the miner demons killed twenty-eight or fifty chinamen. The Rock Springs Massacre began in a large coal mine owned by the Union Pacific; the outnumbered chinamen were shot in the back as they ran to Chinatown, which the demons burned. They forced chinamen out into the open and shot them; demon women and children threw the wounded back in the flames. (There was a rumour of a good white lady in Green Springs who hid China Men in the Pacific Hotel and shamed the demons away.) The hunt went on for a month before federal troops came. The count of the dead was inexact because bodies were mutilated and pieces scattered all over the Wyoming Territory. No white miners were indicted, but the government paid $150,000 in reparations to victims' families. There were many family men, then. There were settlers – abiding China Men. And China Women. Ah Goong was running elsewhere during the Drivings Out of Tacoma, Seattle, Oregon City, Albania, and Marysville. The demons of Tacoma packed all its chinamen into boxcars and sent them to Portland, where they were run out of town. China Men returned to Seattle, though, and refused to sell their land and stores but fought until the army came; the demon rioters were tried and acquitted. And when the Boston police imprisoned and beat 234 chinamen, it was 1902, and Ah Goong had already reached San Francisco or China, and perhaps San Francisco again.

In Second City (Sacramento), he spent some of his railroad money at the theatre. The main actor's face was painted red with thick black eyebrows and long black beard, and when he strode on to the stage, Ah Goong recognized the hero, Guan Goong; his puppet horse had red nostrils and rolling eyes. Ah Goong's heart lept to recognize hero and horse in the wilds of America. Guan Goong murdered his enemy – crash! bang! of cymbals and drum – and left his home village – sad, sad flute music. But to the glad clamour of cymbals entered his friends – Liu Pei (pronounced the same as Running Nose) and Chang Fei. In a joyful burst of pink flowers, the three men swore the Peach Garden Oath. Each friend sang an aria to friendship; together they would fight side by side and live and die one for all and all for one. Ah Goong felt as warm as if he were with friends at a party. Then Guan Goong's arch-enemy, the sly Ts'ao Ts'ao, captured him and two of Liu Pei's wives, the Lady Kan and the Lady Mi. Though Ah Goong knew they were boy actors, he basked in the presence of Chinese ladies. The prisoners travelled to the capital, the soldiers waving horsehair whisks, signifying horses, the ladies walking between horizontal banners, signifying palanquins. All the prisoners were put in one bedroom, but Guan Goong stood all night outside the door with a lighted candle in his hand, singing an aria about faithfulness. When the capital was attacked by a common enemy, Guan Goong fought the biggest man in one-to-one combat, a twirling, jumping sword dance that strengthened the China Men who watched it. From afar Guan Goong's two partners heard about the feats of the man with the red face and intelligent horse. The three friends were reunited and fought until they secured their rightful kingdom.

Ah Goong felt refreshed and inspired. He called out Bravo like the demons in the audience, who had not seen theatre before. Guan Goong, the God of War, also God of War and Literature, had come to America – Guan Goong, Grandfather Guan, our own ancestor of writers, of actors and gamblers, and avenging executioners who mete out justice. Our own kin. Not a distant ancestor but Grandfather.

In the Big City (San Francisco), a goldsmith convinced Ah Goong to have his gold made into jewellery, which would organize it into one piece and also delight his wife. So he handed over a second bag of gold. He got it back as a small ring in a design he thought up himself, two hands clasping in a handshake. 'So small?' he said, but the goldsmith said that only some of the ore had been true gold.

He got a ship out of San Francisco without being captured near the docks, where there was a stockade full of gaoled chinamen; the demonesses came down from Nob Hill and took them home to be servants, cooks, and baby-sitters.

Grandmother liked the gold ring very much. The gold was so pure, it squished to fit her finger. She never washed dishes, so the gold did not wear away. She quickly spent the railroad money, and Ah Goong said he would go to America again. He had a Certificate of Return and his Citizenship Paper.

But this time, there was no railroad to sell his strength to. He lived in a basement that was rumoured to connect with tunnels beneath Chinatown. In an underground arsenal, he held a pistol and said, 'I feel the death in it.' 'The holes for the bullets were like chambers in a beehive or wasp nest,' he said. He was inside the earth when the San Francisco Earthquake and Fire began. Thunder rumbled from the ground. Some say he died falling into the cracking earth. It was a miraculous earthquake and fire. The Hall of Records burned completely. Citizenship Papers burned, Certificates of Return, Birth Certificates, Residency Certificates, passenger lists, Marriage Certificates – every paper a China Man wanted for citizenship and legality burned in that fire. An authentic citizen, then, had no more papers than an alien. Any paper a China Man could not produce had been 'burned up in the Fire of 1906'. Every China Man was reborn out of that fire a citizen.

Some say the family went into debt to send for Ah Goong, who was not making money; he was a homeless wanderer, a shiftless, dirty, jobless man with matted hair, ragged clothes, and fleas all over his body. He ate out of garbage cans. He was a louse eaten by lice. A fleaman. It cost two thousand dollars to bring him back to China, his oldest sons signing promissory notes for one thousand, his youngest to repay four hundred to one neighbour and six hundred to another. Maybe he hadn't died in San Francisco, it was just his papers that burned; it was just that his existence was outlawed by Chinese Exclusion Acts. The family called him Fleaman. They did not understand his accomplishments as an American ancestor, a holding, homing ancestor of this place. He'd gotten the legal or illegal papers burned in the San Francisco Earthquake and Fire; he appeared in America in time to be a citizen and to father citizens. He had also been seen carrying a child out of the fire, a child of his own in spite of the laws against marrying. He had built a railroad out of sweat, why not have an American child out of longing?

The laws

The United States of America and the Emperor of China cordially recognize the inherent and inalienable right of man to change his home and allegiance, and also the mutual advantage of the free migration and emigration of their citizens and subjects respectively from the one country to the other for purposes of curiosity, of trade, or as permanent residents. ARTICLE V OF THE BURLINGAME TREATY, SIGNED IN WASHINGTON, DC, 28 JULY 1868, AND IN PEKING, 23 NOVEMBER 1869

The First Years: 1868, the year of the Burlingame Treaty, was the year 40,000 miners of Chinese ancestry were Driven Out. The Fourteenth Amendment, adopted in that same year, said that naturalized Americans have the same rights as native-born Americans, but in 1870 the Nationality Act specified that only 'free whites' and 'African aliens' were allowed to apply for naturalization. Chinese were not white; this had been established legally in 1854 when Chan Young unsuccessfully applied for citizenship in Federal District Court in San Francisco and was turned down on grounds of race. (He would have been illegal one way or another anyway; the Emperor of China did not give permission for any of his subjects to leave China until 1859.) Debating the Nationality Act, Congressmen declared that America would be a nation of 'Nordic fibre'.

1878: California held a Constitutional Convention to settle 'the Chinese problem'. Of the 152 delegates, 35 were not American citizens but Europeans. The resulting constitution, voted into existence by a majority party of Working Men and Grangers, prohibited Chinese from entering California. New State laws empowered cities and counties to confine them within specified areas or to throw them out completely. Shipowners and captains were to be fined and gaoled for hiring or transporting them. (This provision was so little respected that the American merchant marine relied heavily on Chinese seamen from the Civil War years to World War I.) 'Mongolians, Indians, and Negroes' were barred from attending public schools. The only California fishermen forced to pay fishing and shellfish taxes were the Chinese, who had brought shrimp nets from China and started the shrimp, abalone, and lobster industries. (The taxes were payable monthly.) Those Chinese over eighteen who were not already paying a miner's tax had to pay a 'police tax', to cover the extra policing their presence required. Though the Chinese were filling and leveeing the San Joaquin Delta for thirteen cents a square yard, building the richest agricultural land in the world, they were prohibited from owning land or real estate. They could not apply for business licences. Employers could be fined and gaoled for hiring them. No Chinese could be hired by state, county, or municipal governments for public works. No 'Chinese or Mongolian or Indian' could testify in court 'either for or against a white man'.

At this time San Francisco supplemented the anti-Chinese state laws with some of its own: a queue tax, a 'cubic air ordinance' requiring that every residence have so many cubic feet of air per inhabitant, a pole law prohibiting the use of carrying baskets on poles, cigar taxes, shoe taxes, and laundry taxes.

Federal courts declared some of the state and city laws unconstitutional, and occasionally citizens of a county or city repealed an especially punitive ordinance on the grounds that it was wrong to invite the Chinese to come to the United States and then deny them a livelihood. The repealed laws were often reenacted in another form.

1880: The Burlingame Treaty was modified. Instead of being free, the immigration of Chinese labourers to the United States would be 'reasonably limited'. In return (so as not to bring about limits on American entry into China), the American government promised to protect Chinese from lynchings.

1881: The Burlingame Treaty was suspended for a period of twenty years. (Since 1881 there has been no freedom of travel between China and the United States.) In protest against this suspension and against the refusal to admit Chinese boys to US

Army and Naval academies, China ordered scholars studying in the United States to return home. The act suspending the treaty did have two favourable provisions: all Chinese already resident in the United States in 1882 could stay; and they were permitted to leave and reenter with a Certificate of Return.

1882: Encouraged by fanatical lobbying from California, the US Congress passed the first Chinese Exclusion Act. It banned the entrance of Chinese labourers, both skilled and unskilled, for ten years. Anyone unqualified for citizenship could not come in – and by the terms of the Nationality Act of 1870, Chinese were not qualified for citizenship. Some merchants and scholars were granted temporary visas.

1884: Congress refined the Exclusion Act with An Act to Amend an Act. This raised fines and sentences and further defined 'merchants' to exclude 'hucksters, peddlers, or those engaged in taking, draying, or otherwise preserving shell or other fish for home consumption or exportation'.

1888: The Scott Act, passed by Congress, again forbade the entry of Chinese labourers. It also declared that Certificates of Return were void. Twenty thousand Chinese were trapped outside the United States with now-useless reentry permits. Six hundred returning travellers were turned back at American ports. A Chinese ambassador, humiliated by immigration officers, killed himself. The law decreed that Certificates of Residence had to be shown on demand; any Chinese caught without one was deported.

1889: Chinese pooled money to fight the various Exclusion Acts in the courts. They rarely won. In *Chae Chan Ping* v. *The United States*, Chae Chan Ping argued for the validity of his Certificate of Return. The Supreme Court ruled against him, saying that 'regardless of the existence of a prior treaty', a race 'that will not assimilate with us' could be excluded when deemed 'dangerous to . . . peace and security . . . It matters not in what form aggression and encroachment come, whether from the foreign nation acting in its national character or from vast hordes of its people crowding in upon us.' Moreover, said the Court, 'sojourners' should not 'claim surprise' that any Certificates of Return obtained prior to 1882 were 'held at the will of the government, revocable at any time, at its pleasure'.

153

1892: The Geary Act extended the 1882 Exclusion Act for another ten years. It also decreed that Chinese caught illegally in the United States be deported after one year of hard labour.

Chinese Americans formed the Equal Rights League and the Native Sons of the Golden State in order to fight disenfranchisement bills. Chinese Americans demanded the right to have their citizenship confirmed before travelling abroad.

1893: In *Yue Ting* v. *The United States*, the US Supreme Court ruled that Congress had the right to expel members of a race who 'continue to be aliens, having taken no steps towards becoming citizens, and incapable of becoming such under the naturalization laws'. This applied only to Chinese; no other race or nationality was excluded from applying for citizenship.

1896: A victory. In *Yick Wo* v. *Hopkins*, the US Supreme Court overturned San Francisco safety ordinances, saying that they were indeed designed to harass laundrymen of Chinese ancestry.

1898: Another victory. The Supreme Court decision in *The United States* v. *Wong Kim Ark* stated that a person born in the United States to Chinese parents is an American. This decision has never been reversed or changed, and it is the law on which most Americans of Chinese ancestry base their citizenship today.

1900: Deciding *The United States* v. *Mrs Cue Lim*, the Supreme Court ruled that wives and children of treaty merchants – citizens of China, aliens travelling on visas – were allowed to come to the United States.

1904: The Chinese Exclusion Acts were extended indefinitely, and made to cover Hawai'i and the Philippines as well as the continental United States. The question of exclusion was not debated in Congress; instead, the measure passed as a rider on a routine appropriations bill. China boycotted American goods in protest.

1906: The San Francisco Board of Education ordered that all Chinese, Japanese, and Korean children be segregated in an Oriental school. President Roosevelt, responding to a protest from the Japanese government, persuaded the Board of Education to allow Japanese to attend white schools.

1917: Congress voted that immigrants over sixteen years of age be required to pass an English reading test.

1924: An Immigration Act passed by Congress specifically excluded 'Chinese women, wives, and prostitutes'. Any American who married a Chinese woman lost his citizenship; any Chinese man who married an American woman caused her to lose her citizenship. Many states had also instituted antimiscegenation laws. A Supreme Court case called *Chang Chan et al. v. John D. Nagle* tested the law against wives; Chang Chan et al. lost. For the first time, the 1924 Immigration Act distinguished between two kinds of 'aliens': 'immigrants' were admitted as permanent residents with the opportunity to become citizens eventually; the rest – scholars, merchants, ministers, and tourists – were admitted on a temporary basis and were not eligible for citizenship. The number of persons allowed in the category of immigrant was set by law at one-sixth of one per cent of the total population of that ancestry in the United States as of the 1920 census. The 1920 census had the lowest count of ethnic Chinese in this country since 1860. As a result, only 105 Chinese immigrants were permitted each year.

In *Cheuno Sumchee* v. *Nagle*, the Supreme Court once again confirmed the right of treaty merchants to bring their wives to the United States. This was a right that coninued to be denied to Chinese Americans.

1938: A Presidential proclamation lifted restriction on immigration for Chinese and nationals of a few other Asian countries. The Chinese were still ineligible for citizenship, and the quota was '100'.

1943: The United States and China signed a treaty of alliance against the Japanese, and Congress repealed the Exclusion Act of 1882. Immigration continued to be limited to the 1924 quota of 105, however, and the Immigration and Nationalization Service claimed to be unable to find even that many qualified Chinese. A 'Chinese' was defined as anyone with more than fifty per cent Chinese blood, regardless of citizenship or country of residence. At this time Japanese invaders were killing Chinese civilians in vast numbers; it is estimated that more than ten million died. Chinese immigration into the United States did not rise.

1946: Congress passed the War Bride Act, enabling soldiers to bring Japanese and European wives home, then enacted a separate law allowing the wives and children of Chinese Americans to apply for entry as 'non-quota immigrants'. Only now did the ethnic Chinese population in the United States begin to approach the level of seventy years previous. (When the first Exclusion Act was passed in 1882, there were some 107,000 Chinese here; the Acts and the Driving Out steadily reduced the number to fewer than 70,000 in the 1920s.)

1948: The Refugee Act passed by Congress this year applied only to Europeans. A separate Displaced Persons Act provided that for a limited time – 1948 to 1954 – ethnic Chinese already living in the United States could apply for citizenship. During the post-war period, about 10,000 Chinese were permitted to enter the country under individual private bills passed by Congress. Confidence men, like the Citizenship Judges of old, defrauded hopeful Chinese by promising to acquire one of these bills for $1,500.

1950: After the Chinese Communist government took over in 1949, the United States passed a series of Refugee Relief Acts and a Refugee Escapee Act expanding the number of 'non-quota immigrants' allowed in. As a condition of entry, the Internal Security Act provided that these refugees swear they were not Communists. (Several hundred 'subversives or anarchists' of various races were subsequently deported; some were naturalized citizens who were 'denaturalized' beforehand.)

1952: The Immigration and Nationality Act denied admission to 'subversive and undesirable aliens' and made it simpler to deport 'those already in the country'. Another provision of this act was that for the first time Chinese women were allowed to immigrate under the same conditions as men.

1954: Ruling on *Mao* v. *Brownell*, the Supreme Court upheld laws forbidding Chinese Americans to send money to relatives in China. Before the Communist Revolution, there were no such restrictions in effect; Chinese Americans sent $70 million during World War II. Nor could they send money or gifts through CARE, UNESCO, or church organizations, which provided only for non-Communist countries.

1957: The Refugee Relief Act of 1953 expired in 1956 and was followed by the Act of 1957, which provided for the distribution of 18,000 visas that had remained unused.

1959: Close relatives, including parents, were allowed to enter.

1960: A 'Fair Share Refugee Act' allowed certain refugees from Communist and Middle Eastern countries to enter. Close to 20,000 people who were 'persecuted because of race, religion, or political beliefs' immigrated before this act was repealed in 1965, when a new act allowed the conditional entry of 10,200 refugees annually.

1962: A Presidential directive allowed several thousand 'parolees' to enter the United States from Hong Kong. Relatives of citizens and resident aliens were eligible. President Kennedy gave Congress a special message on immigration, saying, 'It is time to correct the mistakes of the past.'

1965: A new Immigration and Nationality Act changed the old quota system so that 'national origin' no longer means 'race' but 'country of birth'. Instead of being based on a percentage of existing ethnic populations in the United States, quotas were reallocated to countries – 20,000 each. But this did not mean that 20,000 Chinese immediately could or did come to the United States. Most prospective immigrants were in Hong Kong, a British colony. Colonies received one per cent of the mother country's allotment: only 200. 'Immediate relatives', the children, spouses, and parents of citizens, however, could enter without numerical limitations. Also not reckoned within the quota limitations were legal residents returning from a visit abroad.

1968: Amendments to the Immigration and Nationality Act provided that immigrants not be allocated by race or nation but by hemispheres, with 120,000 permitted to enter from the Western Hemisphere and 170,000 from the Eastern Hemisphere. This act limits immigration from the Western Hemisphere for the first time in history. The 20,000-per-country quota remained in effect for the Eastern Hemisphere, no per-country limitation for the Western Hemisphere.

1976: The Immigration and Nationality Act Amendments, also called the Western Hemisphere Bill, equalized the provisions of law regulating immigration from the two hemispheres. The House Committee on the Judiciary in its report on this legislation stated, 'This constitutes an essential first step in a projected long-term reform of US Immigration law.' The 20,000-per-country limit was extended to the Western Hemisphere. The limitation on colonies was raised from 200 to 600.

1978: The separate quotas for the two hemispheres were replaced by a worldwide numerical limitation on immigration of 290,000 annually. On the basis of the 'immediate relatives' clause, about 22,000 Chinese enter legally each year, and the rate is increasing. There are also special quotas in effect for Southeast Asian refugees, most of whom are of Chinese ancestry. In the last decade, the ethnic Chinese population of the United States has doubled. The 1980 census may show a million or more.

Alaska China Men

The China Man also went to Alaska to strike-it-rich in gold mining. At the top of the world, people wrote in their diaries for entertainment; they recorded the weather and described their health, their daily farming, hunting, and cooking, and the executions they witnessed. Many of them wrote about seeing an old Indian put to death in the middle of a public street: The tribe feasted and drank whisky. Then while they drummed on walrus hide, the old father calmly brought out a walrus hide thong. A son or a brother came from behind him, noosed his throat, pushed a foot against his back and broke his neck. There was also a stoning of an Indian woman in Juneau.

The strongest court of law was the miners' meetings, and the code of self-defence was the miners' law. Citizenship was cheaper in Alaska; the Citizenship Judge, who followed the prospectors, only asked for a pinch of gold dust. The white miners voted in 1885 that the chinamen be shipped out for fighting with the Indian miners. Posters and newspapers announced that on a certain day in July, chinamen were to report to the waterfront on Douglas Island. Diaries glowed with the weather: 'It was a beautiful sight, and one of the few days when the channel was smooth the day it was done.' (Beauty was different in those days, the foliage along the edges of Douglas Island was dead because of the sulphur from the gold mills. After the ore was pounded a hundred and twenty times by nine-hundred-pound pistons, the gold was broken free, and the sulphur was slagged on to the land and into the channel.) Demons came from miles around to see the Driving Out done. There were no fights. The whites stood on the shore with guns and tools; the Indians in their colours paddled fifty war canoes into the channel and rowed away 'the entire Chinese population' of one hundred. In Juneau they were put on a schooner to Puget Sound, where they were released.

The area was rid of chinamen except for China Joe, who was a baker in Juneau. He had saved the miners in the Cassiar

District from starvation and bad winters by giving bread away. He had opened his stores to everyone. 'He was the most loved person in Alaska,' a diarist wrote. When he died, Juneau held the largest funeral Alaska had ever seen.

As soon as they touched shore in Puget Sound, the China Men found ways to return and take back their mines, jobs, houses, and girl friends.

So the next year, there had to be another shipping out (unless it only happened once with two versions of the same event and the dates mixed up). This time the white miners went on strike against the Treadwell Mining Company, and ninety Chinese scabs took their jobs. Treadwell blackballed the strikers, who hired rustlers, claim jumpers, trap looters, to get rid of the chinamen. One of these rowdies or bummers wrote in his diary: 'The citizens of Juneau did not approve of the mining company's employing them and appealed to us to aid them in getting rid of the orientals which we did in the month of July.' The China Men asked Treadwell for guns to defend themselves, but the mining company refused to arm them. Some citizens wrote to the governor to send help: 'They are commencing the dynamiting business against the Chinese.' The governor himself came. But one day in July 1886, the demons walked the chinamen at gunpoint to the harbour, no Indians with war canoes this time. They were forced to board an old ship, and the ship was set adrift at sea. Some say there were two old schooners. There was no food or water, and the hundred China Men were so crowded together, they could not lie down. After eight days at sea, they steered the ship to Wrangel, a hundred and fifty miles south of Douglas Island. A white man named Captain Carroll gave them water and food and berths on his ship, the *Ancon*. He offered to sail them home, and they said, Yes, they would take him up on that. 'Take us home,' said the sourdough China Men, 'to Douglas Island.'

The only China Man not set adrift was China Joe, who owned a laundry and a big garden. He had provided vegetables during the bad winters. As French Pete was probably the name of more than one man, as were Dutch John and Missouri Frank and Arkansas Jim and French Charley, Dago Joe, and Indian Joe – one of the Citizenship Judges himself was named French Pete – perhaps any China Man was China Joe.

The making of more Americans

To visit grandfathers, we walked over three sets of railroad tracks, then on sidewalks cracked by grass and tree roots, then a grey dirt path. The roadside weeds waved tall overhead, netting the sunlight and wildflowers. I wore important white shoes for walking to the grandfathers' house.

The black dirt in their yard set off my dazzling shoes – two chunks of white light that encased my feet. 'Look. Look,' said Say Goong, Fourth Grandfather, my railroad grandfather's youngest brother. 'A field chicken.' It was not a chicken at all but a toad with alert round eyes that looked out from under the white cabbage leaves. It hopped ahead of my shoes, dived into the leaves, and disappeared, reappeared, maybe another toad. It was a clod that had detached itself from the living earth; the earth had formed into a toad and hopped. 'A field chicken,' said Say Goong. He cupped his hands, walked away quietly with wide steps and caught it. On his brown hand sat a toad with perfect haunches, eyelids, veins, and wrinkles – the details of it, the neatness and completeness of it swallowing and blinking. 'A field chicken?' I repeated. 'Field chicken,' he said. 'Sky chicken. Sky toad. Heavenly toad. Field toad.' It was a pun and the words the same except for the low tone of *field* and the high tone of *heaven* or *sky*. He put the toad in my hands – it breathed, and its heart beat, every part of it alive – and I felt its dryness and warmth and hind feet as it sprang off. How odd that a toad could be both of the field and of the sky. It was very funny. Say Goong and I laughed. 'Heavenly chicken,' I called, chasing the toad. I carefully ran between the rows of vegetables, where many toads, giants and miniatures, hopped everywhere. Which one was the toad in my hand? Then suddenly they were all gone. But they clucked. So it isn't that toads look or taste like chickens that they're called chickens; they cluck alike! Dragonflies held still in the air, suddenly darted. Butterflies in pairs flew far away from their partners, then together again. I stepped into a green hallway in the corn and sat in a teepee grown of vines over lattices; from ceilings and walls hung gourds, beans, tomatoes, grapes, and peas, winter melons like fat green prickly piglets, and bitter melons like green mice with tails. But the real marvel was the black dirt, which was clean and not dirty at all.

In one corner of the yard was a pile of horse manure taller than an adult human being. 'Aiya! Aiya!' our parents, grandfathers, and neighbours exclaimed, eyes open in wonder as they stood around the pile, neighbours and friends invited especially to view it. 'Come here! Come look. Oh, just look at it!' – I could tell that the adults felt what I felt, that I did not feel it alone, but truly. This pile hummed, and it was the fuel for the ground, the toads, the vegetables, the house, the two grandfathers. The flies, which were green and turquoise-black and silvery blue, swirling into various lights, hummed too, like excess sparks. The grandfathers boxed the horse manure, presents for us and their good friends to take home. They also bagged it in burlap. It smelled good.

Say Goong took my hand and led me to a cavernous shed black from the sun in my eyes. He pointed into the dark, which dark seemed solid and alive, heavy, moving, breathing. There were waves of dark skin over a hot and massive something that was snorting and stomping – the living night. In the day, here was where the night lived. Say Goong pointed up at a wide brown eye as high as the roof. I was ready to be terrified but for his delight. 'Horse,' he said. 'Horse.' He contained the thing in a word – *horse*, magical and earthly sound. A horse was a black creature so immense I could not see the outlines. Grasping Say Goong's finger, I dared to walk past the horse, and then he pointed again, 'Horse.' There was a partition, and on the other side of it – another horse. There were two such enormities in the world. Again and again I looked inside the stalls to solve the mystery of what a horse was. On the outside of the shed was horse shit, on the inside, the source of horse shit.

What I could see in its entirety because inanimate was the vegetable wagon, which was really a stagecoach. I climbed up a wheel and into the seat. I opened the compartments, drawers, and many screened doors. A scale hung in back, and in front were reins and two long prongs.

When I heard hooves clippity-clopping down our street, I ran to the upstairs window and saw two grandfathers and the two horses, which were contained between the prongs. They had blinders cupping their eyes. I had discovered the daily shape of horses. My mother opened the window, and she and I made up a song about grandfathers and horses; we sang it to them in the interplaying rhythm of hooves on the street:

Third Grandfather and Fourth Grandfather,
Where are you going?
Hooves clippity-clopping
four by four,
Where are you going?

'We're going to the north side to sell lettuce,' they said. Or, the horses facing another direction, 'We're going to the feed store,' or 'We're going home.' 'We're going on our route of demonesses.' The grandfathers could understand demon talk; they told us how the demonesses praised the tomatoes all the same size. 'Allee sem,' said the demonesses.

Sometimes under our very windows, the grandfathers fitted nosebags of oats over the horses' muzzles. The water for the horses had run into two buckets from a block of ice that sat melting in the middle of the wagon. The grandfathers sprinkled the vegetables with a watering can while the horses drank. Neighbours who had waited until late in the day for bargains circled the wagon. Through the screens they looked shrewdly at the red, yellow, and green vegetables. The god with the gourd had a gourd like the ones the grandfathers sold. At New Year's, tangerines hung by the branch from the roof, and in the fall, persimmons. In summer the grandfathers sold watermelons, which grew in China too, only there the meat was light pink and nobody we knew had ever tasted it. A railing along the top of the stagecoach kept the sacks of potatoes and yams from rolling off. Our family got what remained for free.

One time I went to the shed to have a look at the horses, and they were gone. 'Where are the horses?' I asked. 'They're gone,' said both my parents with no surprise or emphasis. Not satisfied with the answer, I asked them again and again. Such vastness could not possibly have disappeared so completely. But they said, 'They've been gone a long time.' I walked inside each bare stall. 'Where are the horses? Where are they?' No more horses. 'What happened to them?' 'They've been gone for a long time.' No explanation. Did they trot away down the street without the stagecoach and the grandfathers? Time must have gone by, then, since I'd last come to visit them, though the visits seemed like the same time, no time at all, time just one time, but it must have been later, a last time. I looked inside the first stall, looked again in the other one but found no aliveness there, bright now and not dark with horses. I could see boards and and into corners, no vestige of horses, no hay spilling over the troughs, not a single yellow straw sticking out of a crack, floor not covered with straw and horse shit, everything swept clean. Manure pile gone. I have looked for proof of horses, and found it in the family album, which has photographs of horses with blinders, though the men standing in front of the wagons are not the grandfathers but the uncles, the same ones who later had their pictures taken with cars and trucks.

The stagecoach was still there. I sat in the seat, shook the reins, and looked in the distance for Indians and bisons.

One day Sahm Goong, Third Grandfather, came to our house alone, and he said to my mother, 'Say Goong is standing in the stable.'

'No,' said my mother. 'He's dead.'

'He's in the stable. I saw him. I left him there just now, standing by the wall near the door.'

'What was he doing?'

'Just standing there. Not working.'

'You know he's dead, don't you?'

'Yes. It must be his ghost standing there. He comes to visit me every day.'

'What does he have to say?' she asked.

'Nothing. I talk to him, but he doesn't answer.'

'You tell him to go home,' said my mother. 'Scold him. "Go home!" Loud. Like that. "Go home, Say Goong!" ' They both called him that even though he was my fourth grandfather and not theirs.

Sahm Goong walked back home. He sat on a crate in the

empty stable, the grey floorboards awash with afternoon sun. There in the shade beside the door stood his brother.

'How nice of you to visit me again,' said Sahm Goong.

Say Goong did not reply. He was wearing his good clothes, his new bib overalls, a white shirt, a tie, his cardigan, and his cloth cap, which he had worn when working in the yard or driving the stagecoach. His fine white hair caught the light like a halo.

'Sit down,' invited Sahm Goong, but his brother did not want to. He certainly could not be seen through, and he was not floating; he had his feet on the floor. The high work shoes were polished.

Third Grandfather stood up and walked over to Fourth Grandfather, the two of them the same size. They did not touch each other. 'I am very well, you know,' the live grandfather said. 'My health is good. Yes, the rest of the family is fine too. Though there are a lot of girls. We're all well.' Say Goong did not say a thing. Sahm Goong walked sideways and examined him in profile; he certainly looked as usual. Then Sahm Goong sat down again, looking a moment into the garden. When he looked back, his brother was still there, no shimmering, no wavering, just as solid and real as ever before. The two brothers stayed with each other until suppertime. Then Sahm Goong went in the house to cook and eat.

After dinner he took his flashlight and went again into the shed. He shone it into the place where the ghost had been. He was still there. He turned off the flashlight so as not to glare it in his face and sat in the dark with his brother. When he felt sleepy, he said, 'Good night,' and went back up to bed.

The next morning, he ate breakfast, then watered the yard, left the hose trickling. He went into the stable and did not see his brother, but the next time he checked, there he was again. Again he sat with him for a while. Then he got up and looked into the familiar old face. They were alike, two wispy old men, two wispy old brothers.

'Do you need to say something to me?' Sahm Goong asked.

The ghost did not answer.

'You don't have something to tell me then? No message?' Sahm Goong paced about. 'What are you doing here?' he asked.

What do you want? You don't have something to tell me? No message? Why are you here?' He waited for a reply. 'What do you want?'

But Say Goong's ghost said nothing.

'It's time to go home, then,' said Sahm Goong. He said it louder. 'Go home! It's time for you to go home now. What's the use of staying here any more? You don't belong here. There's nothing for you to do here. Go home. Go back to China. Go.'

There did seem to be a flickering then. All was still, no sound of bird or toad, no aroused insect, only the humming that could have been the new refrigerator. 'Go home,' Sahm Goong said sternly. 'Go back to China. Go now. To China.' His voice was loud in the bare shed.

Say Goong disappeared, as if the vehement voice had filled the space he had been using. He had been startled away, reminded of something. He did not come back again. Later Sahm Goong couldn't say whether he had been looking directly at his brother at the moment of disappearance. He might have looked aside for a second, and when he looked again, Say Goong was gone. A slant of light still came in at the door.

Then Third Grandfather too disappeared, perhaps going back to China, perhaps dead here like his brother. When their descendants came across the country to visit us, we took them to the place where two of our four grandfathers had had their house, stable, and garden. My father pointed out where each thing had stood, 'They had two horses, which lived in a stable here. Their house stood over there.' The aunts and uncles exclaimed, 'Their horses were here, then,' and said it again in English to their children. 'And their house over there.' They took pictures with a delayed-shutter camera, everyone standing together where the house had been. The relatives kept saying, 'This is the ancestral ground,' their eyes filling with tears over a vacant lot in Stockton.

Third Grandfather had a grandson whom we called Sao Elder Brother to his face, but for a while behind his back, Mad Sao, which rhymes in our dialect. Sao firmly established his American citizenship by serving in the US Army in World War II, then sent for a wife from China. We were amazed at how lovely and kind she was even though picked sight unseen. The new couple, young and modern (*mo-dang*), bought a ranch house and car, wore fashionable clothes, spoke English, and seemed more American than us.

But Sao's mother sent him letters to come home from China. 'I'm growing old,' she said or the letter writer said. 'If you don't come home now you'll never see me again. I remember you, my baby. Don't wait until you're old before coming back. I can't bear seeing you old like me.' She did not know how American he had looked in his army uniform. 'All you're doing is having fun, aren't you?' she asked. 'You're spending all the money, aren't you? This is your own mother who rocked you to sleep and took care of you when you were sick. Do you remember your mother's face? We used to pretend our rocker was a boat like a peapod, and we were peas at sea. Remember? Remember? But now you send paper boats into my dreams. Sail back to me.' But he was having his own American babies yearly, three girls and a boy. 'Who will bury me if you don't come back?' his mother asked.

And if she wasn't nagging him to return, she was asking for money. When he sent photographs of the family with the car in the background, she scolded him: 'What are you doing feeding these girls and not your mother? What is this car, and this radio? A new house. Why are you building a new house in America? You have a house here. Sell everything. Sell the girls, and mail the profits to Mother. Use the money for ship fare. Why are you spending money on photographs of girls? Send me the money you give the photographers so I can send you *my* picture, the face you've forgotten.' She did not know that he owned his own camera. His family was one of the first to own a shower, a lawn, a carport, and a car for passengers rather than for hauling.

'You're doing everything backwards,' his mother wrote. 'I'm starving to death. In the enclosed picture, you can see my bones poking through the skin. You must be turning into a demon to treat a mother so. I have suffered all my life; I need to rest now. I'll die happy if you come home. Why don't you do your duty? I order you to come back. It's all those daughters, isn't it? They've turned your head. Leave them. Come back alone. You don't need to save enough money to bring a litter of females.

What a waste to bring girls all the way back here to sell anyway. You can find a second wife here too. A Gold Mountain Sojourner attracts ten thousand rich fat women. Sell those girls, apprentice the boy, and use the money for your passage.' Of course, though Mad Sao favoured his son, there was no question but that, being very American, he would raise and protect his daughters.

'Let me tell you about hunger,' wrote his mother. 'I am boiling weeds and roots. I am eating flowers and insects and pond scum. All my teeth have fallen out. An army drafted the ox, and soldiers took the pigs and chickens. There are strangers in the orchard eating the fruit in its bud. I tried to chase them away. "We're hungry. We're hungry," they kept explaining. The next people through here will gnaw the branches. The sly villagers are hoarding food, begging it, and hiding it. You can't trust the neighbours. They'd do anything. I haven't eaten meat for so long, I might as well have been a nun who's taken a vegetable vow. You'd think I'd be holy by now and see miracles. What I see are the hungry, who wander lost from home and village. They live by swindling and scheming. Two crazed villagers are stealing a Dragon King statue from each other. It goes back and forth and whoever's doorstep it lands on has to pay for a party. There's no goodness and wisdom in hunger. You're starving me. I see you for what you are – an unfaithful son. Oh, what blame you're incurring. All right, don't bring yourself to me. I don't need a son. But send money. Send food. Send food. I may have been exaggerating before, but don't punish me for playing the boy who cried wolf. This time there really is a wolf at the door.' He shut his heart and paid his house mortgage. He did nothing for her, or he did plenty, and it was not enough.

'Now we're eating potato leaves,' she wrote. 'We pound rice hulls into paste and eat it. At least send money to bury me.' (Sao felt the terror in *bury*, the dirt packing the nose, plugging the eyes and mouth.) 'I've wasted my life waiting, and what do I get for my sacrifices? Food and a fat old age? No. I'm starving to death alone. I hold you responsible. How can you swallow when you know of me?' Some letters were long and some short. 'The beggar children who came to the door on your sister's wedding day were the worst-looking beggars in many years,' she wrote.

'Give them food? Huh. I should have kidnapped them and sold them. Except that people don't buy children any more, not even boys. There's a baby on the rich family's doorstep every morning. Oh, it's so pathetic. The mother hides behind bushes to watch the rich lady bring the baby inside. There are people eating clay balls and chewing bark. The arbour we sat under is gone, eaten. No more fish in the rivers. Frogs, beetles, all eaten. I am so tired. I can't drive the refugees off our property. They eat the seeds out of the dirt. There'll not be harvest again.'

Other relatives wrote letters about their hunger: 'We'd be glad to catch a rat but they're gone too,' a cousin wrote. 'Slugs, worms, bugs, all gone. You think we're dirty and depraved? Anything tastes good fried, but we can't buy oil.' 'We're chewing glue from hems and shoes,' wrote another cousin. 'We steal food off graves if people are rich enough to leave some. But who tends the dead any more?' 'Starving takes a long time.' 'No more dogs and cats. No more birds. No mice. No grasshoppers.' 'We've burned the outhouse for fuel. Don't need it anyway. Nothing comes out because nothing goes in. What shall we do? Eat shit and drink piss? But there isn't any coming out.' 'I can't sleep for the hunger. If we could sleep, we'd dream about food. I catch myself opening cupboards and jars even though I know they're empty. Staring into pots.' 'I searched under my own children's pillows for crumbs.' 'Soon I won't be able to concentrate on writing to you. My brain is changing. If only the senses would dull, I wouldn't feel so bad. But I am on the alert for food.' 'There are no children on some streets.' 'We know which weeds and berries and mushrooms and toads are poisonous from people eating them and dying.' 'Fathers leave in the middle of the night, taking no food with them.' 'The dead are luckier.'

When the relatives read and discussed one another's hunger letters, they said, 'Perhaps it's more merciful to let them die fast, starve fast rather than slow.' 'It's kinder either to send a great deal of money or none at all,' they said. 'Do you think people really go into euphoria when they die of hunger? Like saints fasting?'

'How can you leave me to face famine and war alone?' wrote Mad Sao's mother. 'All I think about is you and food. You owe it to me to return. Advise me. Don't trick me. If you're never coming home, tell me. I can kill myself then. Easily stop looking for food and die.' 'The neighbours heard rumours about food inland to the north,' she wrote next. 'Others are following an army their sons joined. The villagers are moving. Tell me what to do. Some people are walking to the cities. Tin miners are coming through here, heading for the ocean. They spit black. They can't trade their tin or money for food. Rich people are throwing money into the crowds. I've buried the gold. I buried the money and jewels in the garden. We were almost robbed. The bandit used the old trick of sticking a pot like his head bulging against the curtain, and when I clubbed it, it clanged. At the alarm he fled. I had nothing to steal anyway.' Hearing that money couldn't buy food relieved Mad Sao of feeling so guilty when he did not send money.

'Since everyone is travelling back and forth, I might as well stay put,' wrote his mother. 'I'm frightened of these hungry eaters and killer soldiers and contagious lepers. It used to be the lepers and the deformed who hid; now the fat people hide.'

'Shall I wait for you? Answer me. How would you like to come home and find an empty house? The door agape. You'll not find me waiting when you get here. It would serve you right. The weather has changed; the world is different. The young aren't feeding the old any more. The aunts aren't feeding me any more. They're keeping the food for their own chlidren. Some slaves have run away. I'm chasing my slaves away. Free people are offering themselves as soldiers and slaves.'

'I'm too old. I don't want to endure any more. Today I gave my last handful of rice to an old person so dried up, I couldn't tell whether it was man or woman. I'm ready to die.' But she wrote again, 'The fugitives are begging for burial ground and make a cemetery out of our farm. Let them bury their skinny bodies if they give me a little funeral food. They ask if Jesus demons have settled near by; they leave the children with them. If you don't have stories that are equally heart-rending, you have nothing better to do with your money than send it to me. Otherwise, I don't want to hear about your mortgage payment or see photographs of your new car. What do you mean mortgage payment? Why are you buying land there when you have land here?'

'If only I could list foods on this paper and chew it up, swallow, and be full. But if I could do that, I could write your name, and you'd be here.'

'I keep planning banquets and menus and guests to invite. I smell the food my mother cooked. The smell of puffed rice cookies rises from tombs. The aunts have left me here with the babies. The neighbours took their children with them. If they find food, they can decide then what to do with the children, either feed them or trade them for food. Some children carry their parents, and some parents carry their children.'

Mad Sao wished that his mother would hurry up and die, or that he had time and money enough to pay his mortgage, raise all his children, and also give his mother plenty.

Before a letter in a white envelope reached us saying that Sao Brother's mother had died, she appeared to him in America. She flew across the ocean and found her way to him. Just when he was about to fall asleep one night, he saw her and sat up with a start, definitely not dreaming. 'You have turned me into a hungry ghost,' she said. 'You did this to me. You enjoyed yourself. You fed your wife and useless daughters, who are not even family, and you left me to starve. What you see before you is the inordinate hunger I had to suffer in my life.' She opened her mouth wide, and he turned his face away not to see the depths within.

'Mother,' he said. 'Mother, how did you find your way across the ocean and here?'

'I am so cold. I followed the heat of your body like a light and fire. I was drawn to the well-fed.'

'Here, take this, Mother,' he cried, handing her his wallet from the nightstand.

'Too late,' she said. 'Too late.'

With her chasing him he ran to the kitchen. He opened the refrigerator. He shoved food at her.

'Too late.'

Curiously enough, other people did not see her. All they saw was Mad Sao talking to the air, making motions to the air, talking to no voice, listening to someone who moved about, someone very tall or floating near the ceiling. He yelled and argued, talked, sobbed. He lost weight from not eating; insomnia ringed his eyes. That's when people began to call him Mad Sao.

He knew how his grandfather had helped Fourth Grandfather

by scolding him on his way. 'Go home, Mother!' he was heard to scold, very firm, his face serious and his voice loud. 'Go home! Go back to China. Go home to China where you belong.' He went on with this scolding for days and nights, but it did not work. She never left him for a moment.

'I'm hungry,' she cried. 'I'm hungry.' He threw money at her; he threw food at her. The money and food went through her. She wept continually, most disturbingly loud at night; though he pulled the covers over his ears and eyes, he heard her. 'Why didn't you come home? Why didn't you send money?'

'I did send money.'

'Not enough.'

'It's against the law to send money,' he told her – a weak excuse. 'But even so, I sent it.'

'I'm not a rich man,' he said. 'It isn't easy in this country either.'

'Don't lie to me,' she said. She pointed towards the kitchen, where the refrigerator and freezer were filled with food, and at the furniture, the radio, the TV. She pointed with her chin the way Chinese people point.

'Since you're here, Mother,' he tried to bribe her, 'you may have all the food I have. Take it. Take it.'

She could see her surroundings exactly, but though she could see food, she could not eat it.

'It's too late,' she mourned, and passed her hand through the footboard of his bed. He drew his feet up. He could not bear it if she should pass her hand through his feet. His wife beside him saw him gesturing and talking, sleepwalking and sleeptalking, and could not calm him.

'I died of starvation,' his mother said. She was very thin, her eye sockets hollow like a Caucasian's. 'I died of starvation while you ate.'

He could not sleep because she kept talking to him. She did not fade with the dawn and the rooster's crowing. She kept a watch on him. She followed him to work. She kept repeating herself. 'You didn't come home. You didn't send money.'

She said, 'I've got things to tell you that I didn't put in letters.' 'I am going to tell them to you now. Did you know that when children starve, they grow coarse black hairs all over their bodies? And the heads and feet of starving women suddenly swell up. The skin of my little feet split open, and pus and blood burst out; I saw the muscles and veins underneath.

'One day there was meat for sale in the market. But after cooking and eating it, the villagers found out it was baby meat. The parents who had sold their children regretted it. "We shouldn't have sold her," they said. The rich people had bought the babies and resold them to butchers.'

'Stop it, Mother,' he said to the air. 'I can't stand any more.'

Night after night, she haunted him. Day after day. At last he drove to the bank. She sat in the back seat directly behind him. He took a lump sum of money out of his savings. Then he ran to a travel agency, his mother chasing him down the street, goading him. 'Look, Mother,' he was heard to say, sounding happier as he showed her the money and papers. 'I'll take you home myself. You'll be able to rest. I'll go with you. Escort you. We're going home. I'm going home. I'm going home at last, just as you asked. I'll take you home. See? Isn't it a wonderful idea I have? Here's a ticket. See all the money I spent on a ticket, Mother? We're going home together.' He had bought an ocean-liner ticket for one, so it was evident that he knew she was a ghost. That he easily got his passport proves that he was indeed an American citizen and in good standing with the Immigration and Naturalization Service. It was strange that at a time when Americans did not enter China, he easily got a visa also. He became much calmer. He did not suddenly scream any more or cry or throw food and money.

The family told him that there were no such things as ghosts, that he was wasting an enormous amount of savings, that it was dangerous to go to China, that the bandits would hold him hostage, that an army would draft him. The FBI would use our interest in China to prove our un-Americanness and deport all of us. The family scolded him for spending a fortune on a dead person. Why hadn't he mailed her the money when she was alive if he was going to spend it anyway? Why hadn't he gone to see her earlier? 'Why don't you give the money to some wretch instead of wasting it on a vacation for yourself, eh?' He reminded them of a ghost story about a spirit that refused ghost money but had to have real money. They shook their heads. When my father saw that Mad Sao would not be swayed, he bought two Parker 51 fountain pens for fifty-five dollars, kept one for himself, and told Mad Sao to deliver the other to a most loved relative in China.

Mad Sao packed a small bag, all the time talking, 'See, Mother? We're on our way home now. Both of us. Yes, I'm going home too. Finally going home. And I'm taking you home. We're together again, Mother.' He hardly heard the live people around him.

All the way up the gangway, he was waving her on, 'This way, Mother,' leading her by the hand or elbow. 'This way, Mother. This way.' He gave her his bed and his deck chair. 'Are you comfortable, Mother?' 'Yes, Mother.' He talked to no other passenger, and did not eat any of the ship's meals, for which he had already paid. He walked the decks day and night. 'Yes, Mother. I'm sorry. I am sorry I did that. Yes, I did that, and I'm sorry.'

He returned his mother to the village. He went directly to her grave, as if led by her. 'Here you are, Mother,' he said, and the villagers heard him say it. 'You're home now. I've brought you home. I spent passage fare on you. It equals more than the food money I might have sent. Travel is very expensive. Rest, Mother. Eat.' He heaped food on her grave. He piled presents beside it. He set real clothes and real shoes on fire. He burned mounds of paper replicas and paper money. He poured wine into the thirsty earth. He planted the blue shrub of longevity, where white carrier pigeons would nest. He bowed his forehead to the ground, knocking it hard in repentance. 'You're home Mother. I'm home too. I brought you home.' He set off firecrackers near her grave, not neglecting one Chinese thing. 'Rest now, heh, Mother. Be happy now.' He sat by the grave and drank and ate for the first time since she had made her appearance. He stepped over the fires before extinguishing them. He boarded the very same ship sailing back. He had not spent any time sightseeing or visiting relatives and old friends except for dropping off the Parker 51. He hurried home to America, where he acted normal again, continuing his American life, and nothing like that ever happened to him again.

*

Another grandfather we had was Kau Goong, the ex-riverboat pirate, our grandmother's brother. When a neighbour boy called him Kau Goong too, I saw rush across the old man's face, pleasure at being the Great Uncle, a title with loft, but he said, 'I'm not *your* kau goong,' scornful of an American boy, a Ho Chi Kuei, who did not know the titles. Kau Goong was the longest-lived and biggest human being I had ever seen, and my mother said that Grandmother was the same size; in fact this was her younger brother. He had to duck under doorways. We tied rags around the pipes in the basement to cushion him when he hit his head; we let strips hang down to warn him. He carried trunks, stones, trees, the railroad ties. He was lucky, and won for us a TV set and a vacuum cleaner, which were raffled off at the Chinese Community Fourth of July Annual Picnic. He also gave us Nabisco wafers, one entire box for each kid. This same Great Uncle had been a murderer in Cuba and a second-storey man in New York, a city he climbed the way King Kong climbed the Empire State Building. That killing must have been done not in stealth but in hand-to-hand fight, no weapons but his enormous hands. A second-storey man, we learned, clamps his mouth shut when jumping so he doesn't bite his tongue off upon landing. At the laundry Kau Goong worked without pay doing the heaviest work, which was pressing overalls and Levis.

Another of his chores was to walk my youngest sister from kindergarten. Once when she came home alone, a wino knocked all afternoon on the doors and windows. She barricaded herself under the dining table with chairs tight all around. When we found her in there among the legs, she was still scared. After that Kau Goong met her at school and walked her to the laundry.

My brothers remember him as a generous old man; he took them to a smoking place where men with silver and wood pipes gave them presents and praised them. The only times he spoke to me were to scold and to give orders. 'Bad girl,' he said.

There was a day when he was shouting for me, probably to do some chore, clean house or wash dishes, rinse the rice, some routine work, which I suddenly did not want to do. I did not want to hear him order me to make a phone call or address an envelope; I would not fill out a form or take something to the laundry or whatever. I did not want to see him or hear him or be in his bossy presence. I dashed downstairs into the basement, where I locked myself into the storeroom, and sat on the stairs under the cellar door as in *The Wizard of Oz*. I liked hiding in the dark, which could be anywhere. The cellar door sloped overhead, a room within the storeroom within the basement. I listened to footsteps above the rafters. He would not come down to the basement, where he had to duck the pipes and walk stooped. I was safely tucked away among the bags of old clothes and shoes, the trunks and crates the grown-ups had brought with them from China, the seabags with the addresses in English and Chinese, the tools, the bags and bottles of seeds, the branches of seeds and leaves and pods hanging upside down, and the drying loofahs. Outside the cellar door, the pigeons purred, the chickens squawked, and a turkey and a dog, a rooster, a train made their noises. In the middle of the basement, the swing my father had hung from a beam bounced and squeaked when Kau Goong walked over it; at night ghosts played on that swing.

I thought over useless things like wishes, wands, hibernation. I talked to the people whom I knew were not really there. I became different, complete, an orphan; my partners were beautiful cowgirls, and also men, cowboys who could talk to me in conversations; I named this activity Talking Men.

But today, interrupting the conversations were the stomping and roaring overhead. 'Children. Children. Where are you?' He sounded angry. But that was his usual voice. The basement ran the length of the house, and his footsteps went everywhere across the ceiling. He was stomping from room to room, opening and slamming doors, closet doors too. I stretched my legs out on the cement and put one elbow on the highest step, my back against one wall and toes against the other. I belonged here; everything was my size. The air smelled of anise from the drying stalks. Kau Goong was calling out our names one by one. I wondered where my brothers and sisters were; one of them ought to be answering by now. If one of them answered, Kau Goong would forget about me. But I heard no reply. Maybe they were hiding in other places – the ledge along the top of the neighbour's goose pen, which was roofless but tall enough for the lazy geese not to fly away, or under the grape leaves on top of the pigeon coop, or

178

on top of wardrobes, behind the boxes. We had many special places. My brothers and sisters were good at chores too, but Kau Goong mostly called me because I was the oldest and took blames. A long time had passed, and he was still calling. He did not give up; he would not forget about it. We had to be there somewhere; the front door had been open, that was how he had got in, and so somebody had to be home.

The longer he looked, I realized, the less plausibly I'd be able to step out of the basement and say, acting natural, 'Yes, Kau Goong, were you calling me?' I tried the appropriate facial expression, erased guile and worry from my face, casually said, 'Here I am.' But then he would say, 'Where have you been?' And then what would I say? I couldn't say, 'I was in the bathroom.' He had checked every room. I couldn't say, 'I was watering the yard,' or 'I was feeding the chickens and rabbits,' because he had made the round of the yard too. I had seen his legs at the basement windows.

Then his footsteps came across the kitchen and down the basement stairs. He would know I was in the storeroom – I had latched the door from the inside. Trapped. How dumb. Stupid. If he found me while I was doing something of use like sweeping out the basement or restacking the lumber or roller skating on the concrete or drawing on the walls, then all would have been right, but to be found doing nothing, to be found hiding, I could not explain. He walked past the storeroom door. Through its screen, I saw him from the shoulders to the waist, the rolled-up sleeves over the long arms. He growled; he lumbered past. I darted out of the corner, unlatched the door, and hid again. Even if he opened the door and looked in, maybe I could count on his eyes not being used to the dark. He walked to the end of the basement. He shouted into the corners. He walked over to the pile of sawdust which we used to outline borders when we played Cities, walked around the Texas rice, the onion pile, the potato pile, and the woodpile of boards and railroad ties. The upright stakes were transfixing vampires. Over where there were treasures buried underneath the front stairs (I had buried some myself in cigar boxes), he roared my name several times. I should either stay hidden or come out. Miraculously, he passed the door again without looking inside. I didn't feel sorry for him

179

calling through an empty house, and it was not as if my name were a tether to me, but I got up, opened the door, and said to his big back, 'Hello, Kau Goong. Did I hear you calling me?' Then scooted around him and ran up the stairs. 'Yes,' he said. From the basement he would only be able to see my feet. 'Oh, here and there,' I mumbled in case he was saying, 'Where were you?' 'I was just on my way to finish my work,' I said, sweeping something into the dustpan I'd grabbed. He did not scold me taking so long to answer. I must have fooled him.

When he was over ninety, and his forehead grown very high, his wife, Great Aunt, wrote to him: 'Now we're surely in our old age. Why don't you come back, and let's spend a few years together before we die.' But in China he would have to have a hole drilled in his head and warm soapy water slooshed through, brainwashed into a Communist. He would have to stand up night after night without sleep until his brain turned Communist. Great Aunt wrote, however, that the Communists had quit breaking up families; men no longer lived in separate houses from women. Some children had been taught to inform on their parents, but some were only pretending they'd do so. Now that families were reuniting, couldn't the two of them also meet again? 'You only have a few years left anyway,' she wrote, 'so don't be afraid of plane crashes or ships sinking. Haven't you had your life of adventure? Now it's time to come home.'

'What are you going to do?' asked my mother, who read him his letters.

'Who knows?' he roared and stomped out of the house to his room at the Benevolent Association, so he wouldn't have to discuss this going back to China.

'What do you think he should do?' MaMa asked. 'If he goes back to China, he'll see his wife again. But he may have to suffer Communism and famines. And we'll never see him again.' We children thought about Kau Goong finding the way street by street to an ocean, then over the Atlantic or the Pacific, then distinguishing the coast of Asia from Africa. Finding was a power not a one of us had, and we too had to go someday on that same quest, for which our mother had made us memorize the directions in syllables. 'If he stays here,' MaMa analysed, 'he'll grow old and never see his wife again, but he'll always have food to eat.' There was no question of Great Aunt coming here, against the law to leave Communist China, also against the law to enter the United States. 'She's so old too,' MaMa said. 'On the other hand, they saw each other when they were young and not again for the rest of their lifetimes; what difference does it make if they don't see each other a little longer? It would only be a sentimental indulgence.' *If, old, but* – terrible words. Gapping, gaping spaces. Two old people with a planet between them, and the planet unfathomable with its hunger and wars and laws.

One day MaMa said, 'He ought to go back,' and I did not see how she came to this conclusion, what bridges of reasoning she took to arrive at it, why this conclusion was better than the other possibility. It must have been Father who had decided and she was doing the announcing. 'You must go back, Kau Goong,' she said. 'Here you're all alone. What use are you here?' She asked him several times, 'What have you decided?' But his growl didn't sound like a Yes or a No. He left the house without talking about the decision he had to make and did not visit again for a week or two.

Then she told us, 'Kau Goong has decided he's not going back.' *Never, forever* – two more terrible words.

'Why?' I asked. 'How did he decide that? Why? How come?'

So Great Aunt, who was also more than ninety years old, saved seventy-five dollars and bribed a farmer, who hid her under the potatoes in his cart, and he smuggled her out of Communist China. 'I could hear the border guard talking with the farmer,' she wrote. 'They even talked about people hiding in sacks – under potatoes. "Eyes among the eyes," they said. Then they laughed, and we went on. A donkey drew the cart. I'm now in Hong Kong. You don't have to worry about Communists any more. They're not of any consideration whatsoever. We can spend our old age in Hong Kong. I'll wait for you here.' I wondered, if she had been hiding under corn would they have said, 'Ears among the ears,' whether Chinese also think corn comes in ears.

More weeks passed while the adults thought over this new development. He has to go now, I thought; he cannot leave her alone and old in a foreign country. But Great Uncle, who was standing by the window, the profile of his big head against the glass and peach trees, the long tendons of his neck stretching, his big Adam's apple bobbing, said, 'I've decided to stay in California.' He said, 'California. This is my home. I belong here.' He turned and, looking at us, roared, 'We belong here.'

My mother wrote Great Aunt about the decision. Not much later, Great Aunt wrote that she had bribed another farmer to smuggle her back into China. Another seventy-five dollars. She said she was not going to spend the rest of her life alone in a strange city. Her return was a clue that Red China couldn't have been as horrible as everyone made out.

Not many years after his decision, Great Uncle grew shorter and thinner, though he was still bigger than most people. He did not appear for dinner one day, and he was dead.

We and the old men sat in rows at the funeral. Some of the old men were: the storekeeper who had torn up his accounts and stopped keeping them when he saw he was not getting ahead, the delivery man who whistled on leaves, the hatchet man who sang opera, the artist uncle who said how paper and pencil are cheap and how inexpensive it is to be an artist, the piano player who lived in the basement and played without depressing the keys so as not to disturb the people upstairs, the Old Man of the North disguised as Uncle Camel Face, the uncle who lived with the Mexican lady, and Uncle Bing Sun Who Laughed Twice (which rhymes). They wore their brown or blue jackets and sweaters; some took off their tweed caps, and others kept them on. Only my father wore a matching suit. I thought about myself dying and about parents dying. We were the only children; the old men admired children.

MaMa sat for a moment, then left, hurried back with four dented buckets filled with sand. She stuck incense sticks any old how into the sand and put the buckets around the coffin. She lit the incense and sat down, having filled the room with smells and broken up the symmetry of the demon mortuary. I looked at the mortician demons, who stood in the back of the room, to see if they were going to upbraid her and remove the buckets. The coffin was brown and very long as if it were made with doors nailed together. He was that tall; he was inside. One old man, then another one, stood up, walked in front of the coffin, and made a speech. They seemed to speak in a higher language than when talking to children; I did not understand most of what they said. Perhaps on this serious occasion, they did not put things into many synonyms until they hit on one a kid could understand. I listened to find out more about Kau Goong's pillages, his plunders, and sackings, and for some details about how he had killed a man, but they did not mention his crimes though he was safe from deportation now. I should have yelled questions at him. I shouldn't have hidden from him. He was almost a hundred years old; Chinese live a long time – to do many things and to make their ages span the legal immigration dates. The old men and a politician told how Kau Goong had come to the Gold Mountain and stayed. He was a Gold Mountain Man. They said 'Gold Mountain' a lot, 'Gum Sahn' many times. 'Long time Califoon,' they said in English.

Mad Sao wept. I did not think that men had feelings; it was women who missed people, minded the distances, the time, and cared about whether or not they saw someone again. But Mad Sao was an unusual man.

After the speeches, the mourners got up to go, but when the demons saw everybody leaving, they started nabbing pallbearers. We hadn't known we were to designate some. My parents asked the old men to carry the coffin, my father asking and my mother tugging them by the sleeves. They were doing us a favour saying Yes, not wanting to do it, reluctant to associate with death. The white demons handed them white gloves, which the men shoved their splintery hands into. There must have been a demon taboo against touching a coffin with one's bare hands. Father, Mad Sao, and four men not in our family each took a coffin handle and, fumbling and stumbling, jostled it between the chairs and out the door. It wasn't like the processions in the movies but like moving furniture, some pallbearers facing forward and some backward, bumping out the door and down the steps, then lifting the big coffin into the hearse.

The limousine unfolded inside; jump seats came up out of the floor and the walls. My mother walked around to the windows in back – we were like the children who ride in station wagons – and gave us strips of white paper the size of dollar bills. 'Throw this money out the window,' she said, but she was unceremonious; I thought it would be better to dole the 'money' out, scatter it in intervals along the way, not just dump it. 'Use it up,' was all she said. We would not have to save any of it. Luxury. We divided the paper evenly amongst us. 'Wait until the car starts so that it'll fly,' we instructed one another.

When the car moved, we flung out a few white bills, budgeting them so that we would not run out before reaching the cemetery. For lack of adult explanations, we children made up what was happening. 'It's for him to spend in heaven,' we said. It may have also been for the waif ghosts lining the streets, or it was like a carrot on a stick to entice Kau Goong, who was lingering behind or hovering overhead, to the cemetery. The hearse, the vegetable trucks, the pickup trucks, and Mad Sao's automobile moved in procession through Stockton. We drove to the places where Kau Goong went when he was alive as if we were following him on his rounds, very slowly, as if gathering him in. His ghost was not to stay at the club where he smoked his water pipe or at the school, where he waited to pick us up. We drove to our house and paused there, engines running. Perhaps he'd come for his things – the trunk and wicker baskets that he had brought from China, his water gourd, his ceramic jug, the rags on the pipes, the TV set, the vacuum cleaner – that is, the invisible duplicates of these things, or perhaps he'd left some of his anima in them and was collecting that. 'We're taking him on a last look,' we explained to one another. 'Or we're looking for him.' We next drove to Chinatown, where we idled in front of the Benevolent Association. In the window of his room on the second floor, the gauze curtains were slightly parted and still. His room overlooked the square where the hoboes and winos slept under the palm trees. On one side of the square was the Chinese school, whose classrooms were also on the second floor; he had heard us at our lessons and seen us lean on the balconies. On the other side of the square was the Catholic church, where the hoboes and winos were lined up for lunch an hour ahead of time; a cop walked by with his dog, and the poor men stiffened to attention like an army. One of them drank water out of the gutter. Beneath Kau Goong's room was the store where the old men sat out on the sidewalk among the big tin cans full of tofu and bean sprouts and live snails and turtles; the bench between the parking meters was empty, the sitters at the funeral. Next to the store was the closed-up place that used to be our gambling house. Next to that was the herbalist's, and at the corner was the Filipino grocery store. At the other corner was the demon liquor store all lit up no matter what time of day or night; in the window, a black scotty and a white scotty, run by batteries behind the cardboard, wagged their tails and tongues. A loudspeaker mounted above the door played country music loud enough for everyone to hear. Once I was crossing the street and heard machine-gun fire full blast and a grenade and a long scream – 'Aaaaaa! ' – then the announcer saying, 'Another GI shot down in battle,' more shooting and the scream again, striking me stock-still in the intersection. We did not drive through the middle of Chinatown, which was the one block with the uncles' businesses on both sides of the street. The cars crossed Washington Street, and from the intersection we looked down Chinatown at the grocery stores, the butcher shops, the shoe store, the restaurants, the candy-and-tobacco store. Leaving Skid Row, we drove to the laundry, where we slowed a moment and then sped on to the highway. The wind twisted the white money, pulled it out of our hands, and carried it away. It went whipping and spinning over the alfalfa fields, and caught in the fruit trees and the tumbleweeds.

We stopped at the Chinese cemetery, which is not on a hillside in China but beside Interstate five on the flat San Joaquin Valley floor. The pallbearing uncles carried the coffin and lowered it into the grave. We may have been one man short, for a demon helped carry. The mortician demons threw their white gloves into the grave, and so the uncles did too. As she does wherever she goes, my mother brought food, which she arranged on the ground around the grave. It was like birthday food, the whole chicken, pork, beef, vegetables. She filled a shot glass with whisky; my father poured it into the grave and bowed three times. She refilled the glass and did that too. Then, according to her directions, starting with my oldest brother, who was younger than I, and ending with the girls, each of us kids poured a glass of the amber and fumy whisky into the blackening dirt and on the coffin, and bowed three times. Whenever we had to do this bowing at political meetings or assemblies at Chinese school, we kids giggled. Now I felt my body slop and shuffle, lean crooked

185

on one foot like an informal American punk – there being something wrong with bowing, something embarrassing, awkward. Not looking at one another, we did some quick nods.

My mother burned Kau Goong's clothes and shoes in the black incinerator at the end of a row of graves. I looked inside the grate; I saw black shoes and red mouths, blood and eyes. She shut the lid before I finished looking. She gave us and the pallbearers red paper with money inside; it was to end the death and begin the luck again.

We went to the big expensive restaurant in the middle of Chinatown, where my parents ordered a moderate amount of food, not like the profusion at wedding banquets. I thought it typical of us to order stingily, but it was only lunch, and we had the grave food left over. As if there were no funeral a moment ago, the adults laughed, talked, ate.

When we got home, we did not burn a pile of leaves and newspapers at the kerb. We were modern. We children had seen such piles and women stoking them. When we asked, 'Is it so that the ghost won't follow you in? Is it so that you're no longer contagious?' the adults scolded, 'It's nothing. Don't talk about it.' We went directly indoors, a relief not to be jumping over fire like Indians or Africans or South Seas Islanders in front of the neighbours and passers-by.

That was the only time our family went to the cemetery. Other families go every year and even twice a year to bring food, flowers, and paper to their relatives. They eat with or for the dead. 'Superstitious backward peasants,' my parents say. 'We don't have that custom in our family,' MaMa says proudly. 'Nothing happens to you after you die. You just disappear. No afterlife. Right?' 'Right,' says BaBa. We treat Kau Goong and any other grandfathers who may be in that cemetery like any American dead.

I had a dream about Kau Goong one morning. MaMa asked, 'What did he say?' I couldn't remember and was tempted to make up something extravagant. 'Sometimes there's a message,' she said. In another family, a grandfather came to one of them in a dream and said that the kids were to bury their parents correctly; after that they would be absolved of all duties to ancestors since they were now Americans.

*

We had an uncle, a second or third cousin maybe, who went back to China to be a Communist. We called him Uncle Bun, which might have been his name, but could also be a pun, Uncle Stupid. He was a blood relative and not just a villager. He was very talkative. In fact, he hardly ever stopped talking, and we kids watched the spit foam at the corners of his mouth. He came to the laundry and sat, or if it was very hot, he stood near the door to talk and talk. It was more like a lecture than a conversation. He repeated himself so often that some of what he said seeped into the ears. He talked about wheat germ. 'You ought to eat wheat germ,' he said, 'because wheat germ is the most potent food in the world. Eat it and you'll stay young for a long time; you'll never get sick. You'll be beautiful and tall and strong, also intelligent. The reason for so much unhappiness and strife is that people have been eating wrong. Meat turns them into animals. Wheat germ, which we can digest easier, can help us evolve into better people. Wheat germ is full of vitamins (*why-huh-ming*), and it is very cheap. A, C, thiamine, riboflavin, niacin, calcium, carbohydrates, fats, iron (*eye-yun*).' He was a scientific and up-to-date man who used English scientific terms. In two weighty syllables, both equally accented, a spondee, he said 'Wheat Germ'. Wheat germ would fatten up my father and also fatten up all the skinny children. Unlike the rest of the men in the family, who were thin and had white hair, this uncle was round and bald with black hair above his ears and around the back of his head. He wore a pearl grey three-piece suit and a necktie with a gold tiepin, the gold chain of his pocket watch linking one vest pocket to the other, the last button of his vest open over his prosperous paunch. He opened his eyes wide to see everything through his round gold-framed eyeglasses.

'Wheat germ – you can put it into any food,' he said. 'Sprinkle it on the rice and strew it on all the accompaniments. Stir it into milk and juices. Drink it in soups and beverages; it melts right in. Mix it with ice cream and strawberries. Combine it with flour. Combine it with rice. Beat it into cakes and pancakes. Scatter it on fried eggs for a crunchy texture. You can eat it by itself. Eat it by the handful, cooked or raw. Add it to cold food or hot food, sauces and gravies. Rain it on vegetables. Coat fish, meat, and fowl with it. Us it as a binder in meatballs and fishcakes. It goes with anything.' Wheat germ. I could not imagine this miracle food, whether it was sweet or salty, what size it was, what it was, what colour, whether it tasted good. Was it a liquid or a solid? Was *germ* the same germ as in *bacteria*? 'Wheat germ is golden brown,' he said, 'though the colour blends with whatever you're cooking. A pinch of it changes regular food into a medicine.' It sounded like a fairy-tale elixir, fairy food. 'You cannot taste or detect its presence in other foods,' he said. 'Yet you can eat it by itself like cornflakes,' which he also pronounced spondaically in his accent, *Coon Flex.* 'Wheat germ is the heart of the wheat,' he said, 'the heart of bread and wheat, which is more nutritious in the first place than rice. It repairs broken parts and tissues.'

'Hum,' said my father and mother.

'We ought to buy some, don't you think?' I asked my parents, hating to ask them to spend more money, but we might be wasting away from the lack of a vital food.

'He's crazy,' my mother said. 'Anything that necessary has to have been invented long ago.'

He bought us some sample wheat germ, which tasted like raw peas or raw oats.

Although he was about my father's age, Uncle Bun, like many of the old men, did not appear to have a job and was able to afford entire mornings, afternoons, days, and evenings sitting and chatting while we worked. Maybe his sons sent money from Chicago. My father did join him talking politics, a man's topic as grey as newspapers. They talked about Sun Yat Sen and Chiang Kai Shek and Mao Tse Tung, about their moves and countermoves, their strategies, the Red Army and the White Army, and the Japanese manoeuvring here, marching there, meeting and retreating, circling, war for years. My father scoffed at Chiang and Mao, at their ineptness. Their inconsistencies made him laugh. Since Sun's death, nobody could unite China.

'The way Chiang solves poverty is to print paper money,' my father said.

'We have to examine the causes of poverty,' said Uncle Bun. 'The world has never experimented to find out if it is rich enough and big enough to support all its people. It probably is. Look at all the rich people who own too much, and you can see there's extra food, land, and money. And certainly, there's always work enough. Only the distribution is wrong; we have to divide up the goods evenly.' We kids divided every five-cent candy bar and all the chores. 'Who really owns the land?' he asked. 'The man who farms it with his sweat and piss or the man whose name is on the paper? And shouldn't the worker on the assembly line own his labour and the results of his labour?'

'The farmers should own the land,' he answered himself. 'The workers should own the factories – and the profits. The rich pigs turn profit into extra cars, ostrich-feather hats, and golf parks. When it ought to be distributed as food among the poor. We have the airplanes and ships and trains for the distribution. The true purpose of the diesel engine is to rush food to everyone on every continent and island. Every child has the right to food.'

'And would the owners, landlords, and bosses voluntarily give away their holdings?' asked my father. 'And the housewives their slaves?'

'Yes!' shouted Uncle Bun. 'Either we educate them, to see the right way, or we, the poor of the earth, will take what's ours by revolution. The takeover by the poor is inevitable. The poor become more and more numerous as the rich become fewer. Haven't you noticed how many poor people there are and how few rich? We will overcome them with our numbers. I get so angry that a boss can deny a worker his job. Why should another man own my muscles and brains and what I make with my hands and my time?' He told again about some fight he had had with the boss at one of his past jobs, his face red and his spit spraying. 'How dare he treat me like that? I'm a man and he's a man. In a fair system, the worker would be the more valuable man, and the supervisor serve him and make his job easier.'

My father had ideas too but merely an observation here and there that changed from day to day. Uncle Bun said the white demons were not the only oppressors, that upper-class Chinese made their money off lower-class ones; the immigrants got twenty-five cents an hour if they were lucky. No day off. We children made exactly twenty-five cents an hour. 'You're in trouble at the cannery if the forelady is Chinese,' my mother agreed. 'She'll make trouble for you to impress the boss.' (*Folaydee, chup-bo* – trouble – *bossu, day offu*, Chinese American words.)

'Actually these aren't dreams or plans,' Uncle Bun said. 'I'm making predictions about ineluctabilities. This Beautiful Nation, this Gold Mountain, this America will end as we know it. There will be one nation, and it will be a world nation. A united planet. Not just Russian Communism. Not just Chinese Communism. World Communism.'

He said, 'When we don't need to break our bodies earning our daily living any more, and we have time to think, we'll write poems, sing songs, develop religions, invent customs, build statues, plant gardens, and make a perfect world.' He paused to contemplate the wonders.

'Isn't that great?' I said after he left.

'Don't get brainwashed,' said my mother. 'He's going to get in trouble for talking like that. He's going to get us in trouble; the barbarians think that Communists and Chinese are the same.'

Even when the uncles were killed during the Revolution and the aunts tortured, Uncle Bun did not change his mind about Communism. 'We have to weigh the death of a few against the lives of millions of poor workers and the coming generations,' he said.

'A fermentation of dreams,' said my father. Uncle Bun should not have said such Communist things against our dead relatives. His fingers followed the gold chain to the gold watch in his vest pocket; he looked at the time and left. BaBa snorted, 'Foolish man. Silly man. Long winded.' 'Long winded', the same metaphor in Chinese and English. 'Fermenting dreams,' said BaBa. 'Dreams fermenting.' I heard in his scorn and words how dreams ferment the way yeast and mould do, how dreams are like fungus.

Next time Uncle Bun came over, he said that Mao himself had had to leave his sick wife and child behind on the Long March, his dedication to Communism that strong. With spit flying, Uncle Bun talked about the glory of the Long March. The lame and weak sacrificed their bodies for use as ladders and fords so that others could leap mountains and rivers. Yes, some of his own family – our family – had given their lives too, though unwillingly. He talked about five-year plans. It frightened me that someone could keep something in mind for five years – keeping track for five years.

'Ah, sad, sad America, which does not respect the poor,' he

said. 'The poor are important. And look, look, even if we distribute everything, and it's spread so thin that we're all poor – that's good. Consider the culture we poor have invented – vegetarianism and fasting, pencil sketches, pottery, singing without instruments, mending, saving and reusing things, quilting, patchwork, the poetry written on leaves, rocks, and walls, acrobatics, dancing, and kung fu, which doesn't require expensive sports equipment. Oh, let's value the poor, who in a way are all of us. Even with money, the rich can't buy good food. They eat white bread and poisoned food. What they ought to do is eat wheat germ.'

Amazing! His two big ideas – wheat germ and Communism – connected.

His ideas had come together neater and neater as the months and years passed. 'Not just China,' he said, 'and not just America, but the world. We will organize the entire world. End world hunger. And we will have world peace.' What scope. What neatness. World peace. How amazingly his ideas connected up.

Then one day, he announced in a whisper, 'The milk demon is poisoning me. The grocer is poisoning me. They have a plot against me. They put poison in my milk and eggs.'

My mother said, 'It's impossible to inject poison into eggs. Look how perfect the shells are.'

But he said, 'Science. Science can do anything.'

When he connected his two big ideas, he touched wrong wires to each other, shot off sparks, and shorted out. He had become a paranoiac. 'They're trying to poison me,' he said, running into the laundry, his red face bursting above the collar and tie. 'I've discovered their plot. They think they can get away with it but because of the sharp senses I've developed on wheat germ, I can detect poisons. I smelled the poison, and did not eat or drink it. I've discontinued milk delivery, and I'm going to buy groceries at a different store.' He looked canny. 'Why do you suppose they're after me?' he asked. 'It must be because I've hit on the truth and discovered the plot against the poor. And so they want to get me.' He entered rooms as if pursued, stepping in and out of doorways, checking behind him, peeping out of windows, and pressing his back to walls. He continually surveyed the street. 'I've noticed a pattern,' he said. 'They put the poison into white food – eggs, bread, milk, vanilla ice cream, flour, sugar, white beans. They're thinking that the seeming purity of white food would fool me, and it would disguise the poison, but I know that they have developed an invisible dissolvable poison. I'm outsmarting them. I'll shop at a different store every day. I'll keep changing stores.'

'He's gone crazy,' my mother diagnosed. 'He's getting crazier. When he comes to the house, and we're at the laundry, you kids don't let him in.'

He became more and more agitated. 'I saw the wholesale demon open a bottle of milk. Yes, I saw him lift the lid. He dropped in a pellet of poison. I could tell by the way he cupped his hand. Then he pressed the lid back on. Sleight of hand. Lately the tops of milk bottles have been looser. That's evidence. And today's evidence is that I saw the wholesale demon tampering with the vacuum seal. He placed the bottle in the exact spot where I had picked my last bottle. They're out to get me because —' and he held his breath on 'because' – 'I am a Communist,' 'FBI,' he whispered. 'Secret police. House Un-American Activities Committee. Coconut. Inside the husk. They've even gotten inside the coconut with their scientific know-how.'

'His head is a coconut,' said BaBa.

Another day Uncle Bun came in, said nothing, sat. His face was red and purple. 'How much did you spend for the kids' bikes?' he asked. 'Where did you get the extra money? Roller skates. Then bikes.' He whirled on my father, poked his face and finger at him. 'Where's my money?' he shouted.

'I don't know,' said BaBa. 'Did you lose your money?'

'Half the money is gone from my savings account,' he shouted. He looked as if he were having a fit, his mouth foaming. Breathing, snorting, bursting, he yelled, 'Where is it?' His round body expanded.

'You shouldn't be accusing me,' said BaBa, and continued ironing. 'Banks are very careful,' he said. 'No one can get your money without your signature and your passbook. Did you lose your passbook and your IDs?'

'No, I didn't lose my passbook and my IDs,' said Uncle Bun, imitating hatefully. 'You took them, and you withdrew my money. You disguised yourself as me. They see a chinaman and can't tell it's not me. You know a lot about handwriting, you forger.' Then he stopped explaining. 'Give me my money,' he shouted. He took his glasses off. Red shot out of his eyes. 'Give me back my money.' He had changed from the jolly roly-poly man; I had not seen him jolly for quite a while. My mother had stopped letting him take the baby for walks, but lately he had not asked to baby-sit her either. 'Thief!' he yelled. As in other emergencies, we kids kept working steadily, acting normal so that the rest of the world would return to normal too. I wished that my father would say soft, cajoling words, even pay him some money, but that was part of the fear too, that my father does not give in. 'You walked into the bank with my passbook, and you took half, thinking that I wouldn't notice. You thought I was going mad and had forgotten how to add and subtract. You're very good at pen and abacus. I see you. I know you. You did it. Give me back the money, or I'll call the cops. Then you'll be sorry.'

He was a hard, perverse man. He might just do that, call the police and get us deported. A man crazy enough to be glad that his relatives had been killed by Communists was capable of treachery.

'Why don't you phone your son long distance in Chicago?' said BaBa. 'Tell him what happened. Or why don't you go to Chicago and stay with him until you feel better?'

'I don't see how I'm going to have money for train fare with you siphoning it. How long have you been dipping in, huh? A little at a time or one lump sum? I'm going to the cops.'

'Why don't you look at the dates in the passbook?' said my father.

'I'm going to the police station,' said Uncle Bun and ran out.

'He may get violent,' said my mother. 'Don't let him in the house.'

He returned to the laundry the next day for further accusations, his open passbook in his hand, pointed at figures, and shouted out numbers. 'Proof!' he said. 'Proof!' and slapped the little book with the back of his hand.

BaBa took the passbook and studied. 'Look. There are no entries in the withdrawal column.'

'Of course not. You didn't do it with this passbook. You did it so that it wouldn't show on this passbook. You told them you had lost the passbook. You filled out a special form.'

'I'll go to the bank with you,' said BaBa. He was taking Uncle Bun very seriously, setting down his iron, offering to take a break from work for him.

'Just watch it,' said Uncle Bun. 'When they see the two of us together, they'll put you in jail. They'll know which is really me.' Which was very crazy; they looked the opposite of each other. When they returned from the bank, Uncle Bun had stopped talking about missing money.

He did come to our house one day when neither of our parents were home. Unfortunately, the front door was wide open, so we couldn't hide and pretend we were out. It would be embarrassing to tell him why he couldn't come in. Being the oldest, I decided that we children would go outside and talk to him on the porch. It was pleasant out there under the grapevines. We stood between him and the red door and asked him questions to distract him. He usually walked right in. 'What exactly is wheat germ?' we asked, but he seemed not as interested in wheat germ as before. 'How's shopping at the new grocery store?' 'Fine. Fine,' he said. 'May I have a drink of water?' he asked. 'We'll get it,' we said, some of us blocking his way while one ran inside, very rude, a guest having to ask for refreshments. He drank the entire glassful quickly. 'You must finish all your water,' he advised us. 'When you have milk, finish all of it. Finish your food. Eat everything. Don't leave scraps. Scraps turn into garbage. Food one moment, garbage the next. Same with paper. Don't blotch it, and if you do, save it for scratch paper. Cross out the mistakes rather than crumple the paper. Make every page count.' He did not go berserk, did not break into the house and throw himself against the sofa like a padded cell, did not act like a maniac at all. He sounded like other adults, advising this, advising that, advising eat.

At the laundry where it would be dangerous to run amok among the hot machines, he announced: ' *They* are not *only* hiding the poison in my food. I am on the verge of discovering the *real* plot. Have you noticed – oh, surely, you must have been alarmed by it – you must have seen how many garbage demons there are in this country?' 'Yes, there are,' said my mother. 'Do you see,' he asked, 'how the white demons are very careful with garbage? And how much garbage there is?'

Now, our family knew a great deal about garbage and how much of it was not garbage at all. On our way home on garbage nights, we visited bins that belonged to the stores and found valuables – mannequin heads and hands, sheet music, hats, magazines, comics, English-language newspapers, a cardboard Eiffel Tower, the black and white scotties, books of rug samples, Christmas card samples, wallpaper, perfectly good boxes. To lower our garbage bill, we left a sack or two of our own garbage – marrowed bones, papers written on front and back, shoes that couldn't be repaired. At the grocery stores, we found carrots and lettuce for our rabbits, the outer leaves for the rabbits. Sometimes we split up to cover the route faster, meeting one another with loot at another corner. So we understood garbage better than most people.

'The white demons are very careful with garbage, aren't they?' said Uncle Bun. 'The city pays men to sweep the gutters and pick up paper with a stick and nail. They attach wire baskets to the signal poles, and on other street corners they have tax-paid trash cans right next to the mailboxes. And every week, regularly, on a highly organized schedule, teams of garbage demons come to each house and collect garbage. Truckloads.' All this we agreed to seeing, and it did not, after all, seem crazy. You could see what he was talking about for yourself. 'Have you ever thought about what they're saving the garbage for?' he asked. 'What are they doing with it? Why are they so diligent? Today I saw children put their candy wrappers in their lunchboxes. And the hoboes who pick up cigarette butts and put them in their pockets – do you assume they're going to smoke them later? There has got to be a purpose behind this storing up and bagging and chuting. Have you seen the buildings with chutes? Garbage from every floor plunges to the basement. The government pays armies of collectors to take it somewhere for a purpose.'

'They take it to the dump,' my mother said. 'They leave it there in heaps, which they burn. They take wet garbage from restaurants and feed it to pigs. Or they use it for fertilizer. They re-pulp paper and make newspaper.'

'Oh, you think so?' he asked. 'Have you ever seen any of this

195

paper-making? Have you ever followed the garbage truck when it leaves your house? Too early in the morning for you to bother, isn't it? Have you seen any of these restaurant pigs?' Then he left very mysteriously, abruptly.

A few days later he again came running into the laundry. He was highly excited and frightened, as if he were being chased. 'I've discovered what they do with the garbage.' He was sweating. 'They're collecting it for me. They're going to feed it to me. They'll capture me and tie me down and shovel it into my mouth. They're going to make me eat it. All of it. It's all for me. You must see what a big plot it is. Everybody is manufacturing garbage constantly, some knowing the purpose and some just because everyone else is doing it. It all ties in with the poisoning, don't you see? The newspapers and radios are in on it too, telling them to buy, buy, and then they turn everything they buy into garbage as fast as they can. They're preparing and saving for the day when they'll shovel it into my mouth. They've been collecting for years, and I didn't see the plot till now. That day is coming soon. They'll make me eat it.'

'Why should they do that to you?' asked my mother.

'Because of my talk about Communism,' he said.

'The garbage is not for you,' said my father. 'The garbage isn't that important. You're not that important. Forget the garbage.'

'You should go to a mind doctor,' said my mother.

He got offended and left. 'You'll be sorry when the day arrives, and you see it all come true. Feeding day.'

His stomach got thinner. He refused most food; he ate only greens and browns, leaving not a scrap, not contributing to the garbage that 'they' would feed him later. 'Paper garbage too,' he said. 'Paper cups, paper plates, paper napkins, Kleenex, gum and gum wrappers.'

At last he said, 'I'm going back to China. I've outsmarted them. I know which day the feeding will be on, and I'll leave before then. It was not like this in China. Remember? In fact, they couldn't poison your milk and bread because we didn't drink milk. And we didn't eat much bread. We used everything thoroughly in China. Remember? There was hardly any garbage. We ate all the food. Remember how we could see with our own eyes that the hogs ate the peelings? If the human beings

196

didn't eat rinds, the animals did, and the fish bones got ploughed into the fields. Remember how paper gatherers collected paper that had writing on it and burned it in word furnaces? Remember we saved the bags and boxes? Why, this—' he picked up a cornflakes box – 'we would have treasured a pretty box like this, such bright colours, such sturdy cardboard. We would have opened the flaps carefully and used it to store valuable and useful things in. We'd have taken good care of it, made it last, handed it down. I'm going back to New Society Village.'

'But New Society Village isn't there any more,' said MaMa. 'It's been Communized. You'd have to sleep in a men's barracks and eat in a dining hall with hundreds of strangers. You'd have to eat whatever they cook. The Communists will take away your bank account.'

'That's right,' he said, and he blinked as if clearing his eyes. 'That's the way the world should be.'

From that decision on, he acted saner and saner, happier, and stopped talking about the garbage except to say, 'I'm returning to China before feeding day.' 'Returning' is not to say that he necessarily had ever been there before.

He talked about how he was using only a part of his money for passage and giving the rest to the new China. If they were suspicious of his years in America and did not let him in, he would sneak in from Hong Kong.

The day he left, he spoke to my youngest sister, who was about three years old. He bent over so that she could hear and see him very well. 'Don't forget me, will you?' he asked. 'Remember I used to play with you. Remember I'm the man who sang songs to you and gave you dimes. What's my name?' She laughed that he would ask her such a silly, easy question. Of course, she knew his name. He coaxed her to say it several times for him. 'You won't forget? Tell me you won't forget.'

'I won't forget,' she said. He seemed satisfied to leave, and we never saw him or heard from him again.

For a while I reminded my sister, 'Do you remember Uncle Bun, the bald fat man who talked a lot? Do you remember him asking you not to forget him.?'

'Oh, yes, the funny man. I remember.'

I reminded her periodically. But one day, I noticed that I had not asked her for some time. 'Do you remember the funny man who talked a lot, the one who smuggled himself into Red China?'

'Who?' she asked.

'Uncle Bun. Remember?'

'No,' she said.

With no map sense, I took a trip by myself to San Francisco Chinatown and got lost in the Big City. Wandering in a place very different from our own brown and grey Chinatown, I suddenly heard my own real aunt calling my name. She was my youngest aunt, my modern aunt just come from Hong Kong. We screamed at each other the way our villagers do, hugged, held hands. 'Have you had your rice yet?' we shouted. 'I have. I have had my rice.' 'Me too. I've eaten too,' letting the whole strange street know we had eaten, and me becoming part of the street, abruptly not a tourist, the street mine to shout in, never mind if my accent be different. She had been talking with a couple of women, to whom I said, 'Hello, Aunt. Hello, Aunt,' mumbling because there are different kinds of aunts depending on whether they're older or younger than one's mother. They'd tease you for being too distant, for addressing them as Lady or Mademoiselle, affectations, and also for being familiar.

'Who is this?' the women asked, one of them pointing at me with her chin, the other with her rolled up newspaper. This talking about me in the third person, this pointing at me – I shoved the resentment down my throat. They do not mean disdain – or they *do* mean disdain, but it's their proper way of treating young people. Mustn't dislike them for it.

'This is my own actual niece come to visit me,' my aunt said, as if I had planned to run into her all along. The women were to understand that I was not just somebody she called a niece out of politeness, but a blood niece. 'Come see my new apartment,' she said to me, turned around, and entered the doorway near which we were standing.

I followed her up the stairs, flight after flight, and along a hallway like a tunnel. But her apartment need not be dismal, I thought; these doors could open into surprisingly large, bright, airy apartments with shag carpets. 'Our apartment is very small,' she warned, her voice leading the way. 'Not like a regular house.

198

Not like your mother's big house.' So she noticed space; I had thought perhaps people from Hong Kong didn't need room, that Chinese people preferred small spaces. Some early mornings if we went down into our basement, we found two straight-backed chairs facing one another, blankets and shawls still cupped in shapes of the women who had sat there. The cord of the electric heater rose to a ceiling socket. Coffee cups and footstools sat on the floor. Our mother and this aunt had stayed up all night, talking again. I might have known from the good times they could have in the basement that it would be the smallest apartment I had seen in my life. The door didn't open up all the way because of a table, which had stuff stored on top and underneath. The half of the table away from the wall was cleared for eating and studying.

'Coffee? Tea?' Auntie asked.

'Coffee,' I said. 'Black.'

'How can you drink it like that? How about some meat? Fish?'

'MaMa has started drinking it black,' I said, giving her the news. 'MaMa has switched to black at her age.'

Big and medium-sized blonde dolls sat and stood on tops of stacks of things. Their pink gauze dresses fluffed against the Cellophane windows of their cardboard boxes. They were expensive dolls with little socks and gloves, purses and hats. I felt very relieved that my cousin, who was about ten or twelve years old, did not have to share one doll, the naked kind that one had to make clothes out of scraps for; she had two bride dolls. My relatives were not badly off, not as poor as we used to be. They had luxuries.

Auntie went into the kitchen, which did not have room for another person. I snooped about at the desk in one corner of the living room; looked at the desk calendar and the statuettes of the guardians of Happiness, Money, and Long Life, read the appointments pinned among the cut-outs of flowers on the wall. It was this aunt who had given my mother a nice set of the guardians mounted on wood and red velvet. There were some Christian pamphlets on a shelf over the desk; I couldn't remember whether this was the aunt who had converted to Christianity and was sending my parents tracts and Bibles or whether it was another aunt in Hong Kong who was sending to both of them. Or maybe she'd been accosted by a missionary working China-town. ('Are you a Christian?' my mother asks periodically. 'No, of course not.' 'That's good. Don't be a Christian. What *do* you believe in?' 'No religion. Nothing.' 'Why don't you take the Chinese religion, then?' And a few minutes later, 'Yes, you do that,' she'd say. 'Sure, Mom. Okay.') Next to the telephone were notebooks, pads, very sharp pencils, a pencil sharpener, another luxury. They had shaving lotion and hand lotion, toiletries on the shelf too.

'The bathroom is over there,' she shouted as if it were a huge house. I went into the bathroom, which was the closet next to the kitchen, to spy some more. They had built shelves with stores of sale toilet paper and soap, which was in fancy shapes prettily boxed. They aren't so poor, I thought. They are above subsis-tence; we have been worse off.

I stood by the kitchen door and watched my aunt cut cake. A corner of the floor was stacked with shiny gallon cans without labels. 'My husband baked these cakes,' she said. *Hus-u-bun*, she called him, a clever solution; some wives get so embarrassed about what to call their husbands, their names and *husband* such intimate words (like *rooster* – or *cock*), that they call him So-and-so's Father. My uncle worked at a famous bakery whose name is stamped on pink boxes that people carry about China-town.

'Cake?' asked my aunt. 'Pie? Chuck-who-luck? Le-mun?'

'I just ate,' I said, which was true, but took a plate anyway. The biggest difference between my aunt and my mother was that my mother would have forced me to eat it. I sat on the sofa, facing the front door. There was another door near the desk; it must have been to the next apartment.

Auntie got herself some chocolate cake and lemon pie and sat next to me. I enjoyed looking at this aunt, who was how my mother would have been if she were the youngest instead of the oldest, the city woman rather than the peasant. She was wear-ing a white blouse with sharp lapels; I also liked the straight grey skirt and intelligent glasses.

'I saw those hoppies they tell about in the newspaper,' she said. 'Some of them talked to me. "Spare change?" That's what they say. "Spare change?" I memorized it.' She held out her hand to show their ways. ' "Spare change?" What does "spare change" mean?' 'They're asking if you have extra money.' 'Oh-h, I see,' she said, laughing. ' "Spare change?" How witty.' She was silly compared to my mother. She giggled and talked about inconsequentials. 'Condo,' she would say. 'Cottage cheese. Football? Foosball?'

But here I was alone with her, and no adults to distract her; maybe I could ask her things, two equal adults, talk the way Americans talk. Talk grown-up. 'Is it hard to endure?' I asked like an old Chinese lady, but because I was not brave enough to hear the answer, quickly said on top of it, 'Where did you go? Were you grocery shopping? Going for a walk? Visiting neighbours?'

'I was coming from the beauty parlour, getting my hair done,' she said, and I wished that I had noticed to compliment her on how nice she looked, but her hair looked the way she always wore it, in stiff black curls. 'Otherwise, it wouldn't be this black,' she said. 'It's really white, you know.' She went to beauty parlours. Another luxury, I enumerated. Leisure.

'Are you working?' I asked because it was odd that she was having her hair done in the middle of a workday. 'Is it your day offu?'

'No. I'm not working any more.'

'What happened to your hotel job? Didn't you have a hotel job? As a maid?' I said *maid* in English, not knowing the Chinese word for *slave*. If she didn't know the word, she wouldn't hear it anyway. Languages are like that.

'I've been fired,' she said.

'Oh, no. But why?'

'I've been very sick. High blood pressure,' she said. 'And I got dizzy working. I had to clean sixteen rooms in eight hours. I was too sick to work that fast.' Something else I liked about this aunt was her use of exact numbers. 'Ten thousand rooms per second,' my mother would have said. 'Uncountable. Infinite.' Half an hour per unit, including bathrooms. 'People leave the rooms very messy,' she said, 'and I kept coughing from the ashes in the ashtrays. I was efficient until I fell sick. Once I was out for six weeks, but when I came back, the head housekeeper said I was doing a good job, and he kept me on.' She worked at a famous hotel, not a flop house in Chinatown. She'd given us miniature cakes of soap whenever she came to visit. 'The head housekeeper said I was an excellent worker.' My mother was the same way, caring tremendously how her employer praised her, never so hurt as when a boss reprimanded her, never so proud as when a forelady said she was picking cleanly and fast. 'He said I speak English very well,' Auntie said. She was proud of that compliment.

'What do you do all day long now that you aren't cleaning hotel rooms?'

'The days go by very slowly. You know, in these difficult times in the Big City mothers can't leave their children alone. The kidnappers are getting two thousand dollars per child. And whoever reports a missing child the FBI turns over to Immigration. So I posted ads, and one in the newspaper too, that I wanted to mind children, but I haven't got any customers. When the mothers see the apartment, they say No.' Of course. No place to run, no yard, no trees, no toys except to look at the dollies. Being poor in Stockton was better than this Big City poverty; we had trees and sloughs and vegetable gardens and animals. Also there were jobs in the fields. 'I could mind four or five children,' she said. 'I'd make as much money as cleaning the hotel. They don't want me to watch their children because I can't speak English.'

'But you do,' I said. 'You know lots of English.' When I could not think of the Chinese for something, she always knew the English word.

She was flattered. 'No, I don't,' she said. 'Now, *you* speak Chinese well,' but I was speaking well because I was talking to her; there are people who dry up language.

'You speak like your mother. She used to sound like a city person, but American people speak peasant accents, village accents, so she talks that way now.'

'Do my mother and father speak alike?'

'Why, yes,' she said, but maybe she couldn't hear the difference; being a city person she lumped the village accents together.

'My own son doesn't talk to me,' she said. 'What's nutrition?'

'It has to do with food and what people ought to eat to keep healthy.'

'You mean like cooking? He's going to college to learn how to cook?'

'Well, no. It's planning menus for big companies, like schools and hospitals and the Army. They study food to see how it works. It's the science of food,' but I did not feel I was giving an adequate explanation, the only word for science I knew was a synonym or derivative of *magic*, something like *alchemy*. 'He could work in public health, and that's a field that has lots of jobs right now. He could work for cafeterias and college dormitories, restaurant chains, mass production food plants that make frozen TV dinners, canned foods, cake mixes.'

'And *engineering*?' she asked.

'Building things, designing them, like designing bridges and mines and electrical things. Do you know what kind of engineering he's studying?'

'No, they shout at me and tell me I'm too stupid to understand. They hardly come home, and when I ask them what they're doing, they say I'm dumb. Oh, my sons have turned out very bad, and after all I've suffered for them.'

I did not want to hear how she suffered, and then I did. I did have a duty to hear it and remember it. She started by telling me how my mother had suffered. 'Oh, the suffering,' she said. 'Think of it. Both of your mother's babies died. How painful it must be to watch your babies die after they can walk and talk and have personalities. Aiya! How hard to endure.'

'What did they die of?'

'Firecrackers. The village women exploded firecrackers to scare germs and bad spirits away, but instead they scared away the babies. They filled the air with smoke so the babies couldn't breathe. And then a few years later, it happened again; when you were a baby, you suddenly stopped breathing, and she pounded on the floor for the downstairs neighbour to help. The fire trucks and the police came, and they revived you. She wrote to me about that.'

'Probably all babies, having recently been nothing, have a tenuous hold on life,' I observed. MaMa would have sat on the floor and held the babies to her or laid them on blankets in the middle of the house. I remembered the floor, the linoleum patterns and smells of it. Under the linoleum I had hidden milk bottle caps, flattening into lovely disks.

In the falling afternoon, I looked out the windows at the neighbours' windows. For a short while light had pushed through the curtains making little suns and a haze. We faced west and caught the last pale sun. The fog rolled between the buildings, and the foghorns were sounding already. My aunt made no move to switch on the lights. Her eyes were very bright. It aggravated me how easily tears came to women her age, not hardened at all by the years. 'I suffered terribly too,' she said. I would never be able to talk with them; I have no stories of equal pain.

Now she was telling her part of the story: When she was born, the blind fortuneteller said that she would be alternately very rich and very poor many times but end up rich. Sure enough, they were poor until her father went to the Gold Mountain, whence he travelled three times; each time he got richer and twice brought back wives. He hired teachers for his daughters, who learned to read and write. Between his trips they were poor. He died when she was ten. She was poor from then until she married a rich man. When Communism transformed the villagers, they chased her family out of their house. She hid with her two boys in the pig house. It was winter, and all they had on were cotton clothes. The boys knew better than to cry, learned instantly. The next morning, she found her husband. He said that the Communists had assigned them a place to live – the leper house. 'That's where you belong,' said the Communists. Lepers, the 'growing yin' people, who have too much cold wind in them, died in there. The rest of the family had disappeared; his mother had run away alone with the gold and jade. They never saw her again. The Communists kept an eye on them in the leper house, waited for them to make a false move. One day her husband caught a pair of doves and hid them to feed the family. 'And do you know how the Communists killed him?'

'I think my mother said they stoned him in the tree where the birds were.'

'They pressed him between millstones,' she said.

Of course. In stories, stones fall crash bang crash bang like pile drivers. It was the sound of harvest and executions. After battle, no matter what farmhouse or courtyard a villain or hero used, when it was time for executions, he always had a device handy – the millstones.

'Aiya,' I said. 'That's horrible. How hard to endure.'

Then she escaped to Hong Kong. She gave her wedding ring to get on the ship, her earrings for food, her necklace to get off the ship. She and the two boys slept on the sidewalks; they ate the rice they begged though the Communists threw sand into it, saying 'Have some salt.' The oldest boy, Big Baby she called him, and her second son, Little Baby, got angry at her when they were hungry or too hot or too cold. 'What did you do today?' she asked them after separating to beg on different streets. 'What do you care?' they said. 'What do you know?'

She noticed a man who was selling shoes alone in a stall. She bade him 'Good morning' daily and thus made his acquaintance. He let her sit in the customer's chair under the awning in rain and in the noon sun. Whenever he shared his lunch with her, she hid some for the boys. One day she said – she said it for me with a giggle – 'Sir, why doesn't your lady come help you work these long hours?' (Hong Kong people are more refined than us and don't say *old lady* for *wife* or *old rooster* for *husband*.)

'I don't have a lady,' he said.

'I'll help you then,' she said, and did so. Soon they got married, the first self-matched marriage in the family. They built the stall up into a store, then added a wholesale outlet, then a factory, and she was rich again. They had a boy and a girl of their own, much younger than the other two.

But she did not forget the accurate blind fortuneteller: a downfall imminent. The people who lived in crates on the hillsides and the boat people who had never touched land would soon rise up and kill the rich people and the British. There are rich people who don't see poor people, but she never stopped seeing them. She took varying routes from home to store so the beggars wouldn't recognize her and mark her. 'The Revolution is coming,' she kept saying, and her husband agreed. 'Yes, it's going to happen,' but went on building his business. Each downfall had been worse than the last – the Japanese, then World War II, then the Revolution. 'The Hong Kong Revolution will be fought with nuclear bombs,' she predicted. Her husband called her a superstitious peasant.

At last she said, 'My name is at the top of the Refugee List. Let's leave for the United States.' But her husband did not want to go; the business was doing very well. He told her that if she went, she would have to go alone. She took the two older boys and left him with the daughter and son. 'Badger him to bring you to the Gold Mountain,' she instructed these two youngest, and left.

'Father,' they said with their little arms supplicating, the boy especially naughty, 'take us to the Gold Mountain. We want to see Ah Ma. Why won't you take us? Do you want us to get killed by Communists? Ah Ba, take us to America and buy us some American toys. You're a selfish father not to take us travelling. All right then. When we're old enough, we're leaving you. We'll go find her. You're cheap, that's why you won't take us.'

My mother showed her the street corners where she was to wait for the farm buses to take her to the tomatoes and grapes.

Yes, life in America was meaner, but no signs of revolution; the beggars in the street were young and fat 'hoppies', who begged for fun. She hoped that this Gold Mountain poverty counted for the next fall in her fortunes. Her husband wrote that he was definitely not about to leave his homeland and his family. And didn't she miss having servants and friends talking her own language? She suggested that he not sell the shoe store but export the shoes to the United States, send them to her here. She had already gotten her American relatives to promise to take cases of sample shoes from store to store. She said a war in Indochina was going to spread to other Asian countries, and the Pentagon would bomb China. She outwrote him. He said, 'All right. I'm coming to the United States, but only to have a look at it and to bring you back.'

He brought the two younger children with him. What luxury, I thought. World travel. No more deciding once and for all on a country sight unseen. He took one look at the Los Angeles International Airport, and said, 'Let's go back.' But she said to give the Gold Mountain a chance. Be a tourist. Take a vacation. For a couple of months he complained how there were no jobs, then how hard he had to work, and how he had to obey a boss. Both of them complained about doing hard work for only a fraction of the money they were making in Hong Kong.

I remember they rented a house with peeling and flaking paint; they did not plaster the cracks, did not hang curtains. They slept on the floor until my sister brought them mattresses.

They used their suitcases instead of dressers. Chinese people are like that, we sisters and brothers told one another – no frills, cheap. My sister bought them sheets, then a bedspread. The two older boys, whom we refused to call Big BiBi and Little BiBi, did not talk to us but looked away if we caught their eyes, answered direct questions Yes or No, and never asked us questions in return. Like old uncles, they talked to our parents in Chinese. They were FOBs all right. Fresh Off the Boat.

The youngest boy was more sociable. He opened our refrigerator door and stood there and ate; he knocked over furniture and sassed his mother in two languages. He asked us questions, and his hair spiked up all over his head as if every hair were listening. 'Why do you look like that?' 'How do they do instant replay so fast?' 'How much money do you make? Yeah, what's your salary?' But when we asked his name, he suddenly stood still. He and his sister looked at one another and down at their shoes. The girl, who was older, pointed to her brother and muttered something, and he turned red. 'What?' I asked. She said it again. It was his Chinese name, and we could hardly hear it. 'Her name is Lucille,' he said. And *Lucille* was easy for him to say and easy to hear. He was proud to be able to give an American name though it wasn't his. So, they'd already learned to be shamed by a Chinese name.

When I Fu, Aunt's Husband, said, 'I'm going back. You do as you please, but I'm going back,' Auntie went with him. They took the two younger children. Our older cousins decided that they would stay in the United States; they were never going back; they would finish school, apply for citizenship, risk getting drafted – it was worth it. How foreign they were. Another generation of heartless boys leaving their family. Only my mother and aunt showed regret at leaving each other.

My mother nagged her nephews if they took any time off from work and study whatsoever. 'My own children study all the time,' she scolded, to which the FOBs replied, 'They must not be very bright if they have to study that hard.' She told us that retort, stirring up suspicions, establishing a pecking order, which must have been the way in China. They lived down in our basement with a bare light bulb. They were not to put their belongings in our closets or drawers, nor to ride our bikes or watch our

TV or listen to the radios. MaMa said, 'They're not my children.' When they came home from school or from the grocery store, where they worked for twenty-five cents an hour, they were to go to the cellar.

Meanwhile in Hong Kong, Auntie was enjoying another one of her high fortunes. But one day I Fu stood up from a customer's feet and told a clerk to finish up. A surge of chemicals or light had rushed through him. He went back to his office and unlocked his desk. He walked to the bank. The walk he took was magical: Inanimate objects glowed, but, oh, the animate – the trees and flowers and bugs and dogs were spraying colours. Human beings flared haloes around their heads and the rest of their bodies. Bands of light connected couples. He explained later how he understood the stopping quality of red light and the go of green. The city was not making a general roar or hum. His ears separated out the sounds of various motors, the gas pipes and water mains under the city, each bicycle wheel, the way the rubber peeled off the asphalt. It was a good thing it had been a sunny seaport day and not San Francisco; a foghorn would have melted him with sorrow. He passed a bookstore. Jets of coloured lights jumped along the books' spines; he wanted to stop and see whether *Red Chamber Dream* and Communist books were red, the Clear River poems blue and green, Confucius's writings a white light, and the *I Ching* yellow or saffron, but he had to hurry on. The seats, handlegrips, and pedals of the pedicabs and bicycles pulsed like fire. The newspapers were aflame in reds and oranges. He passed a drugstore and saw the little drawers leaking squares of light.

At the bank, he filled out a withdrawal slip with the very figure that was the last balance in his account. He said later those digits had had a numerological significance. He took the money in cash – and money had its own brilliance. It was so much money, the bank let him keep the canvas bag to carry it in. The teller and manager asked if he were certain he didn't want a cheque or money order, and he said Yes. He liked the feeling of the Yes escaping warm out of his body. He also liked voices warming his ears. He would have to remember to go to the theatre more often. He carried the money through the streets. He was certain that thieves would not snatch it; he was choreographing the movements of people and the weather. Time and fate were his invention and under the control of his will. He walked into a part of Hong Kong where he had never gone before, but he knew where to go. Fences made out of air guided his way. He entered the correct building and in the elevator knew which floor to choose. He walked through a particular door into a particular room. There were several men he had never seen before, but he knew just which one to approach and what to say. He gave this man all the money he had in the world. He walked out. Free of money. Free of burden. Purpose fulfilled. He flew home. 'I can control the weather,' he said earnestly. 'You can too.' His wife and the employees kept asking if he were all right. They planted in him the possibility of his not being all right.

'You look sick,' his wife said.

'Stop saying that,' he said, and he crashed down to normal. 'I've been robbed,' he said. 'I've been robbed. I was drugged by the bandits that prey on Gold Mountain Sojourners. They slipped a drug into my lunch. And their post-hypnotic suggestion was for me to take all the money out of the bank. I gave it all to them. We're ruined. Why didn't you stop me?'

'What are you talking about?' my aunt asked. 'That's impossible. A drug, you say? Hypnosis? How could I have stopped you? Is there such a drug? You gave all our money away? All of it? It wasn't gambling?'

'It was like sleepwalking,' he said. 'I could see everything; the world was the same, but the story behind it was different. I thought strangely. I thought it was a friend I gave the money to, that he was doing me a favour taking it.' According to the passbook, which he found in his pocket, the account had been closed out. 'Our life savings.'

Husband and wife dashed outside, trying to trace where he had walked. They ran about asking if anyone had seen him come this way. 'Did you see me go by a little while ago?' 'The bookstore,' he said. 'I remember it. And that drugstore.' The unknown neighbourhood had disappeared as if the bandits had set it up, then taken the buildings away. They ran to the bank, which was closed. They went to the police station, though they knew that the police were themselves crooks.

They and a policeman were at the doors when the bank opened

in the morning. The teller who had waited on I Fu confirmed that he had been at that window the day before, and he had withdrawn all his money. 'Was there anyone with him?' his wife asked. 'Did you see anyone behind him? Could there have been someone behind him with a gun?' The tellers had not seen anyone. I Fu told the bank manager that he had been drugged or hypnotized to take out all his money and give it away. The bank manager could do nothing about that. 'We don't insure against that,' he said. Hong Kong was full of criminals, tricksters, shysters, cheaters, con artists, plotters. People made their living by eating other people, by catching pigs. At lunch, a customer who followed him to the back room might have waved a hand over I Fu's food, and the drug had poured down a sleeve or slipped out of a button or a hinged ring. 'Maybe so,' said the policeman. Pig-catching was a game among the southern people. The shoe clerks and his relatives were probably in on it too, and the police too.

'We shouldn't have left the United States,' Auntie complained. 'American police and American people are honest.'

When I Fu made change for the last customer of the day, when the bell dinged in the cash register, the spell came over him again. He scooped up the bills and put them in a shoe box. 'Where are you going?' cried Auntie, alarmed at his pinpointy, jumpy eyes. 'Where are you going? Stop it. You're doing it again. You told me to stop you. It's come over you again. Snap out of it. Put the money back. Give it to me. Wake up.' She clapped her hands and shook him, but he pushed her aside 'with superhuman strength,' she said. 'Hold him,' she called to the customers and employees. 'He's under a spell. Don't let him go. He's got all the petty cash we have left in the world.'

'Leave me alone,' he said. 'It's my money.' He broke from their grasp and ran through the streets. The after-work crowds moved aside and closed behind him.

'Stop him. Stop him,' Auntie and the employees called, but the people did not want to grab the wild man. Auntie hunted for him, but he had entered a side street into another world. She went back to the store, terrified at what the thieves were capable of.

I Fu returned, walking slowly; he looked fatigued, having been run about like a puppet. 'Let's sell the shoe business,' he said, giving in at last, 'and go back to the United States.' 'Return,' he said. 'Return to the United States.'

'Be warned not to travel to China,' Auntie told me. 'Chinese are crooks. Travellers disappear and are never heard of again.'

My aunt and uncle sold their businesses before someone could trick them into signing them away. With that money, they went for the second time to the Gold Mountain, where they arrived no better off than other immigrants. They would never go back; they said good-bye properly, good-bye for ever.

'He got the job at the bakery, and I got the one at the hotel,' said Auntie. 'But I've been sick and can't work any more.'

'You look well.'

'I get dizzy when I work. By the time I carry my vacuum cleaner and linens up the stairs, I'm so dizzy I have to lie down on the landing. High blood pressure. I'll not fly in an airplane again.'

'Do you keep seeing a doctor?'

'Yes.'

'The doctor gave you some pills?'

'Yes, but I'm not taking them. It's not the blood pressure that makes me dizzy; it's the pills. I've discovered a cure. The Chinatown women, who all have high blood pressure, say that fresh, unprocessed, pure honey is good for hypertension, and I've been drinking it by the quart. I'm going to get your mother started on the pure honey cure too. I feel so much better on the honey than the pills. Too many side effects with the pills.'

'Is that honey in the cans in the kitchen?'

'Yes, I like to stock up when a fresh supply comes into Chinatown. It comes from a special farm with special bees.'

'I think you ought to keep taking the pills,' I said. 'How does the honey have that effect?'

'I'm not sure. Maybe it smooths out the blood so it takes less pressure to move through the veins.'

There was no use talking her out of it. I would have to persuade my mother to continue taking the pills along with the honey.

'I'm glad you've decided to quit your job,' I said. 'You're lucky to be able to stay home and be a housewife.'

'But I need a job badly, very badly. My husubun insists on one thing,' she said. 'He makes six hundred dollars a month. Exactly three hundred goes to China. He's a rescuer. Out of our three hundred dollars, we have to pay rent, food, clothes, everything. So you see why I have to get a job. He's been saying that I don't know how to save money, that I spend too much. He's so stingy; ever since I lost my job, he's been doing the grocery shopping himself. I had to refuse to cook until I got control of the grocery money again. I went on strike.' She laughed. 'Sometimes when the two of us are carrying the groceries home, he puts his bag down on the sidewalk and walks away swinging his arms free. I have to hurry home with my bag and run back for his before somebody takes it. Men from Kwangtung are arrogant like that. Independent.'

'I'll cook if you stay for dinner,' she added.

'I have to go,' I said.

'Well, I know there isn't much room to play,' she said, as if I were a child, or perhaps she meant 'stroll' or 'tour'.

'No, it's not that. I have some tasks that I have to do. Was your apartment in Hong Kong bigger than this one?'

'No. No. About this size.' Oh, such relief that the Chinese life they keep regretting leaving is no better than this.

'Do you want to move outside Tang People's Street?' I asked.

'No. No. Here my husubun can walk to and from work. He can wake up five minutes before the bakery opens and get there on time. And I can talk to the neighbours. The children walk across the street to Chinese school.' I hoped that she was drawing the conclusion that she and her family were well off, that they were living in this room by choice, in a way.

'Stay for dinner,' she urged. 'There won't be good food, but stay.'

'I can't,' I said. 'I have work to do.'

'Then let me phone my husubun to bring home a cake for you.'

'No, thank you. You don't need to do that. I just ate some cake.'

'You can give it to someone, your brothers and sisters.' She picked up the phone (another luxury, I counted) and called the bakery. 'Bring a cake for my niece,' she said. 'The best kind – lemun kuk.' 'The bakery is just around the corner,' she said to me. 'He'll get off work in five minutes and be here in another minute or two.'

It would only be polite to stay and say hello to my uncle. Also I wanted to take a good look at him after what I had heard about him. I did feel nervous that he would walk in angry at me for causing him to have to carry a lemon cake through the streets. A request right before closing time. What if he had to whip together a lemon cake on his own time or humble himself to ask the boss for a remainder cake, or, worse yet, if he had to take it out of his pay? My mother would want me to protest a gift, argue and tussle, my aunt and I trying to give the cake away, running back and forth, her yelling, 'All right, then, I take it back. No cake for you,' tucking it into clothes, hiding it in bags, throwing it in and out of windows, pushing the windows up and down, pulling the box back and forth until I gave up and took it. Being rude because young and American, taking advantage of that, I planned to say 'Thank you' and take the cake.

I Fu arrived at the front door at exactly 5.05, as I could see by the alarm clock on the desk. Watching the knob turn, I thought, What if he were filled with years of gall, furious from kneeling at people's feet and carrying groceries? He would be mad at me for making my aunt sit all afternoon, no dinner started. But he seemed ordinary, handing over the cake box, a man not particularly burdened by money, smiling, not wide-eyed on drugs, the *Gold Mountain Times* under his arm. I stood up, old enough to have manners without being told. 'How do you do, I Fu?' I said, shaking his hand. He did not look like a tough businessman who had built and lost a shoe empire or one who could marry a flirtatious beggarwoman from off the street or dash through Hong Kong giving away bags of money. He asked me what I was doing in the Big City. He sat down, asked if I wanted to eat anything. Then he couldn't resist any longer, rolled the rubber band off his newspaper, shook it open, and began to read, exactly as my father would have done. He looked just like my father behind the newspaper, the very same newspaper, skinny legs and hands sticking out.

'Why don't you come visit my parents at Christmas time?' I invited my aunt, figuring out a way to leave.

Just then the door opened again, and my girl cousin came home. She glanced at me, startled, and headed straight for the locked door, which I had thought led to the next apartment. She bent and unlocked it with one of the keys on the chain around

213

her neck. I could see inside; it was the children's room, larger than the rest of the apartment, girl's stuff in one half, boy's stuff in the other.

'Lucille,' scolded my aunt. 'Say hello to Big Sister.'

'Hello,' she said, her whole body leaning to get into her own room.

'Lucille is returning from Chinese school,' said Auntie.

The only times I had ever gotten Lucille to sit down with me was when playing games; she methodically set out to win everything on the board, only talking to clarify a rule.

'I was trying to explain to Big Sister what your brothers are studying at college,' said Auntie.

'Nutrition and engineering,' said my cousin.

'I see,' I said, wishing my aunt would let her go. I Fu could have said something from behind the newspaper, like 'I'm a baker and didn't have to study nutrition,' but he didn't.

'Where's your youngest son?' I asked my aunt, and while she answered, Lucille went quickly inside her room and locked it.

'In the streets I guess,' Auntie said. 'Sometimes he doesn't come home until all the stores and restaurants are closed.' He was only about ten years old.

'What does he do out there all night?'

'I don't know. Explores.'

'Aren't you afraid of kidnappers and gangs getting him?'

'Yes, of course, but there's nothing we can do about him.'

I asked her, 'Will you walk me a short distance and point out which way I ought to go?' I said good-bye to my uncle, who looked up and said, 'Leaving so soon?' My cousin did not come out of her room. Auntie and I walked for a block and a half until I recognized where I was, though the night and the street lights were coming on. We stood on a corner and shouted good-byes, me carrying a box of food with a red string, so Chinese, shouting and carrying food, shouting good-bye.

Once MaMa telephoned her brother after not having seen him for fifty years. This was the Singapore uncle who had spent his first fortune throwing a party for friends in Hong Kong. ('Americans get steadily richer building up their savings; Chinese save for years, then spend it all and go into debt for a party.') She told me to be ready to get up at five a.m. to do the dialling. They had written letters agreeing on this day, 2 January, when it would be a cheap time and eight p.m. in Singapore. 'Oh, the size of the world,' she exclaimed. 'Look at that time difference. That's not three hours but fifteen hours apart. How far away.'

I heard the alarms go off all over the house at four thirty a.m. and leapt out of bed for nervousness. Wrapped in my blanket, I dialled the operator. After hearing my uncle's phone ring once, I handed the receiver to my mother. She heard a ring and handed it back to me. 'Here, you talk to him.' 'No,' I yelped, 'I've never met him. He's your brother. You talk to him.' Besides, I didn't want to scare him. My parents' friends hang up when we forget to answer with a Chinese accent.

The index finger of my mother's hand that held the phone tapped involuntarily against her cheek; it was the only part of her that shook. 'Happy New Year, Wah,' she yelled in her loudest voice, no titles, just his name, her baby brother, named after the Chinese Republic. 'Is this Wah? Are you well? You're all well, aren't you? Everyone well. Yes, we're all fine too. Yes, very good. Everyone is good. Do you celebrate this New Year's day? Ours is very festive. All my children come back, eating at everybody's houses every day. We go from one of my children's house to another's eating. No, I can't come visit you. Five years ago I could have visited you. But I'm old now. Yes, I'm old now too. Are you old? Do you work hard? Did you just now come home from work? How hard do you work? I still work. Yes. Yes. Thirty employees, huh? That's good. Yes, my children are all working. Everyone working. Happy New Year. Yes, you have a good year too. Good year, good business, good health. Your son has his own corporation? Why don't you come visit me? No, I don't fly. Yes, we're all well. Doing well. Fine. Good jobs. It's five a.m. here. What time is it there? It's January second now. What day is it there? You're home from work? Let me talk to your wife.' Then she talked to his first wife, repeating just about everything. My father said, 'Nine minutes,' and she said, 'That's enough. Be well. Good-bye,' and hung up.

'Well,' she said, 'nothing significant said.' She tried repeating the conversation to us. 'He employs thirty people. He says that he wishes his children were smart. They're horses and oxen, he said. His son is in the construction business too, but has a different company. He says it's eight p.m., January second there in Singapore.' I noticed she had not asked him how his second wife was, nor how the children of that family were. 'Fifty years since we've talked, and we didn't say anything important,' she said.

'That's the nature of phone calls,' my father said. 'You just hear each other's voices. That's enough.'

'You can call again next year, you know,' I said. 'You can call again any time.'

The Wild Man of the green swamp

For eight months in 1975, residents on the edge of Green Swamp, Florida, had been reporting to the police that they had seen a Wild Man. When they stepped towards him, he made strange noises as in a foreign language and ran back into the saw grass. At first, authorities said the Wild Man was a mass hallucination. Man-eating animals lived in the swamp, and a human being could hardly find a place to rest without sinking. Perhaps it was some kind of a bear the children had seen.

In October, a game officer saw a man crouched over a small fire, but as he approached, the figure ran away. It couldn't have been a bear because the Wild Man dragged a burlap bag after him. Also, the fire was obviously man-made.

The fish-and-game wardens and the sheriff's deputies entered the swamp with dogs but did not search for long; no one could live in the swamp. The mosquitoes alone would drive him out.

The Wild Man made forays out of the swamp. Farmers encountered him taking fruit and corn from the turkeys. He broke into a house trailer, but the occupant came back, and the Wild Man escaped out a window. The occupant said that a bad smell came off the Wild Man. Usually, the only evidence of him were his abandoned campsites. At one he left the remains of a four-foot-long alligator, of which he had eaten the feet and tail.

In May a posse made an air and land search; the plane signalled down to the hunters on the ground, who circled the Wild Man. A fish-and-game warden 'brought him down with a tackle', according to the news. The Wild Man fought, but they took him to gaol. He looked Chinese, so they found a Chinese in town to come translate.

The Wild Man talked a lot to the translator. He told him his name. He said he was thirty-nine years old, the father of seven children, who were in Taiwan. To support them, he had shipped out on a Liberian freighter. He had gotten very homesick and asked everyone if he could leave the ship and go home. But the officers would not let him off. They sent messages to China to find out about him. When the ship landed, they took him to the airport and tried to put him on an airplane to some foreign place. Then, he said, the white demons took him to Tampa Hospital, which is for insane people, but he escaped, just walked out and went into the swamp.

The interpreter asked how he lived in the swamp. He said he ate snakes, turtles, armadillos, and alligators. The captors could tell how he lived when they opened up his bag, which was not burlap but a pair of pants with the legs knotted. Inside, he had carried a pot, a piece of sharpened tin, and a small club, which he had made by sticking a railroad spike into a section of aluminium tubing.

The sheriff found the Liberian freighter that the Wild Man had been on. The ship's officers said that they had not tried to stop him from going home. His shipmates had decided that there was something wrong with his mind. They had bought him a plane ticket and arranged his passport to send him back to China. They had driven him to the airport, but there he began screaming and weeping and would not get on the plane. So they had found him a doctor, who sent him to Tampa Hospital.

Now the doctors at the gaol gave him medicine for the mosquito bites, which covered his entire body, and medicine for his stomach-ache. He was getting better, but after he'd been in gaol for three days, the US Border Patrol told him they were sending him back. He became hysterical. That night, he fastened his belt to the bars, wrapped it around his neck, and hung himself.

In the newspaper picture he did not look very wild, being led by the posse out of the swamp. He did not look dirty, either. He wore a checkered shirt unbuttoned at the neck, where his white undershirt showed; his shirt was tucked into his pants; his hair was short. He was surrounded by men in cowboy hats. His fingers stretching open, his wrists pulling apart to the extent of the handcuffs, he lifted his head, his eyes screwed shut, and cried out.

There was a Wild Man in our slough too, only he was a black

man. He wore a shirt and no pants, and some mornings when we walked to school, we saw him asleep under the bridge. The police came and took him away. The newspaper said he was crazy; it said the police had been on the lookout for him for a long time, but we had seen him every day.

The adventures of Lo Bun Sun

We had a book from China about a sailor named Lo Bun Sun, who as a child had a calling to go to sea. His father, a man from a foreign country, ordered him and his two brothers to settle down working in the family business. But Lo Bun Sun did not enjoy the business nor did he learn a trade or study law. He signed on a ship. 'Heaven will not bless you,' his father said.

A storm came upon his ship, which sprang a leak. He escaped in a lifeboat, and from there watched the ship sink. Other sailors told him that this unfortunate first voyage was a warning that he give up the sea, but he signed on another ship, which was besieged by pirates. After escaping from them, he bought land in Brazil and planted sugarcane. But one day he became tempted to go to sea again, this time on a slave-trading ship. The ocean reared black waves that knocked the sailors off the decks. Masts snapped, and the ship broke against the reef of an unknown shore. The deck splintered under Lo Bun Sun, and he dropped into the water. Waves big as buildings fell on him whenever he surfaced, and drove him under.

Then he had a sense of coming back from a distance. His dream was that he had been flying but clutching something in his hand; he had tried to open his fingers to drop it, but the burden had pulled him down to this beach. The storm had thrown the ship here also, its stern in the air and its head in the sea. No shipmates had landed with him, not even their bodies.

He put his forehead against the ground and thanked the heavenly beings for protecting him. After resting some more, he swam to the wreckage. With pieces of topmast and spars, he fashioned a raft, on which he loaded sacks of grain – rice, barley, and wheat. In the bread room, he filled his pockets with biscuits. Eating as he worked, he help himself to ink, paper, and pens, barrels of flour and bolts of cloth, clothes of men and officers, tools – an adze, hatchets, axes, a saw; he took tobacco and rum, guns, pistols, muskets, and shot.

And happily a dog and two cats, glad to see him, came out of hiding. The dog swam; Lo Bun Sun carried one cat in his arms, and the other jumped from the wreck on to the raft. Also for delight, the illustrator had drawn rats climbing down ropes; the rats had wonderfully long tails and whiskers.

The first night, Lo Bun Sun covered himself with a piece of sail and slept in a tree.

He set up a work schedule, rescuing things against the next obliterating wave. Every day he worked during the daylight hours just as if he had a job, stopping only to eat at set meal-times. He ate the beef jerky and drank water from the ship's barrels; he ate lemons and pickles also. According to the drawings, the clay water jugs and wine jugs, the water gourds, and vinegar jugs leaned together in rows and stacks padded with straw; one or two jugs had broken into graceful shards.

MaMa repeated exactly what things Lo Bun Sun took from the ship (this was one of the more boring tales she read – no magicians, no beautiful ladies, no knights, or warrior poets): rice, barley, wheat flour, clothes, bolts of cloth, ink, pens, and paper, biscuits, jerked beef, water, fruit and vegetables, guns, pistols, muskets, bullets, adze, hatchet, axe, saw, tobacco, rum, a dog, two cats.

He also found a chest of gold coins, and although he had not seen a place to spend money, lugged it on to the raft.

One morning, he awoke and the ship was gone. No man-made hulk served as a marker against all that sea. He might have been born on the island.

He walked around the island and saw no signs of another human being. He decided on places to build two houses. One was a dry cave ('such as the cave I lived in when the Japanese bombed China'). He bolstered the roof and sides with planks and planted a wall of stakes, which sprouted and grew around the entrance. The other house was in the woods on an opposite part of the island; if enemies found it, they would be satisfied, diverted. He called his dwellings castles.

A rescue ship would probably come any moment now. Food

grew plentifully on the island, and Lo Bun Sun had taken abundant stores from the shipwreck, yet he did not loaf and tan himself on the beach; neither did he nap or play. Lo Bun Sun worked. He was never idle; never lazy. He farmed the island. There is drudgery in his name: *Lo* is 'toil', what one does even when unsupervised; he works faithfully, not cheating. *Lo* means 'naked', man 'the naked animal', and *lo* also sounds like the word for 'mule', a toiling animal, a toiling sexless animal. *Bun* is the uncle who went to China to work on a commune. And *sun* is like 'body' and also 'son' in English and 'grandson' in Chinese. *Sun* as in 'new'. Lo Bun Sun was a mule and toiling man, naked and toiling body, alone, son and grandson, himself all the generations. There is still another meaning of *lo*, the *lo* in 'lohan'; like 'arhat', like 'bodhisattva'. There were eighteen lohans, two of them Chinese and sixteen Hindu, personal disciples of the Buddha who enjoyed an easy life like the life on the island of lotus eaters.

Lo Bun Sun marked the days with notches on a board, but on the first busy days when he was hurrying to unload the wreck, he had not yet started this system and might have been thrown off a day.

After physical labour, he wrote in his diary, with which he kept his spirits up. He would leave a record. He ruled a page down the middle and listed the advantages and disadvantages of his island life. The two columns were entitled 'Evil' and 'Good'. One of the Evils was the desolation; that he had not drowned was the balancing Good. Other Goods were food and water and the tropical weather that made up for his dearth of clothes. An Evil was that he had no one to talk to. His Good list outstripped the Evil list; Good may always preponderate in this method of reckoning.

Another way he wrote was: 'I really ought to stop complaining because I could be writing that . . .' He began fictions about raving death, starvation, and mutilation, but stopped to continue chronicling his chores, which were endless. He built a table for writing and eating. He preserved eggs in vinegar and some in wine. He spread wild grapes to dry for raisins. He built barricades. He opened a turtle and admired its thirty gold eggs in the shell bowl. (*Lo* also connotes the mystic markings on the tortoise shell.)

When he felt poorly, he drank liquor in which he had soaked tobacco, a mixture also good for rubbing bruises. He grew beans and made tofu and bean sauce. He shot and snared goats; he penned the kids in corrals for domestication.

From the start, he worried about using up his ink and paper, so he decided he would record only 'the most remarkable events of my life'. He wrote how he planted rice in dry ground, and it did not grow. Then he planted the seeds in boxes, where the shoots remained from twenty-five to fifty days. Next to a stream, he dug pools and built clay walls into dams and sluices to make paddies of water and soil two to four inches deep, which he stirred, *lo* connoting 'dike' and 'libation', and he transplanted the young plants by hand. One day he counted thirty panicles of rice, and he wrote that down. 'Miracle. Miracle.' He reaped the heavy tops, handshocked and dried them. Then he carefully ground the brown hulls with rocks. The husks blew away like insect wings. The rice straw was thatch for his roof, slippers, an umbrella, a raincoat; he wove a winnow for next harvest. He searched the ground at the feet of the cut shafts and picked the grains that had fallen; this he used for seed. (My father came to listen to this part of the story, and he told it again, retelling the gleaning several times.) Birds also picked the seed grain, but he scared them away by shooting three birds, which his dog retrieved, and hanging them in the field. From planting to harvest was one year.

Lo Bun Sun shaped pots out of clay and baked them in the sun, which was not hot enough. He built an oven of rocks sealed with clay. When he saw how well it fired, he began decorating the pots. He dipped them in a mixture of mud and beach sand, which melted into a glaze. He wove nets around the outsides of wet pots; the grass burned off, leaving decorations. Sometimes he wove baskets around the cooled pots; he tied the straw into handles.

He made bread without yeast. There was a picture of him with a hand on his stomach; he was sniffing the loaves from which savoury steam arose in wavy lines. The same oven baked bread as well as pottery because of vents that regulated the temperature.

He built a boat and rowed around the island. The waves took

him farther and farther out. He had to fight his way back, desiring his island. 'There's no miserable condition of mankind that heaven can't make worse,' he wrote.

He knocked a young parrot out of a tree, and after some years taught it to say his name so that he would hear a voice other than his own, a voice calling him by name. 'Poor Lo Bun Sun,' it said. 'Poor, poor Lo Bun Sun. Where are you? Where have you been? How come you here? Poor Lo Bun Sun, and how did I come here?'

If there were migratory geese on the island, he could have bound a letter to the leg of a goose.

More years passed, and he used up the brushes, inks, and paper. How to replace the Four Valuable Things? When the rice stalks dried to a pale yellow, he crisscrossed them in a woven mat. The squares were the right size for a word each. He also soaked rice straw, pounded it, and pressed the mash into sheets. And there was a tree whose bark peeled off in layers; he called it a paper bark tree. He sewed its pages into notebooks. If he had not found these things, he could have written on stones. He could have written on leaves. For brushes he used goat hairs.

Making good ink took years of experimentation. He hunted for berries dark enough; he crushed leaves, opened reeds, bled trees, but the sap ran clear or amber and sticky or milky. (Plants with milky sap are poisonous to eat.) He tried swamp mud. He caught squid offshore to see if the black in them was ink. But no dirt or flower or blood flowed correctly and lasted. He wrote with oil and dipped the paper in berry stain. What he ate, he fed to parrot, dog, cats, goats, and fields, and he also wrote with it. At last, he discovered the juice of the sandalwood, whose bark and flowers he crushed to produce red. And he found woad, whose leaves look like arrows and writing brushes, and he wrote in indigo. He used red and purple; he was king of his own island.

Still more years went by, and now he was dressed entirely in straw and skins, straw coat, goatskin vest and pants, straw shoes. His pants were open at the knees for movement. He carried a straw umbrella in the sun and a skin umbrella in the rain; the hair was on the outside of the umbrella so the water ran off. Hair grew long on his face and head. A picture showed him trimming his hair with the scissors he treasured, looking at his mirror face and talking to himself. The sea continued empty and the nights black.

One day while patrolling the beach, where the crabs rolled seaweed bubbles across the sand, Lo Bun Sun saw something that sent a burning fear up his spine – a human footprint. He ran to one of his fortifications. He chattered, 'It can't be. It can't be.' After starving for human company for twelve years, he did not shout, 'Where are you? Who are you? Hey, where are you? Come on out. Welcome. Welcome. I'm here. I'm over here.' Instead, he became scared and henceforth timid on his island. His eyelid began to twitch. He took up the musket, which he always kept loaded anyway, and never again walked abroad without it. He stuck loaded pistols and rifles into gunports in his walls. For days he shivered in his cave, peeked through cracks in every direction, jumped at noises of winds and animals. He had another look at the print. Perhaps he had construed a human foot rather than paw or hoof or claw because of his loneliness. In need of human company, he had imagined the five toes and a heel. But, no, there it was – unmistakably the imprint of a naked human foot. The drawing showed Lo Bun Sun kneeling propped against his musket and regarding a footprint, inky like a baby's on a birth certificate. 'It must be my own,' he said aloud, but the footprint was bigger than his foot. He clapped his hand over his mouth like a Japanese; he did not know how loud or soft was normal any more. He returned to puzzle over the footprint until the wind and rain wore it away. From then on in case some accident disabled him, he planted two or three years' supply of grain.

For more than a decade, he thought about the footprint and sometimes thought he had dreamed it. But one dawn he saw a light on the beach and crept up hidden behind rocks and trees to see who was there. Around a campfire in the warm climate, nine black demons danced and ate. Then they rowed off, leaving the beach strewn with human bones, heads, hands, and feet.

Lo Bun Sun fortified his hiding places. He planted vegetables in small separate patches and split his goats into small herds. He tied the muskets on tripping lines so that he could pull seven triggers in two minutes. He established burrows, covers, and camouflages everywhere, and planted twenty thousand trees in all. The cannibals might come when he was doing his chores or sleeping. He comforted himself by recalling a hero, Kao Chung, who overcame the cooking-and-eating sea monster, and then ate its food on the beach. Several more times in later years, the black demons held their ghastly feasts, and Lo Bun Sun found the remains. Once he also found a wrecked galleon and the body of a drowned sailor.

Thirteen and a half years after the footprint and twenty-five and a half years after his arrival, five canoes landed. From his watchtower in a tree, Lo Bun Sun looked through his spyglass at the black figures against the yellow sand. In the ink drawings, they were silhouettes and far away, so we could not study facial expressions. They slaughtered one prisoner and dressed the meat in front of the others. Suddenly a prisoner broke loose, his ropes falling from him. Two or three savages gave chase – all running directly towards Lo Bun Sun's hiding place. The savages swam a creek, where one pursuer was left behind because he could not swim. Standing between the pursued and pursuers, Lo Bun Sun shot the oncoming cannibals. One of the wounded men returned to the others, who quickly paddled off. The poor man who might have been eaten fell to his knees. He lifted Lo Bun Sun's foot and set it on his head. This was the first human being Lo Bun Sun had touched and who had touched him in over a quarter of a century. One of the cannibals had only been wounded, and when Lo Bun Sun pointed to him, the rescued savage cut his head off. 'I name you Sing Kay Ng,' said Lo Bun Sun, 'because I saved your life on a Friday.' 'Sing Kay Ng,' he pointed to the savage. 'You name Sing Kay Ng. My name Teacher.'

Sing Kay Ng buried the dead men, then took his first lesson in the Teacher's language. Lo Bun Sun pointed at everything – 'Goat. Jar. Fence. Man.' Sing Kay Ng pointed to the graves and gestured: 'Let's dig them up and eat them.' Lo Bun Sun acted as if he were vomiting. He let Sing Kay Ng know that he would kill him if he offered him any human meat or showed his cannibal tastes in any way again.

Sing Kay Ng understood the calendar, the arc his arm made from horizon to horizon, sunrise to sunset to sunrise, one mark. They walked on the island measuring off a distance, which Lo Bun Sun said was one li. 'One hundred and twenty li away,' said

Sing Kay Ng. 'I come from land one hundred and twenty li in that direction.' The people fought, and the winners brought the losers here for eating. In his country, it was the custom to worship The Old Man Who Had Made Everything. 'All things do say "O" to him,' he said. He said that he had a father.

Lo Bun Sun gave his servant and pupil a notebook and a brush with a gold cap and many brushes in bamboo tubes so that he too could record his thoughts and life. Every day the Naked Toiling Mule and Friday sat like two scholars at their desks, reading, studying, writing, recording plantings, harvests, bird migrations, the seasons, the weather, and how many goats had kids.

Lo Bun Sun armed Sing Kay Ng for hunting. Also they would be in league should the cannibals return. ' "A real hero will take on a village," ' Lo Bun Sun taught.

Three years later, twenty-one savages and three prisoners, two of whom looked like Lo Bun Sun and one like Sing Kay Ng, came sailing to the island in a fleet of canoes. The companions fired from their ambuscade, killing seventeen cannibals and wounding one, three escaping by boat. When the boat was out of sight, the victors came out and untied the prisoners. Suddenly Sing Kay Ng was jumping up and down and shouting in his own language, 'O joy! O glad!' He was embracing the man who looked like himself, and when he untied him, they held each other and wept. It was his father. The father praised Sing Kay Ng for waiting all these years on this island to save him. What a good son he had raised.

One of the other prisoners was a sea captain who had lost his ship in a mutiny. 'I have loyal men on the mainland,' he said. 'If I can just reach them, I'll come back here and take you home.' Arming themselves from Lo Bun Sun's store, the captain and Sing Kay Ng's father took the wounded cannibal as a hostage and left in a canoe.

Another ship came to the island, and Lo Bun Sun was in such a rush, he left on it. He took with him one of his parrots, his goatskin cap, an umbrella, his money, and his man, Sing Kay Ng, and returned to his native land.

'But that isn't the end of the story,' said my mother. At about sixty years of age Lo Bun Sun found a wife and had two sons and a daughter. When his wife died, he went to sea again. He and Sing Kay Ng had many adventures in barbarous lands; they fought wolves, bears, and bandits. Once, surrounded by a wolf-pack, they remembered that the fiercest beasts are terrified by the voice of man; at their shouting, the wolves retreated.

A nostalgia for his island came over Lo Bun Sun, and he sailed back there without telling Sing Kay Ng their destination. Sing Kay Ng recognized it on sight, clapped his hands, and cried, 'O yes, O there, O yes, O there,' pointing to the site of one of their houses and dancing like mad. The island was now inhabited by mutineers and savages, who had formed a society. They felt no need for rescue, nor did their children have any curiosity about their ancestral countries.

And Sing Kay Ng found his father again; he had seen him from a distance so far at sea that Lo Bun Sun could descry no human shape even through his perspective glass. Sing Kay Ng embraced his father, kissed him, stroked his face, hugged him again, picked him up and set him down under a tree, lay down by him, then stood and looked at him for a quarter of an hour at a time, stroked his old feet and kissed them, and got up again and stared at him. He walked along the beach leading his father by the hand as if he were a lady. He went back and forth to the ship, fetched him a lump of sugar, a drink, a cookie. He danced about him, and he talked and talked, telling him of his travels.

The island was warring with another island, and the ship became caught in the war. A thousand canoes attacked the ship. Lo Bun Sun ordered Sing Kay Ng to go on deck and talk to the attackers in their own language and translate. Three hundred arrows flew at him, and Sing Kay Ng was killed. He was buried at sea with an eleven-gun salute. After more adventures, Lo Bun Sun returned to the land where he was born; he retired at the age of seventy-two.

The American father

In 1903 my father was born in San Francisco, where my grandmother had come disguised as a man. Or, Chinese women once magical, she gave birth at a distance, she in China, my grandfather and father in San Francisco. She was good at sending. Or the men of those days had the power to have babies. If my grandparents did no such wonders, my father nevertheless turned up in San Francisco an American citizen.

He was also married at a distance. My mother and a few farm women went out into the chicken yard, and said words over a rooster, a fierce rooster, red of comb and feathers; then she went back inside, married, a wife. She laughs telling this wedding story; he doesn't say one way or the other.

When I asked MaMa why she speaks different from BaBa, she says their parents lived across the river from one another. Maybe his village was America, the river an ocean, his accent American.

My father's magic was also different from my mother's. He pulled the two ends of a chalk stub or a cigarette butt, and between his fingers a new stick of chalk or a fresh cigarette grew long and white. Coins appeared around his knuckles, and number cards turned into face cards. He did not have a patter but was a silent magician. I would learn these trick when I became a grown-up and never need for cigarettes, money, face cards, or chalk.

He also had the power of going places where nobody else went, and making places belong to him. I could smell his presence. He owned special places the way he owned special things like his copper ashtray from the 1939 World's Fair and his Parker 51. When I explored his closet and desk, I thought, This is a father place; a father belongs here.

One of his places was the dirt cellar. That was under the house where owls bounced against the screens. Rats as big as cats sunned in the garden, fat dust balls among the greens. The rats ran up on the table where the rice or the grapes or the beans were drying and ate with their hands, then took extra in their teeth and leapt off the table like a circus, one rat after another. My mother swung her broom at them, the straw swooping through the air in yellow arcs. That was the house where the bunny lived in a hole in the kitchen. My mother had carried it home from the fields in her apron. Whenever it was hopping noiselessly on the linoleum, and I was there to see it, I felt the honour and blessing of it.

When I asked why the cellar door was kept locked, MaMa said there was a 'well' down there. 'I don't want you children to fall in the well,' she said. Bottomless.

I ran around a corner one day and found the cellar door open. BaBa's white-shirted back moved in the dark. I had been following him, spying on him. I went into the cellar and hid behind some boxes. He lifted the lid that covered the bottomless well. Before he could stop me, I burst out of hiding and saw it – a hole full of shining, bulging, black water, alive, alive, like an eye, deep and alive. BaBa shouted, 'Get away.' 'Let me look. Let me look,' I said. 'Be careful,' he said as I stood on the brink of a well, the end and edge of the ground, the opening to the inside of the world. 'What's it called?' I asked to hear him say it. 'A well.' I wanted to hear him say it again, to tell me again, 'Well.' My mother had poured rust water from old nails into my ears to improve them.

'What's a well?'

'Water comes out of it,' BaBa said. 'People draw water out of wells.'

'Do they drink it? Where does the water come from?'

'It comes from the earth. I don't think we should drink it without boiling it for at least twenty minutes. Germs.'

Poison water.

The well was like a wobble of black jello. I saw silver stars in it. It sparked. It was the black sparkling eye of the planet. The well must lead to the other side of the world. If I fall in, I will come out in China. After a long, long fall, I would appear feet first out of the ground, out of another well, and the Chinese would laugh to see me do that. The way to arrive in China less obtrusively was to dive in head first. The trick would be not to get scared during the long time in the middle of the world. The journey would be worse than the mines.

My father pulled the wooden cover, which was the round lid of a barrel, back over the well. I stepped on the boards, stood in the middle of them, and thought about the bottomless black well beneath my feet, my very feet. What if the cover skidded aside? My father finished with what he was doing; we walked out of the cellar, and he locked the door behind us.

Another father place was the attic of our next house. Once I had seen his foot break through the ceiling. He was in the attic, and suddenly his foot broke through the plaster overhead.

I watched for the day when he left a ladder under the open trap door. I climbed the ladder through the kitchen ceiling. The attic air was hot, too thick, smelling like pigeons, their hot feathers. Rafters and floor beams extended in parallels to a far-away wall, where slats of light slanted from shutters. I did not know we owned such an extravagance of empty space. I raised myself up on my forearms like a prairie dog, then balanced sure-footed on the beams, careful not to step between them and fall through. I climbed down before he returned.

The best of the father places I did not have to win by cunning; he showed me it himself. I had been young enough to hold his hand, which felt splintery with calluses 'caused by physical labour', according to MaMa. As we walked, he pointed out sights; he named the plants, told time on the clocks, explained a neon sign in the shape of an owl, which shut one eye in daylight. 'It will wink at night,' he said. He read signs, and I learned the recurring words: *Company*, *Association*, *Hui*, *Tong*. He greeted the old men with a finger to the hat. At the candy-and-tobacco store, BaBa bought Lucky Strikes and beef jerky, and the old men gave me plum wafers. The tobacconist gave me a cigar box and a candy box. The secret place was not on the busiest Chinatown street but the street across from the park. A pedestrian would look into the barrels and cans in front of the store next door, then walk on to the herbalist's with the school supplies and saucers of herbs in the window, examine the dead flies and larvae, and overlook the secret place completely. (The herbs inside the hundred drawers did not have flies.) BaBa stepped between the grocery store and the herb shop into the kind of sheltered doorway where skid-row men pee and sleep and leave liquor bottles. The place seemed out of business; no one would rent it because it was not eyecatching. It might have been a family association office. On the window were dull gold Chinese words and the number the same as our house number. And delightful, delightful, a big old orange cat sat dozing in the window; it had pushed the shut venetian blinds aside, and its fur was flat against the glass. An iron grillework with many hinges protected the glass. I tapped on it to see whether the cat was asleep or dead; it blinked.

BaBa found the keys on his chain and unlocked the grating, then the door. Inside was an immense room like a bank or a post office. Suddenly no city street, no noise, no people, no sun. Here was horizontal and vertical order, counters and tables in cool grey twilight. The place smelled like cat piss or eucalyptus berries. Brass and porcelain spittoons squatted in corners. Another cat, a grey one, walked into the open, and I tried following it, but it ran off. I walked under the tables, which had thick legs.

BaBa filled a bucket with sawdust and water. He and I scattered handfuls of the mixture on the floors, and the place smelled like a carnival. With our pushbrooms leaving wet streaks, we swept the sawdust together, which turned grey as it picked up the dirt. BaBa threw his cigarette butts in it. The cat shit got picked up too. He scooped everything into the dustpan he had made out of an oil can.

We put away our brooms, and I followed him to the wall where sheaves of paper hung by their corners, diamond shaped. 'Pigeon lottery', he called them. 'Pigeon lottery tickets.' Yes, in the wind of the paddle fan the soft thick sheaves ruffled like feathers and wings. He gave me some used sheets. Gamblers had circled green and blue words in pink ink. They had bet on those words. You had to be a poet to win, finding lucky words from last night's games: 'white jade that grows in water', 'red jade that grows in earth', or – not so many words in Chinese – 'white waterjade', 'redearthjade', 'firedragon', 'waterdragon'. He gave me pen and ink, and I linked words of my own: 'rivercloud', 'riverfire', the many combinations with *horse*, *cloud*, and *bird*. The lines and loops connecting the words, which were in squares, a word to a square, made designs too. So this was where my father worked and what he did for a living, keeping track of the gamblers' schemes of words.

We were getting the gambling house ready. Tonight the gamblers would come here from the towns and the fields; they would sail from San Francisco all the way up the river through the Delta to Stockton, which had more gambling than any city on the coast. It would be a party tonight. The gamblers would eat free food and drink free whisky, and if times were bad, only tea. They'd laugh and exclaim over the poems they made, which were plain and very beautiful: 'Shiny water, bright moon.' They'd cheer when they won. BaBa let me crank the drum that spun words. It had a little door on top to reach in for the winning words and looked like the cradle that the Forty-niner ancestors had used to sift for gold, and like the drum for the lottery at the Stockton Chinese Community Fourth of July Picnic.

He also let me play with the hole puncher, which was a heavy instrument with a wrought-iron handle that took some strength to raise. I played gambler punching words to win – 'cloudswallow', 'riverswallow', 'river forking', 'swallow forking'. I also punched perfect round holes in the corners so that I could hang the papers like diamonds and like pigeons. I collected round and crescent confetti in my cigar box.

While I worked on the floor under the tables, BaBa sat behind a counter on his tall stool. With black elastic armbands around his shirtsleves and an eyeshade on his forehead, he clicked the abacus fast and steadily, stopping to write the numbers down in ledgers. He melted red wax in candle flame and made seals. He checked the pigeon papers, and set out fresh stacks of them. Then we twirled the dials of the safe, wound the grandfather clock, which had a long brass pendulum, meowed at the cats, and locked up. We bought crackly pork on the way home.

According to MaMa, the gambling house belonged to the most powerful Chinese American in Stockton. He paid my father to manage it and to pretend to be the owner. BaBa took the blame for the real owner. When the cop on the beat walked in, BaBa gave him a plate of food, a carton of cigarettes, and a bottle of whisky. Once a month, the police raided with a paddy wagon, and it was also part of my father's job to be arrested. He never got a record, however, because he thought up a new name for himself every time. Sometimes it came to him while the city sped past the barred windows; sometimes just when the white demon at the desk asked him for it, a name came to him, a new name befitting the situation. They never found out his real names or that he had an American name at all. 'I got away with aliases,' he said, 'because the white demons can't tell one Chinese name from another or one face from another.' He had the power of naming. He had a hundred dollars ready in an envelope with which he bribed the demon in charge. It may have been a fine, not a bribe, but BaBa saw him pocket the hundred dollars. After that, the police let him walk out the door. He either walked home or back to the empty gambling house to straighten out the books.

Two of the first white people we children met were customers at the gambling house, one small and skinny man, one fat and jolly. They lived in a little house on the edege of the slough across the street from our house. Their arms were covered with orange and yellow hair. The round one's name was Johnson, but what everyone called him was Water Shining, and his partner was White Cloud. They had once won big on those words. Also *Johnson* resembles *Water Shining*, which also has *o, s,* and *n* sounds. Like two old China Men, they lived together lonely with no families. They sat in front of stores; they sat on the porch. They fenced a part of the slough for their vegetable patch, which had a wooden sign declaring the names of the vegetables and who they belonged to. They also had a wooden sign over their front door: TRANQUILLITY, a wish or blessing or the name of their house. They gave us nickels and quarters; they made dimes come out of noses, ears, and elbows and waved coins in and out between their knuckles. They were white men, but they lived like China Men.

When we came home from school and a wino or hobo was trying the doors and windows, Water Shining came out of his little house. 'There's a wino breaking into our house,' we told him. It did occur to me that he might be offended at our calling his fellow white man a wino. 'It's not just a poor man taking a

drink from the hose or picking some fruit and going on his way,'
I explained.

'What? What? Where? Let's take a look-see,' he said, and
walked with us to our house, saving our house without a fight.

The old men disappeared one by one before I noticed their
going. White Cloud told the gamblers that Water Shining was
killed in a farming accident, run over by a tractor. His body had
been churned and ploughed. White Cloud lived alone until the
railroad tracks were levelled, the slough drained, the blackbirds
flown, and his house torn down.

My father found a name for me too at the gambling house.
'He named you,' said MaMa, 'after a blonde gambler who always
won. He gave you her lucky American name.' My blonde name-
sake must have talked with a cigarette out of the side of her
mouth and left red lip prints. She wore a low-cut red or green
gambling dress, or she dressed cowgirl in white boots with baton-
twirler tassels and spurs; a stetson hung at her back. When she
threw down her aces, the leather fringe danced along her arm.
And there was applause and buying of presents when she won.
'Your father likes blondes,' MaMa said. 'Look how beautiful,'
they both exclaimed when a blonde walked by.

But my mother keeps saying those were dismal years. 'He
worked twelve hours a day, no holidays,' she said. 'Even on New
Year's, no day off. He couldn't come home until two in the
morning. He stood on his feet gambling twelve hours straight.'

'I saw a tall stool,' I said.

'He only got to sit when there were no customers,' she said.
'He got paid almost nothing. He was a slave; I was a slave.' She
is angry recalling those days.

After my father's partners stole his New York laundry, the
owner of the gambling house, a fellow ex-villager, paid my
parents' fares to Stockton, where the brick buildings reminded
them of New York. The way my mother repaid him – only the
money is repayable – was to be a servant to his, the owner's,
family. She ironed for twelve people and bathed ten children.
Bitterly, she kept their house. When my father came home from
work at two in the morning, she told him how badly the owner's
family had treated her, but he told her to stop exaggerating.
'He's a generous man,' he said.

The owner also had a black servant, whose name was Harry. The rumour was that Harry was a half-man/half-woman, a half-and-half. Two servants could not keep that house clean, where children drew on the wallpaper and dug holes in the plaster. I listened to Harry sing 'Sioux City Sue'. 'Lay down my rag with a hoo hoo hoo,' he sang. He squeezed his rag out in the bucket and led the children singing the chorus. Though my father was also as foolishly happy over his job, my mother was not deceived.

When my mother was pregnant, the owner's wife bought her a dozen baby chicks, not a gift; my mother would owe her the money. MaMa would be allowed to raise the chicks in the owner's yard if she also tended his chickens. When the baby was born, she would have chicken to give for birth announcements. Upon his coming home from work one night, the owner's wife lied to him, 'The aunt forgot to feed her chickens. Will you do it?' Grumbling about my lazy mother, the owner went out in the rain and slipped in the mud, which was mixed with chicken shit. He hurt his legs and lay there yelling that my mother had almost killed him. 'And she makes our whole yard stink with chicken shit,' he accused. When the baby was born, the owner's wife picked out the scrawny old roosters and said they were my mother's twelve.

Ironing for the children, who changed clothes several times a day, MaMa had been standing for hours while pregnant when the veins in her legs rippled and burst. After that she had to wear support stockings and to wrap her legs in bandages.

The owner gave BaBa a hundred-and-twenty-dollar bonus when the baby was born. His wife found out and scolded him for 'giving charity'.

'You deserve that money,' MaMa said to BaBa. 'He takes all your time. You're never home. The babies could die, and you wouldn't know it.'

When their free time coincided, my parents sat with us on apple and orange crates at the tiny table, our knees touching under it. We ate rice and salted fish, which is what peasants in China eat. Everything was nice except what MaMa was saying, 'We've turned into slaves. We're the slaves of these villagers who were nothing when they were in China. I've turned into the servant of a woman who can't read. Maybe we should go back to China. I'm tired of being Wah Q,' that is, a Sojourner from Wah.

My father said, 'No.' Angry. He did not like her female intrigues about the chickens and the ironing and the half-man/half-woman.

They saved his pay and the bonuses, and decided to buy a house, the very house they were renting. This was the two-storey house around the corner from the owner's house, convenient for my mother to walk to her servant job and my father to the gambling house. We could rent out the bottom floor and make a profit. BaBa had five thousand dollars. Would the owner, who spoke English, negotiate the cash sale? Days and weeks passed, and when he asked the owner what was happening, the owner said, 'I decided to buy it myself. I'll let you rent from me. It'll save you money, especially since you're saving to go back to China. You're going back to China anyway.' But BaBa had indeed decided to buy a house on the Gold Mountain. And this was before Pearl Harbor and before the Chinese Revolution.

He found another house farther away, not as new or big. He again asked the owner to buy it for him. You would think we could trust him, our fellow villager with the same surname, almost a relative, but the owner bought up this house too – the one with the well in the cellar – and became our landlord again.

My parents secretly looked for another house. They told everyone, 'We're saving our money to go back to China when the war is over.' But what they really did was to buy the house across from the railroad tracks. It was exactly like the owner's house, the same size, the same floor plan and gingerbread. BaBa paid six thousand dollars cash for it, not a cheque but dollar bills, and he signed the papers himself. It was the biggest but most run-down of the houses; it had been a boarding house for old China Men. Rose bushes with thorns grew around it, wooden lace hung broken from the porch eaves, the top step was missing like a moat. The rooms echoed. This was the house with the attic and basement. The owner's wife accused her husband of giving us the money, but she was lying. We made our escape from them. 'You don't have to be afraid of the owner any more,' MaMa keeps telling us.

Sometimes we waited up until BaBa came home from work.

In addition to a table and crates, we had for furniture an ironing board and an army cot, which MaMa unfolded next to the gas stove in the wintertime. While she ironed our clothes, she sang and talked story, and I sat on the cot holding one or two of the babies. When BaBa came home, he and MaMa got into the cot and pretended they were refugees under a blanket tent. He brought out his hardbound brown book, with the grey and white photographs of white men standing before a flag, sitting in rows of chairs, shaking hands in the street, hand-signalling from car windows. A teacher with a suit stood at a blackboard and pointed out things with a stick. There were no children or women or animals in this book. 'Before you came to New York,' he told my mother, 'I went to school to study English. The classroom looked like this, and every student came from another country.' He read words to my mother and told her what they meant. He also wrote them on the blackboard, it and the daruma, the doll which always rights itself when knocked down, the only toys we owned at that time. The little *h*'s looked like chairs, the *e*'s like lidded eyes, but those words were not *chair* and *eye*. ' "Do you speak English?" ' He read and translated. ' "Yes, I am learning to speak English better." "I speak English a little." "How are you?" "I am fine, and you?" ' My mother forgot what she learned from one reading to the next. The words had no crags, windows, or hooks to grasp. No pictures. The same *a*, *b*, *c*'s for everything. She couldn't make out ducks, cats, and mice in American cartoons either.

During World War II, a gang of police demons charged into the gambling house with drawn guns. They handcuffed the gamblers and assigned them to paddy wagons and patrol cars, which lined the street. The wagons were so full, people had to stand with their hands up on the ceiling to keep their balance. My father was not gaoled or deported, but neither he nor the owner worked in gambling again. They went straight. Stockton became a clean town. From the outside the gambling house looks the same closed down as when it flourished.

My father brought his abacus, the hole punch, and extra tickets home, but those were the last presents for a while. A dismal time began for him.

He became a disheartened man. He was always home. He sat

in his chair and stared, or he sat on the floor and stared. He stopped showing the boys the few kung fu moves he knew. He suddenly turned angry and quiet. For a few days he walked up and down on the sidewalk in front of businesses and did not bring himself to enter. He walked right past them in his beautiful clothes and acted very busy, as if having an important other place to go for a job interview. 'You're nothing but a gambler,' MaMa scolded. 'You're spoiled and won't go looking for a job.' 'The only thing you're trained for is writing poems,' she said. 'I know you,' she said. (I hated her sentences that started with 'I know you.') 'You poet. You scholar. You gambler. What use is any of that?' 'It's a wife's job to scold her husband into working,' she explained to us.

My father sat. 'You're so scared,' MaMa accused. 'You're shy. You're lazy.' 'Do something. You never do anything.' 'You let your so-called friends steal your laundry. You let your brothers and the Communists take your land. You have no head for business.' She nagged him and pampered him. MaMa and we kids scraped his back with a porcelain spoon. We did not know whether it was the spoon or the porcelain or the massage that was supposed to be efficacious. 'Quit being so shy,' she advised. 'Take a walk through Chinatown and see if any of the uncles has heard of a job. Just ask. You don't even need to apply. Go find out the gossip.' 'He's shy,' she explained him to us, but she was not one to understand shyness, being entirely bold herself. 'Why are you so shy? People invite you and go out of their way for you, and you act like a snob or a king. It's only human to reciprocate.' 'You act like a piece of liver. Who do you think you are? A piece of liver?' She did not understand how some of us run down and stop. Some of us use up all our life force getting out of bed in the morning, and it's a wonder we can get to a chair and sit in it. 'You piece of liver. You poet. You scholar. What's the use of a poet and a scholar on the Gold Mountain? You're so skinny. You're not supposed to be so skinny in this country. You have to be tough. You lost the New York laundry. You lost the house with the upstairs. You lost the house with the back porch.' She summarized, 'No loyal friends or brothers. Savings draining away like time. Can't speak English. Now you've lost the gambling job and the land in China.'

Somebody – a Chinese, it had to be a Chinese – dug up our loquat tree, which BaBa had planted in front of the house. He or she had come in the middle of the night and left a big hole. MaMa blamed BaBa for that too, that he didn't go track down the tree and bring it back. In fact, a new loquat tree had appeared in the yard of a house around the corner. He ignored her, stopped shaving, and sat in his T-shirt from morning to night.

He seemed to have lost his feelings. His own mother wrote him asking for money, and he asked for proof that she was still alive before he would send it. He did not say, 'I miss her.' Maybe she was dead, and the Communists maintained a bureau of grandmother letter writers in order to get our money. That we kids no longer received the sweet taste of invisible candy was no proof that she had stopped sending it; we had outgrown it. For proof, the aunts sent a new photograph of Ah Po. She looked like the same woman, all right, like the pictures we already had but aged. She was ninety-nine years old. She was lying on her side on a lounge chair, alone, her head pillowed on her arm, the other arm along her side, no green tints at her earlobes, fingers, and wrists. She still had little feet and a curved-down mouth. 'Maybe she's dead and propped up,' we kids conjectured.

BaBa sat drinking whisky. He no longer bought new clothes. Nor did he go to the dentist and come back telling us the compliments on his perfect teeth, how the dentist said that only one person in a thousand had teeth with no fillings. He no longer advised us that to have perfect teeth, it's good to clamp them together, especially when having a bowel movement.

MaMa assured us that what he was looking forward to was when each child came home with gold. Then he or she (the pronoun is neutral in the spoken language) was to ask the father, 'BaBa, what kind of a suit do you want? A silk gown? Or a suit from the West? An Eastern suit or a Western suit? What kind of a Western suit do you want?' She suggested that we ask him right now. Go-out-on-the-road. Make our fortunes. Buy a Western suit for Father.

I went to his closet and studied his suits. He owned two grey suits, dark blue ones, and a light pinstripe, expensive, successful suits to wear on the best occasions. Power suits. Money suits. Two-hundred-dollars-apiece New York suits. Businessmen-in-the-movies suits. Boss suits. Suits from before we were born. At the foot of the closet arranged in order, order his habit, were his leather shoes blocked on shoe trees. How could I make money like that? I looked in stores at suits and at the prices. I could never learn to sew this evenly, each suit perfect and similar to the next.

MaMa worked in the fields and the canneries. She showed us how to use her new tools, the pitters and curved knives. We tried on her cap pinned with union buttons and her rubber gloves that smelled like rubber tomatoes. She emptied her buckets, thermoses, shopping bags, lunch pail, apron, and scarf; she brought home every kind of vegetable and fruit grown in San Joaquin County. She said she was tired after work but kept moving, busy, banged doors, drawers, pots and cleaver, turned faucets off and on with *ka-chunks* in the pipes. Her cleaver banged on the chopping block for an hour straight as she minced pork and steak into patties. Her energy slammed BaBa back into his chair. She took care of everything; he did not have a reason to get up. He stared at his toes and fingers. 'You've lost your sense of emergency,' she said; she kept up her sense of emergency every moment.

He dozed and woke with a jerk or a scream. MaMa medicated him with a pill that came in a purple cube lined with red silk quilting, which cushioned a tiny black jar; inside the jar was a black dot made out of ground pearls, ox horn, and ox blood. She dropped this pill in a bantam broth that had steamed all day in a little porcelain crock on metal legs. He drank this soup, also a thick beef broth with gold coins in the bottom, beef teas, squab soup, and still he sat. He sat on. It seemed to me that he was getting skinnier.

'You're getting skinny again,' MaMa kept saying. 'Eat. Eat. You're less than a hundred pounds.'

I cut a Charles Atlas coupon out of a comic book. I read all the small print. Charles Atlas promised to send some free information. 'Ninety-seven-pound weakling', the cartoon man called himself. 'I'll gamble a stamp,' he said. Charles Atlas did not say anything about building fat, which was what my father needed. He already had muscles. But he was ninety-seven pounds like the weakling, maybe ninety pounds. Also he kicked over chairs like in the middle panel. I filled in the coupon and forged his signature. I did not dare ask him how old he was, so I guessed maybe he was half as old as his weight: age forty-five, weight ninety. If Charles Atlas saw that he was even skinner than the weakling, maybe he would hurry up answering. I took the envelope and stamp from BaBa's desk.

Charles Atlas sent pamphlets with more coupons. From the hints of information, I gathered that my father needed lessons, which cost money. The lessons had to be done vigorously, not just read. There seemed to be no preliminary lesson on how to get up.

The one event of the day that made him get up out of his easy chair was the newspaper. He looked forward to it. He opened the front door and looked for it hours before the mailman was due. The *Gold Mountain News* (or the *Chinese Times*, according to the English logo) came from San Francisco in a paper sleeve on which his name and address were neatly typed. He put on his gold-rimmed glasses and readied his smoking equipment: the 1939 World's Fair ashtray, Lucky Strikes, matches, coffee. He killed several hours reading the paper, scrupulously reading everything, the date on each page, the page numbers, the want ads. Events went on; the world kept moving. The hands on the clocks kept moving. This sitting ought to have felt as good as sitting in his chair on a day off. He was not sick. He checked his limbs, the crooks of his arms. Everything was normal, quite comfortable, his easy chair fitting under him, the room temperature right.

MaMa said a man can be like a rat and bite through wood, bite through glass and rock. 'What's wrong?' she asked.

'I'm tired,' he said, and she gave him the cure for tiredness, which is to hit the inside joints of elbows and knees until red and black dots – the tiredness – appear on the skin.

He screamed in his sleep. 'Night sweats,' MaMa diagnosed. 'Fear sweats.' What he dreamed must have been axe murders. The family man kills his entire family. He throws slain bodies in heaps out the front door. He leaves no family member alive; he or she would suffer too much being the last one. About to swing the axe, screaming in horror of killing, he is also the last little child who runs into the night and hides behind a fence. Someone

244

chops at the bushes beside him. He covers his ears and shuts his mouth tight, but the scream comes out.

I invented a plan to test my theory that males feel no pain; males don't feel. At school, I stood under the trees where the girls played house and watched a strip of cement near the gate. There were two places where boys and girls mixed; one was the kindergarten playground, where we didn't go any more, and the other was this bit of sidewalk. I had a list of boys to kick: the boy who burned spiders, the boy who had grabbed me by my coat lapels like in a gangster movie, the boy who told dirty pregnancy jokes. I would get them one at a time with my heavy shoes, on which I had nailed toe caps and horseshoe taps. I saw my boy, a friendly one for a start. I ran fast, crunching gravel. He was kneeling; I grabbed him by the arm and kicked him sprawling into the circle of marbles. I ran through the girls' playground and playroom to our lavatory, where I looked out the window. Sure enough, he was not crying. 'See?' I told the girls. 'Boys have no feelings. It's some kind of immunity.' It was the same with Chinese boys, black boys, white boys, and Mexican and Filipino boys. Girls and women of all races cried and had feelings. We had to toughen up. We had to be as tough as boys, tougher because we only pretended not to feel pain.

One of my girl friends had a brother who cried, but he had been raised as a girl. Their mother was a German American and their father a Chinese American. This family didn't belong to our Benevolent Association nor did they go to our parties. The youngest boy wore girls' dresses with ruffles and bows, and brown-blondish ringlets grew long to his waist. When this thin, pale boy was about seven, he had to go to school; it was already two years past the time when most people started school. 'Come and see something strange,' his sister said on Labor Day. I stood in their yard and watched their mother cut off his hair. The hair lay like tails around his feet. Mother cried, and son cried. He was so delicate, he had feelings in his hair; it hurt him to have his hair cut. I did not pick on him.

There was a war between the boys and the girls; we sisters and brothers were evenly matched three against three. The sister next to me, who was like my twin, pushed our oldest brother off the porch railings. He landed on his face and broke two front teeth on the sidewalk. They fought with knives, the cleaver and a boning knife; they circled the dining room table and sliced one another's arms. I did try to stop that fight – they were cutting bloody slits, an earnest fight to the death. The telephone rang. Thinking it was MaMa, I shouted, 'Help. Help. We're having a knife fight. They'll kill each other.' 'Well, do try to stop them.' It was the owner's wife; she'd gossip to everybody that our parents had lost control of us, such bad parents who couldn't get respectable jobs, mother gone all day, and kids turned into killers. 'That was Big Aunt on the phone,' I said, 'and she's going to tell the whole town about us,' and they quit after a while. Our youngest sister snuck up on our middle brother, who was digging in the ground. She was about to drop a boulder on his head when somebody shouted, 'Look out.' She only hit his shoulder. I told my girl friends at school that I had a stepfather and three wicked stepbrothers. Among my stepfather's many aliases was the name of my real father, who was gone.

The white girls at school said, 'I got a spanking.' I said we never got spanked. 'My parents don't believe in it,' I said, which was true. They didn't know about spanking, which is orderly. My mother swung wooden hangers, the thick kind, and brooms. We got trapped behind a door or under a bed and got hit anywhere (except the head). When the other kids said, 'They kissed me good night,' I also felt left out; not that I cared about kissing but to be normal.

We children became so wild that we broke BaBa loose from his chair. We goaded him, irked him – *gikked* him – and the gravity suddenly let him go. He chased my sister, who locked herself in a bedroom. 'Come out,' he shouted. But, of course, she wouldn't, he having a coat hanger in hand and angry. I watched him kick the door; the round mirror fell off the wall and crashed. The door broke open, and he beat her. Only, my sister remembers that it was she who watched my father's shoe against the door and the mirror outside fall, and I who was beaten. But I know I saw the mirror in crazy pieces; I was standing by the table with the blue linoleum top, which was outside the door. I saw his brown shoe against the door and his knee flex and the other brothers and sisters watching from the outside of the door, and heard MaMa saying, 'Seven years' bad luck.'

246

My sister claims that same memory. Neither of us has the recollection of curling up inside that room, whether behind the pounding door or under the bed or in the closet.

A white girl friend, whose jobless and drunk father picked up a sofa and dropped it on her, said, 'My mother saw him pushing *me* down the stairs, and *she* was watching from the landing. And I remember him pushing *her,* and *I* was at the landing. Both of us remember looking up and seeing the other rolling down the stairs.'

He did not return to sitting. He shaved, put on some good clothes, and went out. He found a friend who had opened a new laundry on El Dorado Street. He went inside and chatted, asked if he could help out. The friend said he had changed his mind about owning the laundry, which he had named New Port Laundry. My father bought it and had a Grand Opening. We were proud and quiet as he wrote in gold and black on big red ribbons. The Chinese community brought flowers, mirrors, and pictures of flowers and one of Guan Goong. BaBa's liveliness returned. It came from nowhere, like my new idea that males have feelings. I had no proof for this idea but took my brothers' word for it.

BaBa made a new special place. There was a trap door on the floor inside the laundry, and BaBa looked like a trap-door spider when he pulled it over his head or lifted it, emerging. The basement light shone through the door's cracks. Stored on the steps, which were also shelves, were some rolled-up flags that belonged to a previous owner; gold eagles gleamed on the pole tips.

We children waited until we were left in charge of the laundry. Then some of us kept a lookout while the rest, hanging on to the edge of the hole, stepped down between the supplies. The stairs were steep against the backs of our legs.

The floor under the building was grey soil, a fine powder. Nothing had ever grown in it; it was sunless, rainless city soil. Beyond the light from one bulb the blackness began, the inside of the earth, the insides of the city. We had our flashlights ready. We chose a tunnel and walked side by side into the dark. There are breezes inside the earth. They blow cool and dry. Blackness absorbed our lights. The people who lived and worked in the four storeys above us didn't know how incomplete civilization is, the street only a crust. Down here under the sidewalks and the streets and the cars, the builders had left mounds of loose dirt, piles of dumped cement, rough patches of concrete tamping down and holding back some of the dirt. The posts were unpainted and not square on their pilings. We followed the tunnels to places that had no man-made materials, wild areas, then turned around and headed for the lighted section under the laundry. We never found the ends of some tunnels. We did not find elevators or ramps or the undersides of the buckling metal doors one sees on sidewalks. 'Now we know the secret of cities,' we told one another. On the shelves built against the dirt walls, BaBa had stacked boxes of notebooks and laundry tickets, rubber stamps, pencils, new brushes, blue bands for the shirts, rolls of wrapping paper, cones of new string, bottles of ink, bottles of distilled water in case of air raids. Here was where we would hide when war came and we went underground for guerilla warfare. We stepped carefully; he had set copper and wood rat traps. I opened boxes until it was time to come up and give someone else a chance to explore.

So my father at last owned his house and his business in America. He bought chicks and squabs, built a chicken run, a pigeon coop, and a turkey pen; he dug a duck pond, set the baby bathtub inside for the lining, and won ducklings and goldfish and turtles at carnivals and county fairs. He bought rabbits and bantams and did not refuse dogs, puppies, cats, and kittens. He told a funny story about a friend of his who kept his sweater on while visiting another friend on a hot day; when the visitor was walking out the gate, the host said, 'Well, Uncle, and what are those chicken feet wiggling out of your sweater?' One morning we found a stack of new colouring books and follow-the-dot books on the floor next to our beds. 'BaBa left them,' we said. He buried wine bottles upside down in the garden; their bottoms made a path of sea-colour circles. He gave me a picture from the newspaper of redwoods in Yosemite, and said, 'This is beautiful.' He talked about a Los Angeles Massacre, but I wished that he had not, and pretended he had not. He told an ancient story about two feuding poets: one killed the other's plant by watering it with hot water. He sang 'The Song of the Man of the Green Hill', the end of which goes like this: 'The dishevelled poet beheads the great whale. He shoots an arrow and hits a suspended flea. He sees well through rhinoceros-horn lenses.' This was a song by Kao Chi, who had been executed for his politics; he is famous for poems to his wife and daughter written upon leaving for the capital; he owned a small piece of land where he grew enough to eat without working too hard so he could write poems. BaBa's luffa and grapevines climbed up ropes to the roof of the house. He planted many kinds of gourds, peas, beans, melons, and cabbages – and perennials – tangerines, oranges, grapefruit, almonds, pomegranates, apples, black figs, and white figs – and from seed pits, another loquat, peaches, apricots, plums of many varieties – trees that take years to fruit.

The *Li Sao*: an elegy

In the epic elegy *Li Sao*, or *Lament on Encountering Sorrow* (also translated *Sorrow After Departure* and *Sorrow in Estrangement*), Ch'ü Yüan, who is Kwut Ngin in our dialect, China's earliest known poet, a Homer, told how he wandered in exile. He lived during the Warring States period when China was twelve states.

('All Chinese know this story,' says my father; if you are an authentic Chinese, you know the language and the stories without being taught, born talking them.)

Ch'ü Yüan, who was born on a Tiger day, was a minister in the Chou Kingdom. He advised the king not to go to war against Ch'in, but the king listened to the warmongers and fought a losing war. Because he had expressed an unpopular opinion, Ch'ü Yüan, also called Ch'ü P'ing, meaning 'Peace', was banished. He had to leave the Centre; he roamed in the outer world for the rest of his life, twenty years. He mourned that he had once been a prince, and now he was nothing. And the people were so blind, they thought he was a wrongdoer instead of the only righteous man left in the world. His love for his country was not returned. He sang poems wherever he went, haggard and poor, always homesick, roving from place to place on foot like an old beggar. Paintings show him floating above the tips of trees and horned houses, over other people's heads, his gown blowing with the clouds at his feet.

He braided a gown out of cress leaves and lilies, and travelled south into the barbarous lands. He met the Goddess of the Hsiang River and the Lady of the Hsiang River, the wonderful women on either side of the water, who decorated him with clinking jade stones, winterthorn, orchids, angel herbs, and selineas. Flying horses, swift green dragons, and phoenixes with gold plumes pulled his chariot, which was a winged dragonboat made of jade and ivory and entwined with ivy leaves. He rowed with cedar oars and flew orchids for flags; orchids were woven in the rigging, and the boat was harnessed to the whirlwind. He left the land of grey plane trees. He drank dew from lotus leaf and magnolia cups. His food was aster petals. Which may all be a way of saying that he had nothing but the outdoors, the mist, the rivers, stones, lightning (his gold whip), and his imagination and dreams. He reached heaven's gate and climbed the roof of the world.

He had many adventures. He followed the phoenix to the uttermost parts of the earth, crossed and recrossed the sky. No home anywhere. He saw the entire world, but not his homeland. He crossed the quicksand; he crossed the burning river red as blood. The Emperor of the West helped him, and the Great Emperor of the East listened to his odes of sacrifice. His steeds drank at the lake where the sun bathes. He brushed the sun with a golden bough. The Lady of the Clouds took him to nine continents and four seas. The Princess of the West, however, declined to meet him, and the falcon refused to act as go-between; the capricious turtledove offered to go, but sent the phoenix, who failed him. Some say he cast his jade pendant on the earth, where it blossomed; some say he cast his jade pendant into the Hsiang River. He sang to the goddess who dries her hair in the rising sun. He gave spiced rice to the wizard who makes circles with green feathers, shoots the dog star with a shaft, casts rainbows, and pours cassia wine from the North Star. He travelled on the nine waters and among the islands with the God of the Yellow River, who rides on a white tortoise beneath the water. He visited the Dragon Halls, purple and pearly red palaces with walls that glittered like fish scales.

When winter came, he journeyed in thunder and rain. The monkeys and hyenas moaned at night, and he cried that he could not find his king and home. 'Time runs like water and takes my youth,' he wrote. He told the God of Law how he had been wronged and exiled; the king had gone hunting and the queen had been stolen by a false friend. His king did not aid the suffering people. 'I am the phoenix dispossessed,' said Ch'ü Yüan. In all these travels, he could not find one uncorrupted human being. He was once rich and handsome with moth-wing eyebrows; now he had no reputation and was misunderstood by Southern Savages. 'I am the naked roaming saint whose head was shaved like a slave's.' The distance between him and home grew farther each day. 'My old wife has gone to a strange district; wind and snow separate us.' 'Birds fly back to last year's nest; foxes face the hill to die, but I cannot go home.' 'No go-between anywhere.' He was an orphan who travelled everywhere because one place was denied him.

He wrote a poem made of one hundred and seventy questions with no answers. 'Soothsayers who use tortoise shell and yarrow,' he asked, 'what is the order of creation?' 'Who built the sky?' 'Where does it end?' 'What supports the sky?' 'Shall I be one of the common herd or a skylark?' 'Why do I try to bank up the waters in the dark sea when I am not a great whale?' 'Can I convince people one by one about what is right?' The soothsayer said, 'I cannot help you.' The Witch of the Future, to whom he gave mistletoe, asked him, 'Why do you want just that one country?'

From his dragonboat, he looked down at his home and realized that escape and return were equally impossible.

At last he walked along the Tsanglang River while reciting poems. He met a fisherman and told his story again. He had seen the entire corrupt world, and 'the crowd is dirty', but he had never given up the ideal of good government. 'The crowd is drunk; I alone am sober, I alone am clean, so I am banished. The world has gone bad. Even the reliable orchid has changed.'

'Why should you be aloof?' asked the fisherman. 'When the water's clear, I wash my tassels, but when it's too muddy for silk, I can still wash my feet.'

Upon hearing these words, Ch'ü Yüan decided that he would use the river too. He sang all his poems and his elegy, his requiem. He danced at the edge of the river to make his last moments happier. He threw himself into the water and drowned. 'There is no wisdom in the world,' says the commentary to the *Li Sao*. 'Its people are too corrupt to deserve a man like this.'

After he drowned, the people realized his sincerity and their loss. Too late, they felt guilt for their waywardness. They tried to call him back. Poets stood by the river and told him how uncomfortable death was: 'Return, O Soul,' they sang, 'from the empty places and the wrong things. Do not go where the titans live who are a thousand cubits tall, and ten suns eat stone, bronze, and gold. Don't wander among the Blackteeth. Don't go where the demons sacrifice men's flesh and grind their bones. Return, O Soul, from the land where cobras move like grass, and foxes rule for a thousand miles. Don't sink into the thousand-mile quicksand or the pool that thunders. Don't go where red ants grow big as elephants and black wasps big as gourds. No crops grow in the dead lands, and human beings eat thorns and weeds. Return from the land of icebergs like mouths. Don't go to the heaven where tigers guard nine gates, serpents have nine heads, and the giant with the nine heads tears up nine thousand forests. Stay away from the devil with the tiger's forehead and three eyes. Stay away from the eater of human beings.'

Then they enticed him with the pleasures of earth: 'Return to earth. Return to earth where you have your own room with no surprises, your home warm in winter and cool in summer. Return to the porch with the balustrade and enter again the doors with the red squares. Return, O Soul, to the earth's great halls, domes, towers, and terraces. Remember the flowers and the birds, wild ducks, black cranes, wild geese.' They chanted food poems and long, long lists of food: 'Pepper with honey, steak, bitter melon soup, lamb, turtle, sugarcane juice.' They reminded him of his clothes, the red belts, the silks. 'Remember candles and early wheat, salt, vinegar, ginger, and water.' They sang about girls as mouthwatering as salt plums and lemons. 'Come back and listen to the singing girls, who have made new songs. Play the urn and drum. Do the wind dance. Play the drums for war songs. Walk in the fields and sing the rustic songs from sea countries. Look again at the actresses playing warriors. Play chess. Hunt the rhino. Return, O Soul. Return.'

The people threw rice into the river for his ghost to eat. They did this every year on the anniversary of his death, and they raced dragonboats up and down the river in memory of his travels or in search of him. Ch'ü Yüan was such a smart man that one day he managed to send his ghost out of the river and say, 'Oh, you foolish people. The fish are eating the rice, and I'm going hungry. Wrap it in leaves for me.' For a change they listened to him. And so on the fifth day of the fifth month, we eat rice and barley cooked in sausage and pork and salted eggs and beans, and a yellow gelatin, shaped by ti leaves. Not just Chinese but the people in Korea, Japan, Vietnam, Malaysia, and America remember Ch'ü Yüan the incorruptible.

The brother in Vietnam

My mother holding my hand, I went through a curtain into a dark, out of which came explosions and screams, voices shouting things I did not understand. In a rectangle of light – which grew and shrank according to how close or far away I thought it – men with scared eyes peered over the top of a big hole they were in. Helmets weighed down their skulls. Their cheekbones were black. The men ran, clutching guns, and fell, and crawled. The explosions rolled them screaming on the ground. I saw the undersides of their boots. Their faces and hands were not flesh-colour. Everyone wore the same outfits. The colour had gone out of the world. I stumbled tangle-legged into my mother's skirt and the curtain and screamed with the soldiers.

Suddenly they were all gone like a dream, and I was crying in the street. Years later I figured it had only been a movie, a war movie, an old sepia-tone. 'Did you take me to an American movie when I was a baby?' I've asked. Usually my father took us to American movies, my mother to Chinese movies, where she could visit with friends during the boring parts, and children played and shouted without getting ejected. MaMa said, 'You cried so much that the usher ghost threw me out of the theatre.' I worried about making her waste money on a ticket, and so she diverted me from the actual horror – I had seen a vision of war.

There has always been war, whether or not I knew about it. My tall parents even taller standing on ladders and covering the windows with black curtains, playing theatre in the bright interstice, had been thinking about war. The curtains fell long and black, but the inside of the room shone. My father cut a picture out of a magazine and pinned it on the wall. The yellow light came from it. 'You look like this,' he said, or 'This girl looks like you.' She was shining because of her golden hair, a golden girl.

It couldn't have been the blonde curls that made her look like me, so it must have been the round face with the fat cheeks. 'Shirley Temple also looks like this girl.' I had been diverted again, and for some years the importance of that day seemed the blonde girl when those were blackout curtains for World War II.

There is no word like *vision* for what one hears. I heard *earthquake* – it may have been during an earthquake – and listened to the world, which was a blue and green sphere with lines of meridians, spinning against a wood fence. It did not clatter against the fence but hummed. 'The earth,' I said, and did not say 'quake' because of the mightiness of it, *earth* the same word as *world* in 'World War II'.

About the fourth and fifth things I remember – and each thing has to do with war – were my two youngest brothers being born. My sister and brother and I were alone; the adults were in a room across the hall. They had said, 'Stay here,' but did not shut us in. My sister and I were standing on the bed when we noticed that through a crack at the doorjamb coincidentally lined up with the crack of the door across the hall, we could see into that other room, which was filled with light. MaMa was squatting over a basin, and blood was pouring from her. So that was how babies were born. Our room turned white, and through the window flew a white Christmas card like a dove and landed on the floor. It had fluttered in the air. Forgetting about what we had seen through the cracks, my sister and I picked up the card. It was very beautiful with snow and sparkles. 'There's no envelope,' we said. 'No stamp. No name. No mailman. How could it come through the window?' I checked the window; someone must have snuck up to the open window and thrown the card in. But screen and glass were shut tight against the winter. 'You saw it too, didn't you?' my sister and I asked each other, our brother only about a year old and no help. 'Yes, it flew through the glass near here.' We pointed out the pane, one of the top ones. 'How did this card come into the room?' we asked when an adult entered. 'The baby's born,' said the adult. That baby was my brother who was born on Christmas day. Later the adults said that they found him naked under a pine tree, but I knew what I had seen: blood and a flash of white flying, a flash of flying white.

258

In addition to his American name, this new brother was named Han Bridge like a bridge between Han and here. We're Han People from the Han Dynasty. Bridge is the name of my brothers' generation. The Chinese name of the brother who waited with us is Incorruptible Bridge or Pure Bridge.

Two years later when our youngest brother was born, I knew days and hours in advance that we were going to have another brother. My mother and the lady doctor locked themselves in a bedroom. I was in charge of my sister and two brothers and decided that we had to arrange to see this birth. Each of us carried a crate or a stool outside and lined it up on the porch under the window (where the card had flown in). We climbed up in a row and saw the doctor lift a white bundle like a snowdrop on a hook. A foot stuck out. The baby had been born. He was being weighed. We heard him cry. Joy swelled the world. We jumped up and down and sang a song the animals in fables sing when they are happy. ' "Jump like a squirrel. Bob like a bluejay. Tails in the air. Tails in the air." ' We added our own lines, 'The baby's born. The baby's born.' Our parents motioned for us to come inside.

This youngest brother was long, thin, and red with very black hair; the other brother had been pale. His fists were tight like fern curls. I prised the fingers open, careful not to break one; there was lint in there already. I put my finger in his hand so that it would feel as if he were holding my hand. MaMa said that a tightfisted baby is lucky because his father saves money, and the baby will also save money. I was glad to see that he had that good useful trait to keep him safe. BaBa named him Bright Bridge, also translated Severe Bridge.

'Where did the baby come from?' I asked the doctor as I walked her to the door.

'I brought him in my black bag.' Adults were always diverting us from the awful. They wanted to protect us, as I wanted to protect the baby, who a moment ago had been nothing and could easily slip back.

I made sure the windows were locked over the baby's crib, and patrolled those locks and latches. I watched the winos and hoboes. Once, we found one of my brothers sitting in the lap of a black man, who was sitting on the sidewalk. I saw burglars carry off the tuba from the Filipino Marching Band's basement.

I watched shadows in the neighbours' windows strangling one another. Feet dangled from ceilings and trees. A big grey bomb slowly covered the skies between houses, but it was only a Navy blimp. Airplanes flew over, but their bomb hatches stayed shut. *Life* magazine showed black and white photographs of dead bodies, limbs, and heads in impossible positions, rib cages barely covered with skin, faces that one could not stop staring at. Piles of skeletons with teeth and eye sockets and hair. 'Is this real?' 'Yes, it's real.' 'What happened to these people?' 'They were killed in the war.'

The Chinese magazines had war cartoons. In the first panel an ugly man in the cockpit of an airplane laughed as he divebombed villagers and water buffaloes. 'What is he, MaMa?' 'He's an enemy person.' So that was what the enemy looked like. He had an evil black pointed moustache, a skullcap, and goggles. She did not say enemy people were Japanese, so for a time, I thought they were from outer space. In the next panel an enemy bayoneted an old man, spurting his blood. A bayonet was a gun that shot knives. An enemy threw two naked babies into the air, and another enemy caught one on his bayonet. The second baby fell to the ground and smashed. A booted enemy stepped on its head. The mother had her arms raised towards the babies. Then the mother was in a cage, the father in another cage, a crowd of children in another, the mother's and father's and children's arms reaching towards one another through the bars. The cells were like cages for ducks and chickens at market. In one panel the huge mother was grimacing, her stomach bloated. She was drinking from a jug. MaMa explained that the Japanese were forcing her to drink water until she burst. They would bounce on her stomach and it would explode. They were torturing her children in front of her, and stopped whenever she drank. If she peed, she had to drink her own urine. The children's mutilation was so gruesome, the cartoonist did not show it.

The adults told us how the Japanese tortured the American soldiers they captured: They tied the prisoner to a stake, and while slicing and poking, they cut an opening in his side and knotted a rope to one of his large intestines. A Japanese, pretending to be friendly, loosened the rope that bound his hands and feet. The American ran, and the rope pulled his guts out in a stream behind him. The Japanese laughed, as they did at the bursting mother and the skewered baby.

While watching for lurkers come to kidnap the babies, I saw many first stars, and wasted them wishing for peace. I was careful to define *peace* so the tricky gods didn't make the earth peaceful by killing everything on it. War used up the magic rings, bracelets, wands, the fairies with dandelion skirts, the fish I let go. I wrote a spell, a one and zeroes all the way around the rims of the lamp shades on my parents' nightstands, turned on the lights, and said, 'I wish MaMa and BaBa to live as many years as I have written around this lamp.' Black ribbons, black wreaths, and pennants with stars hanging in windows and on doors meant the sons of those houses had been killed in war.

Each time we went to the Confucius Hall for meetings and Chinese movies, everybody together bowed three bows, and everybody on stage lit three sticks of incense, the first to wish happiness to the ruler, the second for World Peace, and the third, good harvest. Sun Yat Sen's and Chiang Kai Shek's pictures were on the stage next to the American and Chinese flags. (My father's small picture was among the other founders' in the foyer.) We sang the Chinese National Anthem, and heard hours of speeches about war and the obligations of us Wah People, then pledged money to help China.

At the parades, where tanks and rockets rolled by and soldiers and sailors marched, Chinese Americans carried a giant red Chinese flag that covered the street for people to throw money on. The dragon in those days came to our houses. We tied lettuce and new dollar bills from the porch eaves, and the dragon jumped for its food. All this money was used for rescuing war refugees.

The houses where the Japanese American families lived were shut down, and the gardens overgrown as if enchanted. We kids explored empty houses and called them haunted. We walked around the yards, climbed in doors and windows, wandered about the rooms, sat on the furniture. A boy fell through a floor. And once we saw a foot step out of a doorway. We ran from it and lost one of the girls, who sat on a kerb bent over with a stomach-ache. The foot was in white socks and oxfords.

All the talk was about war and death. Even the story about

the squirrel and the blue jay was about their burying a friend. Buried. Fa Mu Lan bled from sword wounds until her armour was soaked red. Ngok Fei's arms were tied behind his back, and the blood squeezed out from the wooden collar around his neck. Grandfather was bayoneted in the head for patriotically withholding information from a Japanese soldier. My mother's family, which had four girls, had saved the only boy, the youngest, Uncle Wah, who dodged the draft. He had been fifteen years old, maybe only fourteen, Chinese adding a year, when they gave him all their money and helped him escape to Singapore.

' "The superior man minds his own business; fools concern themselves with public matters," ' said the adults, talking politics. ' "Fan Kuei was a butcher before becoming a general." ' ' "Warlords confiscate the land, and kidnap the farmer to guard some obscure border." ' ' "To go to war is to mingle with the desert sands." '

'Armies enter the village with draft lists, and there are dots against our names,' sang Tu Fu. 'Boys come back with their hair white.' He wrote that giving birth to daughters is better than sons. 'We can still give her in marriage, keep her as a neighbour, but a son is buried without ceremonies among the hundred grasses.' 'Soldiers ravage and burn even the print blocks.' He sang a threnody for a woman sewing the head back on her husband's dead body. 'A wife of a soldier is a wisteria clinging to an old tree.' 'A woman married to a soldier is rabbit silk clinging to wild chrysanthemum and hemp.'

Soldiers wrote their poems on the paper money they'd been paid and let the money fly away in the wind at crossroads.

In his last five poems before he died in battle, Wang Tsan, a poet with eidetic memory in Ts'ao Ts'ao's army witnessed the final days of the Han Dynasty. He saw a woman throw her child into yellow weeds, which were studded with skulls. While he wandered in the embers and ashes of once-tall cities, he cupped his hands like blinders beside his eyes.

There was a farmer in Mei Chia village, who knew that he would be drafted. Recruiters told the hungry farmer about the food, clothes, and shoes the army would give him free. He could send all the pay home to his mother. Whichever army reached the village first would force him to fight on its side or shoot him for an enemy, so he might as well volunteer. His mother told him that she did not want that money. But the farmer said he would have to get some sleep if he was to go to war in the morning. That night as he lay sleeping, his mother stabbed his eyes out with her two hairpricks.

Freedom from the draft was the reason for leaving China in the first place. The Gold Mountain does not make war, is not invaded, and has no draft. The government does not capture men and boys and send them to war.

My father was exactly the right age for the draft. So was Uncle Bun's son and Big Brother Sao. Everybody suggested ways to get out of war. Certain butchers were supposed to be efficient cutting off the trigger finger with one blow of the cleaver. 'He's faster than a surgeon.' There were diets to get thinner and diets to get fatter. So-and-so had gained ten pounds on the day of the physical by eating ten pounds of bananas. They discussed the advantages and dangers of staying awake for a week drinking coffee. They rehearsed flunking ear tests – not to turn around when a tester whispered behind them, for example.

'There was a poet who took a drug that paralysed his vocal cords. I wonder what drug that was.'

'Chlorine bleach and ammonia. The effect, unfortunately, is permanent.'

'What you do to foil the X-ray machine is drink ink straight. Then the photograph comes out black.'

'Is ink poisonous?'

'A brother in Los Angeles drank ink. He's gotten out of the draft, and he's still healthy. Wouldn't you rather die drinking ink than be blown up by a land mine?'

Borax, alum, rat poison. Run for twenty miles a day while smoking cigarettes.

I sniffed at the undiluted ink; it smelled metallic sweet. The men were brave and desperate to drink it. It made my teeth clench.

'Drink two quarts before the X-rays.'

They experimented how to make more phlegm, how to ruin the stomach, how to control temperature and blood pressure by will power and breath.

'That inking the X-rays is not going to work,' my father said. 'It's only a superstition; it won't work.' He was interested because he had been drafted.

BaBa did not sleep after he got drafted. I planned to be always awake too, alert, on guard. I would make time pass deliberately, like a slow train, but suddenly my mother and two of the children and I were on a train. Our father was not with us; we were travelling with the owner of the gambling house. He was the most powerful of the Stockton Chinese, an American citizen, an English speaker; he dealt with white people on our behalf. They knew him as a good citizen and Chinese community spokesman. The seat did not fit; I stood on it or in the aisle. Everything moved. We did not have to walk on top of the train, nor did we have to sneak aboard a boxcar. We were going where the tracks went, to Sacramento, Second City. 'Look,' said my mother. 'Sheep. Look at the sheep.' I was standing at the window, but did not see anything until she said 'Sheep,' and they appeared, white in the sun. I looked at her, and when I turned back, they were gone. The train whistled regularly ahead of us. At bends the engine and the caboose looked like other trains. We were on our way to rescue BaBa from the United States Army.

In Second City we took taxis and walked to places that were like train stations. We sat on benches waiting, or stood against MaMa on sidewalks and in hallways. We waited in lobbies decorated with posters of Army, Navy, and Marine demons. The baby didn't cry. Father's employer went away to talk to generals; then he also waited. BaBa was somewhere inside this city. Homeless and fatherless, I did not see how we were going to find the train tracks again. My mother said, 'I'm going to go into the general's office and beg him not to take your father. I'll say, "These children's lives depend on him." Then all of you cry, "BaBa. BaBa. Don't take our BaBa away from us."-' I would hang on to her coat, my sister to her hand, my brother be the babe in arms.

MaMa was wearing her black New York coat with the black fur collar; I wore my maroon coat with the brown fur collar, and my sister, her powder blue coat with the grey fur collar.

This waiting was like when villagers waited in the landlord's courtyard to pay taxes. The other reason for leaving China was the taxes paid with grain. There was a story about a widow who paid with the heads of her two children. The peasants cried Aiya when she poured their heads out of a rice bag. 'Here are your taxes,' she said as the heads rolled out at the feet of the landlord. Landlords and generals and governments 'pare and peel the ignorant country people'. Families had to sell the mother or a sister, leave her there at the landlord's.

At last, suddenly, BaBa came out of a door, laughing and talking. Time rippled again. He told MaMa what had happened to him: 'We had to take all our clothes off, and file past the doctor demon. The white man in front of me was white and fat – rolls of fat. And there I was next to him – skinny with rows of ribs. The doctor flunked us both at once. Too fat and too skinny. He took one look at us, and said, "Four F." Mr Too Fat and Mr Too Thin. We pointed at each other and laughed.' He told this miracle many times.

All of us together again, we found the train and went home. As soon as we got in the door, MaMa started fattening him up, but it never worked. She had been using her old doctoring skills poisoning him, and his weight had dropped permanently. 'I poisoned him to keep him out of World War II,' she says. 'Now all these years, I've been trying to plump him up with food and medicine, but he stays skinny. His metabolism is ruined. He eats a lot but doesn't gain weight.'

The cousins who were not clever enough to avoid the war – in fact some foolhardy ones enlisted – sent pictures from Europe. They looked like the good soldiers in the movies. Uncle Bun's son, who had been the most enthusiastic about drinking ink and shooting off toes, had posed for a studio portrait of himself in a helmet with antennae. His hands in gauntlets held a machine with nozzles; the hose was draped around his neck. Big Brother Sao, an officer, wore a creased hat in some pictures and a brimmed hat in others; he is looking sideways into the camera to show off the bars on his collar. A Boston cousin was among a group of soldiers kneeling and standing in front of their tent. Their hair was inside hats and helmets, and they wore rumpled uniforms. My mother said they were army doctors. I kept asking which were men and which women, but she didn't know either. We guessed the pretty ones were women. The ones with beard stubbles and big knuckles were definitely men. The one that was our cousin had the chin strap of his helmet unbuckled, and it hung down jauntily and war-wearily. If he had not written which one he was, we would not have been able to pick him out; he did not look peculiarly Chinese. It must have been the uniform. Another cousin sent a picture of himself leaning against a palm tree; he looked like he was in a war musical.

One cousin was in the Fourteenth Service Squad, the Chinese American Air Force Battalion, the first American soldiers into China. What they found in Chungking was a city of primitive natives who did not understand Cantonese. The soldiers hired them as houseboys, carriers, and road builders. Two by two the Chinese carried bombs tied to a pole between them. They moved fifty-gallon drums of fuel. The Chinese Americans drove their trucks on the new road while thousands of natives built it before them. Men, women, and children broke rocks into gravel so fast the drivers did not have to step on their brakes.

We had a family portrait taken to send to the faraway relatives. One brother was dressed in a kid army uniform with a leather strap across his chest and another brother in a baby navy uniform with white middy collar and white short, his sweet knees showing.

We went to a movie where the attendants gave each kid a free picture of an atomic bomb explosion. Smoke boiled in a yellow and orange cloud like a brain on a column. It was a souvenir to celebrate the bombing of Japan. Since I did not own much, I enjoyed the ownership of the VJ picture. At the base of the explosion, where the people would have been, the specks didn't resolve into bodies. I hid the picture so the younger children could not see it, to protect them against the fear of such powerful evil, not to break the news to them too soon. Occasionally, I took it out to study. I hid it so well, I lost it. I drew billows and shafts of light, and almost heard the golden music of it, the gold trumpets with drums of it.

For a while after the soldiers in the family came home, they looked like their photographs; they wore the uniforms visiting. But then they put on their regular slacks and white shirts. Their hair grew out, and their wives trimmed it with home clippers. Their noses rounded out, the bridges receding, and their tight jaws softened. They did not walk from the shoulders like football players and boxers any more. They started speaking Chinese again. Big Brother Sao's eyes began looking at things far away again.

The one family of AJAs, Americans of Japanese Ancestry, on our block came out of relocation camp. They did not seem capable of killing ten million Chinese civilians, but then these were Americans and not Japanese. We had not broken into their house; it had stood shut for years. They pruned the bushes back into neat balls; they preferred ornamentals over vegetables. They gave us their used comic books, and were the only adults who gave us toys instead of clothes for Christmas. We kids, who had peasant minds, suspected their generosity; they were bribing us not to lynch them. The friendlier they were, the more hideous the crimes and desires they must have been covering up. My parents gave them vegetables; we would want them to be nice to us when the time came for us Chinese to be the ones in camp. No matter how late we walked home from the laundry, as we passed their house, they switched on their porch light to light our way.

A comic book they gave us each month was *Blackhawk*, which is about a squadron of allied pilots. Chop Chop was the only Blackhawk who did not wear a blue-black pilot's uniform with yellow and black insignia. He wore slippers instead of boots, pyjamas with his undershirt showing at the tails, white socks, an apron; he carried a cleaver and wore a pigtail, which Chinese stopped wearing in 1911. He had buck teeth and slanted lines for eyes, and his skin was a muddy orange. Fat and half as tall as the other Blackhawks, who were drawn like regular human beings, Chop Chop looked like a cartoon. It was unclear whether he was a boy or a little man. He did not pilot his own plane but rode behind the main Blackhawk, the American. 'Very clever, these Chinese,' Blackhawk kept saying; 'I always said little Chop Chop is the smartest of the Blackhawks.' And not being clever myself, I took these words as compliments. Tall dragon ladies with cigarette holders said, 'I'd kill for a kiss from those lips,' meaning Blackhawk's or André's. I thought I had to learn to like Chop Chop; it was certainly true that we used cleavers, and we admired fat people, and I for one was short. We decided the

Japanese family must not have known what those comics meant, or they wouldn't have bought them.

The cousins who had gone to war didn't talk about what they had seen or done, just as the AJAs did not mention the camps. They must have been too ashamed. They might have talked among themselves, and shut up in front of an outsider like me, not a soldier, not an AJA. The stories unfit for children must have been worse than guts hanging out, legs and brains hurtling through the air, cities and countries bombed into insanity, my own cousins killing Germans and Italians. I wouldn't tell children such things either.

The next enemy was the Communists. Our parents agreed that we should not meet at a designated place should Stockton be bombed but be free to escape with our teachers if we were at school or to run with the neighbours. But we children privately planned to meet at the big tree, wait for each other there, come back to the tree years later if we got lost in the city altered by bombing. The scary thing about going to school was that I might come home to find a bomb crater, or the house would be empty. I would walk from room to room calling, and then the sun would go down. The AJA children must have come home from school and waited on the porch for their parents to open the door, but they had been taken to camp.

Grandmother and the aunts wrote letters on the deaths of every last uncle. If the uncles could have figured out what the Communists wanted of them, they would have complied, but Communism made no sense. It was something to do with new songs, new dances, and the breaking up of families. Maybe it had to do with no sex; the men were separated from the women. Children were put into motherless, fatherless camps for training; they were taught to report on their parents instead of guarding family secrets. The Communists were not simply after property; they wanted the people to say certain things. They had to sing ugly Communist songs. 'Stoop and scoop, stoop and scoop,' they sang, and genuflected, swooping their red scarves from air to ground. The aunts waved their kerchiefs vigorously; they memorized fast and sang aloud, but still they had to kneel on ground glass, and their thumbs were broken. They did whatever they thought the Communists wanted, but the Communists were not satisfied. Communists were people who had gone crazy and perverted. They made order by rationing food, a cup of oil per family per week. They held court trials, which they thought were the same as entertainment and theatre. The torturers asked riddles with no correct answers. The uncles had listened to the answers of the people ahead of them, but the Communists wanted peculiar responses; the same answer did not fit everyone. Communist schools taught from strange books. The uncles had been kept awake at night to study. 'If Uncle doesn't get some sleep soon, he's going to die. He's working from four a.m. to eleven p.m., then has to study how to be a Communist in his spare time. If he doesn't memorize a page a day perfectly, he can't have his dinner.' The Communists were monkeys trying to be human beings; they were pretending to explain and reason, putting on serious faces. They were saying nonsense, pretending they knew the classics when they were not teaching from real books. Communist schools, Communist books, Red art work, Red courts, theatres, customs were almost like real ones but off. The shrewd villagers were not fooled. The Japanese had tortured people for the fun of it; the Communists wanted something else: their monkey civilization. Neighbours informed against one another to prove they were true Communists. The number of people the Communists killed was sixty million.

After the uncles were killed, the aunts fled to Hong Kong, Canada, and the United States. That the Communists were holding their distant cousins as hostages did not deter them.

'I wish the Japanese had won,' my mother said.

For the Korean War, we wore dog tags and had Preparedness Drill in the school basement. We had to fill out a form for what to engrave on the dog tags. I looked up 'religion' in the *American-Chinese Dictionary* and asked my mother what religion we were. 'Our religion is Chinese,' she said. 'But that's not a religion,' I said. 'Yes, it is,' she said. 'We believe in the Chinese religion.' 'Chinese is our race,' I said. 'Well, tell the teacher demon it's Kung Fu Tse, then,' she said. The kids at school said, 'Are you Catholic?' 'No.' 'Then you're Protestant.' So our dog tags had *O* for religion and *O* for race because neither black nor white. Mine also had *O* for blood type. Some kids said *O* was for 'Oriental', but I knew it was for 'Other' because the Filipinos, the Gypsies, and the Hawaiian boy were Os. Zero was also the name of the Japanese fighter plane, so we had better watch our step. The teachers gave us anti-Communist comic books and Civil Defense pamphlets about atomic bomb attacks. We did a scientific experiment about chain reactions by arranging matches in triangles, the first match burning and lighting two, and those two igniting four, and so on until the whole world was on fire. The earth would quake and split in half.

'The War,' I wrote in a composition, which the teacher corrected, 'Which war?' There was more than one.

Before the letter writers stopped complaining about the Communists, the Vietnam war had begun. The government said that Vietcong weapons came from China. We ought to bomb China into the Stone Age, the generals said. Soon the war would be Chinese Americans against Chinese. And my brothers old enough to be drafted.

One brother got married a few months before the draft exemption for married men was cancelled. But one brother enlisted in the Navy and the other was commissioned as an officer in the Air Force.

I drove my youngest brother to the airport in the middle of the night. He didn't want the flowers I brought; he had already refused to carry the chickens and puddings that MaMa had cooked. He was in his uniform like the middy that he wore in his baby picture. He said not to wait for him to board or for the plane to take off. 'Go on,' he said. 'Don't wait around.' So I only got to see him check his luggage. As I drove past the terminal, I saw him sitting by himself on a cement bench under a light.

The brother tried to get into the Coast Guard, which he thought rescued surfers and sailboats and directed traffic around buoys. He drove to Santa Cruz and Monterey, and there were no openings; everybody else who did not want to go to war had had the same idea. Then the Coast Guard were sent to Vietnam to fight on the rivers there.

The Japanese and Chinese Americans warned one another what would happen if they got captured: the Vietnamese would flay Asian Americans alive. Unless you die of shock, you're still alive after being skinned. You had to die fighting. Imagine the eyes looking out of a skinless body. During World War II the United States had tactfully sent the 442nd Go-For-Broke AJAs to Europe, not Asia or the Pacific. But for this war, there was not that special consideration.

The rumour also went that the brother's draft board was channelling hippies and blacks into the infantry. And 'Orientals' belonged over there in Asia fighting among their own kind. The only way that he would be able to get classified as a Conscientious Objector was to have a religion, and he did not have one. He did not want to end up a medic in this immoral war anyway.

While deciding what to do, as time ran out, the brother did his job, which was teaching high school. He had been teaching for months, but had not gotten over his surprise at how dumb the students were. Most of them had an IQ of 100, the average, which permitted them to read by sounding out each word. The human race was not smart.

During Current Events, he told his class some atrocities to convince them about the wrongness of war. The students looked at the pictures of napalmed children and said, 'Sure, war is hell.' Where had they learned that acceptance? He told them the worst torture he knew: the Vikings used to cleave a prisoner-of-war's back on either side of the spine, and pull the lungs out, which fluttered like wings when the man breathed. This torture was called the Burning Eagle. The brother felt that it was self-evident that we ought to do anything to stop war. But he was learning that upon hearing terrible things, there are people who are, instead, filled with a crazy patriotism.

'Who owns electricity?' a boy with an 85 IQ and a third-grade reading level asked one day. The brother recognized a 'teachable moment', as these happy seconds were called in college. He explained how water, electricity, gas, and oil originally belonged to nobody and everybody. Like the air. 'But the corporations that control electricity sell it to the rest of us,' he said. 'Well, of course they do,' said the student; 'I'd sell the air if I had discovered it.' 'What if some people can't afford to buy it?' 'Whoever discovered it deserves to be paid for it,' said the stubborn boy. 'It's Communist not to let him make all the money he can.' Although the students could not read or follow logic, they blocked him with their anti-Communism, which seemed to come naturally to them, without effort or study. He had thought that it was self-evident that air, at least, belongs to all of us. The students' parents were on welfare, unemployment, and workmen's compensation, but they defended capitalism without knowing what it was called.

'Can you invent a plan where a person can always find a job, and with that job make a living?' the brother asked. 'How do we go about making food instead of bombs?' 'What steps can we take to stop the war in Vietnam?'

'You think like that because you're a Communist,' the kids replied. 'That's a Communist question.' Any criticism he had of America they dismissed as his being gookish.

Students were dropping out, not in protest like college students but to volunteer for the Army, Navy, and Marines. He had a few months, a few weeks, days to educate them before they got killed or killed others in Vietnam. Or until he himself had to go. He had to make up words of advice on the spot. Supposedly men, the drop-outs came back to the hallways to show off their sturdy uniforms and good shoes. They looked more substantial, taller, smoothed out, as if some kind of potential had been fulfilled. 'Take care of yourself,' he told them. To those who dropped out to work on assembly lines, he said, 'Find out what you're making.'

In the one class that wasn't remedial, strange things happened to the literature. After the lessons on how to fill out employment forms, cheques, income tax forms, drivers' licence and health insurance applications, after reading and discussing the motor vehicle code, he introduced *Romeo and Juliet* with a movie of it, models of the Globe, role-playing, and the sound track from *West Side Story*. But upon its reading, *Romeo and Juliet* became a horror story about children his students' age whispering, tiptoeing, making love, and driven mad in the dark. They killed and were killed in dark streets and dark rooms. They married in the dark. Plague infested the country, and drugs poisoned instead of cured. Children were buried alive among their ancestors' bones, with which Juliet feared she would dash in her brains. She was locked in a tomb with her dead husband, a young suicide, and her cousin festering green. The brother could not shift the emphasis; he felt he had spoiled the love story for a generation of students.

Between classes he found secret torn books hidden underneath shelves and stuffed behind other books. Somebody had jammed books behind the radiator and up the air vent, 'Fuck you, basturds' scrawled on their pages. Books that he had bought for a classroom library were ripped in half along the bindings.

The students shamed by Remedial Reading covered their books with paper bags or oil cloth. The remedials had no brotherly feeling towards one another. 'Dummy,' they said. 'Stupid.' 'Shut up, Stupid.' There were hardly any girl remedials; when girls landed in those classes, they improved quickly and got out.

His students stole anything. They shot up bowling alleys, and beat up hippies and whores ('Hors Welcome' they painted on their cars). One boy collected German helmets, bayonets, knives ('with real bloodstains'), swastikas, atrocity and Hitler photos, flags, iron crosses, grenades. He had big hands but quit football practice for the brother's private reading lessons. When the poor boy stayed at third-grade, 3.0, reading level, he banged his head against the wall. His file said that he had had two older brothers who died when they reached third grade; one drowned and the other fell off a roof. One boy tied rocks around the necks of dogs and watched them struggle and drown. He bragged about killing two tied together. He also jumped dogs and slit their throats. One boy had three babies by three different girl friends, and persuaded all of them to keep the children; the brother gave him three Doctor Spock books. One student was a vampire boy, who wore a cape and would not go out into the sun. The others pulled him away from the shade along the walls, tore off his clothes, held him down, and trained magnifying glasses on his skin. Many students acted like animals: One, Benjie, lowered his heavy head snarling over his papers, peeped and spied over his left arm so nobody could cheat off his poor paper. He held his pencil straight up and down in a fist that stuck out of an unravelling sweater sleeve. His eyebrows jerked; growls came from inside his arms. Whenever his pencil broke, he walked all the way around the room to the sharpener, and wrote *fuck* and *chink* on the blackboards.

'Why does he think he's so smart?' Benjie asked, pointing with his middle finger at a yearbook picture of the student body president. 'People who get *A*s don't have fun. They're fairies.

Fuckin' fairies. That guy's such a fairy, if I hit him, he'd fall over like anybody else. Is it true about that ten-year-old kid who's going to college?'

'Yes,' said the brother, 'but there are hardly any people like him. He's sort of a freak of nature.'

'If I hit him, he'd fall over.' He threw something, then retreated behind his arms, came out again. 'You don't think I'm smart, do you? You think I'm dumb. Stu-pee-do.'

'No, you're not so dumb. In three months you went from third-grade books to fourth-grade books. That's very fast. Three more months and you can read fifth-grade books. Two year's improvement in one year. At that rate in about two years you'll catch up to twelfth grade. You are the most improved person in the class.'

'Most improved means I started out the dumbest. In a class of stupidos. But I'm in the twelfth grade right now. Eighteen years old. I ain't no dumb Mexican from Mexico. I been speaking English all my life. All my life.' He put his head down inside the cave of his arms.

The next day he said, 'Is it true about that three-year-old kid studying physics in Korea?'

'Yes.'

Benjie hit himself hard on the face.

To give the students something they would read, the brother brought them a pile of comic books. 'They're coming out with the first black superheroes,' he said. 'Too bad, though, they're starting to make Oriental villains again with yellow skin and long fingernails.'

'That's supposed to be a chink?' Benjie asked, interested. 'You're making a mistake this time. That doesn't look like no chink.' He took the comic book and read it. 'Don't feel bad. I just read it all the way through. That's not a chink. They draw him ugly to show how bad he is, that's all.' Fu Manchu. The Mandarin. Yellow Claw. The brother was touched at Benjie's trying to protect his feelings.

The first of the brother's students to go to Vietnam was Alfredo Campos, who was twenty-one years old, the age at which the brother had graduated from college. Alfredo had emigrated alone from Mexico when he was nineteen. He was going to school to get a job away from the grape fields. He asked the brother to help him write letters to his eleven brothers and sisters, who practised English for coming to the United States someday. But suddenly, in the middle of the semester, Alfredo dropped out and went to Vietnam. 'I send honour to you, Teacher,' he wrote from there. 'I send congratulations to you, my Teacher, on Christmas Day.' His sister, who was eighteen, took his place in class. She brought slides he had sent from Vietnam.

The brother showed the pictures to the class: A puff of orange smoke was artillery fire. A row of tanks fired into what looked like a prairie. Guns mounted on wheels taller than men shot at a mountain. Rows of shit-coloured helicopters blotched the sky. No dead bodies, though. Alfredo and his prisoner smiled side by side at the camera; they were both small, dark boys. Alfredo and a Vietnamese girl friend, who was dressed in a leopard mini-skirt, stood with their arms around each other's waist. Children cut his hair and shined his shoes; they did not seem to heed their broken arms and missing legs. He and his buddies, all Latins, toasted his former classmates with beer and made *V*s with their fingers. Women rummaged through garbage cans marked PROPERTY OF USA. The sun made everybody's eyes squint.

The brother did not say anything. The students also did not say much. He showed the slides to all five of his classes, and therefore got to see them himself five times. He didn't find anything to say about them. It was just as well; it would be unfair to say anything, Alfredo being in the war, more fair to let the students draw their own conclusions seeing actual pictures of Vietnam taken by somebody they knew.

The third or fourth time around, the pictures seemed very happy, very attractive: Alfredo, grown, not lonely, almost married to a large and happy leopard-skinned wife. The sun shining orange in their cottage. Smoking an after-dinner cigarette while children played at his feet. Children laughing around his head, all their faces catching the light. Many friends, compadres. In winter Alfredo had jungles, not leafless trees in concrete. Even the prisoner was smiling. A lovely day. Sunshine and palm trees. The old woman held up half a potato and laughed.

The brother had to answer Alfredo's letters. 'Dear Alfredo,' he wrote, and could not think of the next thing to say. 'I hope you are well,' he wrote because that was the truth. He did hope he was well. 'Take care of yourself,' he wrote, but not 'Take *good* care of yourself'; Alfredo might have to kill someone in order to do that. He did not write, 'I showed your slides to the class'; he did not want to encourage him to take more dramatic shots. The brother kept writing the same letter: 'I am fine. I hope you are too.' He did not send any war or history books or peace pamphlets; Alfredo might let down his guard at a crucial moment and not defend himself. He did not mention religion though he knew Alfredo had one; if he put doubt into him, maybe he would hesitate at the wrong moment and get shot. Nor did he ask if he had killed anybody yet.

The schools started atomic attack drills again. The teachers had to sign a paper to be Civil Defense deputies. The brother did not turn it in, as he had not submitted his loyalty oath. Nobody noticed. If the principal said a code sentence on the PA system, 'The fire department will be inspecting Buildings C and D at two o'clock today,' it meant that a bomb was really coming. The students were not to know so that they wouldn't panic. For drill, the brother was assigned to take his group to the weight room, where the PE Department stored the body-building equipment. He sat in the dark with the remedials and waited for the all-clear bell. The boys rolled the weights about, lifted them in the wrong postures, dropped them on the wood floor, punched one another. He would not like being trapped under rubble with them. He'd be the only rational, unselfish adult there, the only one with an idea of order, responsible for the safety of all of them, the only one who would question cannibalism. No, these would not be the people he would wish to die with. 'Stop throwing the barbells,' he ordered.

He could not escape induction. He did not have physical disabilities. He was not married. He was not in a job vital in defence. The Army would not assign him to some easy NATO duty like guarding a German border. They'd send a gook to fight the gook war. He had to do something, not leave his fate to the draft lottery, an all-or-nothing gamble. The chances had narrowed to two: go to Canada or enlist in the Navy. He decided against Canada though he had relatives in Vancouver China-

276

town, Pender Street. He had no friends there. He had never met those relatives. He did not want to live the rest of his life a fugitive and an exile. The United States was the only country he had ever lived in. He would not be driven out.

So he enlisted in the Navy for four years. The Air Force was more apt to drop bombs. On the ocean, he would not have his heart broken at the sight of Vietnamese grandmothers and babies.

He arrived at his decision by reasoning like this: In a country that operates on a war economy, there isn't much difference between being in the Navy and being a civilian. When we ate a candy bar, drank grape juice, bought bread (ITT makes Wonder bread), wrapped food in plastic, made a phone call, put money in the bank, cleaned the oven, washed with soap, turned on the electricity, refrigerated food, cooked it, ran a computer, drove a car, rode an airplane, sprayed with insecticide, we were supporting the corporations that made tanks and bombers, napalm, defoliants, and bombs. For the carpet bombing. Everything was connected to everything else and to war. The Peace Movement published names of board members of weapons factories; they were the same people who were bankers and university trustees and government officials. Lines connected them in one interlocking system. The Pacifists' boycott lists included so many ordinary things, we couldn't live day-to-day Americans lives without adding to the war. Universities, funded with government grants, were inventing eerie new weapons: cobalt bombs, cluster bombs, scatter bombs, porpoise delivery systems, shrapnel that couldn't be X-rayed, fires that water did not put out, spider-web sensors that picked up body heat and relayed its presence to computers and from computers to satellites to bombers. Fragmentation bombs, 'guavas', embedded pellets that sent out radio signals to be traced to hideouts. Seismologists were not just studying the natural quaking of the earth but the impact of bombs. Electronics companies in the United States and the Far East, headed by retired admirals and generals, were building missiles, firebombs, and nuclear weapons for warfare on land and under water. Bugs monitored conversations miles away. Engineers and psychologists were researching police systems for riot control in American cities. Computer companies were keeping track of everyone by cross-indexing our banking and social security numbers, drivers' licences, airline tickets, birth certificates, gaol records, and purchases. The metals and stones of the abundant continent were being changed into weapons, which were funnelled to Vietnam.

The way to contribute less to the war was to go on welfare and eat out of garbage bins in back of grocery stores. Women were having babies at home to help them escape the draft in future wars or this war, which might not end by the time they grew to adolescence. There were drop-outs in a wagon train leaving California for Alaska, a Texas wagon train having already reached Canada. People were living in caves in Nevada and in the California north woods. A family from Hawai'i had had all their teeth replaced with metal ones; they went to live on a secret island for ever. Families and friends bought boats and would live on the sea. The brother knew people leaving for the New Hebrides, Honduras, New Zealand. But he enlisted.

He resolved that in the Navy he would follow orders up to a point short of a direct kill. He would not shoot a human being; he would not press the last button that dropped the bomb. But he would ride the ship that brought the bombs, which his taxes had already paid for. If ordered to shoot at a human target, he would then go AWOL to Canada or Sweden. But up until then, he would be a Pacifist in the Navy rather than in gaol, no more or less guilty than the ordinary stay-at-home citizen of the war economy.

When the new Secretary of Defense called the Chinese 'the enemy of the world' and predicted all-out nuclear war before 1970, the brother stopped reading newspapers. There wasn't any news; it would be news if the war ended. The news didn't change; only the numbers kept going up.

When the brother handed in his resignation, the principal told him that he would get credit for being in the service; he would rise four years on the salary schedule just as if he'd been teaching all along. The school would have a job for him later, give him preference. 'You don't have to do that,' he said. He did not tell his students where he was going or that he was leaving. The last thing he tried to teach them was: 'The military draft is not an American tradition. Protest against it is a longer tradition.'

His mother said, 'Bring a wife home. Look for a Chinese girl, but Japanese are okay too, Koreans okay. Just as long as she has a soft smile.' His father stood at the door waving good-bye. 'Good-bye,' he said. 'So long,' like leaving for college.

Basic training wasn't bad; he had expected worse, like in *DI* with Jack Webb. He did not have to fight and die like Prewitt and Maggio. Nobody called him chink or gook or slope or Commie. The only personal racial harassment was when the Company Commander stopped in front of him and hollered, 'Where you from?' and he had to shout out his home town, Sir. 'Louder. Where you from?' 'Stockton, California, Sir.' 'Where is that?' 'West Coast, Sir.' 'What country?' 'USA, Sir.' Each time the chief shouted at him, it wasn't about his shoe shine or his attitude but 'Where from?' 'Stockton, California, USA.' The chief didn't ask anyone else about his home town. It was a racial slur, all right, as though he were saying, 'Remember you're not from Vietnam. Remember which side you're on. You're no gook from Vietnam.' That's right, he wasn't. Fat men got the worst chewing out; the Company Commander called them girls – pussies, twats, sows, cunts, girls, ladies – and assigned them to run extra laps. His fellow man was like the remedials.

For the first five weeks, the recruits, or 'boots', were not allowed to talk during meals. At the brother's first dinner conversation, a big man across from him spread a hand and said, 'See this? You know what it's for?'

'What?'

'It's to make this.' He made a fist and nodded at it.

'Nah,' said the brother. 'It's to put good food in your mouth, not this swill.' They were eating the same chili sauce they cleaned the metal urinals with. Heads over their plates, which they encircled with one arm, the men stoked their mouths.

The brother lost his appetite. From the first day of boot camp when the recruits were marched to breakfast, he did not want the food. No food tasted any better or worse than any other. Peanut butter, french fries, chocolate did not taste good. He had lost the sensation of hunger. His stomach did not growl no matter how long he did without food. Not eating gave him some extra time, privacy; there were men who had nothing better to do than line up in front of the mess hall long before mealtime.

He would use his insensitivity to advantage; he would not have to plan his life around food. He had not eaten for days when it occurred to him that his appetite was unreliable; he could not depend on it to keep alive. He would never get hungry. 'I have to eat to keep myself alive,' he said aloud at table; he would remember better by saying it to those around him. He would have to use his reason instead of his instinct to eat and stay healthy. Each day, regularly, he would eat three meals, enough of each kind of food whether he wanted it or not. 'I've got to keep eating,' he said. He would eat by reason rather than appetite. He calculated what foods a body needed and ate them. He would take care of himself until his appetite returned. 'Eat vegetables,' he grumbled. 'Eat salad. Why do they feed us canned peas and carrots. Why can't they get fresh vegetables to San Diego?'

Whether anybody listened or not, he muttered from morning till night. 'They get us up at five-thirty before our brains can start functioning,' he said. 'My brain feels like wet cement. I can't see. Here I'm getting up, and I didn't even go to sleep yet. I didn't even have any dreams. Sorry. No dreams to tell. When I get out of the Navy, I'm never going to make a bed again. They're turning us into housewives. Make beds. Fold clothes. Shine shoes. Sweep. Swab. The Navy is housework. And the Navy is gym class. Hell is staying in PE for ever.' He mumbled while marching, 'Foot blisters. Bone bruises. Shin splints. Slave labour.' He mumbled while swimming, 'Abandon ship. Sharks at my underbelly. The ocean covered with black oil and the oil igniting. Ears clogged with chlorine.' Actually he was making up the sharks; the reasons for the training were not given. 'Can't shit in peace,' he said, sitting in the head while twenty people stared awaiting their turn, no doors and walls around toilets. 'I'm getting dumber,' he said. 'I can feel it, the IQs are leaking away. Everybody here is so dumb.' 'Yeah,' people agreed, 'they sure are.' He was ordered to mutter numbers in the tear-gas training room, to feel the gas burn before running out. He talked even in his sleep. 'Cut it out,' said the men in the next bunks or 'racks', but he didn't hear them because he'd stuffed erasers in his ears.

Recruit training wasn't the first time he had handled a gun. Each New Year's Eve, his father took a heavy box out of its hiding place, lifted the lid, unwrapped the wads of cloth, and took out the black pistol. The brothers and sisters passed it around with barrel upturned. Their father oiled it and loaded it. They followed him outside, and at midnight he fired one shot in the air over the slough, a year ending and a year beginning at that bang. On the rifle range, shooting at bull's-eyes, the rifle became so hot that when the brother looked at his hand, a flap of skin was rolled back. It did not hurt.

Because he could type, he escaped some of the clean-up. He was not as badly off as the others. He was older and had had something going for him before the Navy. Office work was in addition to other duties; he lost time the Navy allotted for letter-writing or study. He made schedules, and wrote out permits, attendance, and duty rosters. No exciting orders to kill Vietnamese.

On the last day of boot camp, his group voted him Champion Complainer. There were men who admitted that they hadn't taken a shit the entire ten weeks. He did not think he was any more full of hate and a desire to kill than before. Nor did his appetite return. At restaurants and at home on leave, he had no appetite for his favourite foods. If only the war were as easy as recruit training, he could take it.

Then for a while he was shuffled from one base to another without there seeming to be a plan. At a sort of holding barracks for homosexuals, his orders were to keep them from 'bed-hopping', though they didn't seem ill. He sat at his lookout's desk watching TV or writing letters or reading. He didn't catch anybody.

One area he avoided was the dependants' housing, which he stumbled upon one lunchtime. Navy wives in curlers and bedroom slippers sat on benches, two facing benches in front of each doorway. Arms folded, they yelled at their kids in the accents of many nations and regions, but even the black women looked colourless. These were women and children who were loved. 'The attack plans are not going to work,' a family man had confided during man-your-stations drill. 'If an enemy ever attacks this place, nobody is going to man his station. Do you think I'm coming to this desk during an attack? I'll be with my wife and kid. And everybody else will be with his wife and kids.' As a single man, the brother had not considered dependants.

Next he was assigned to a ship, an aircraft carrier. The beams and cables of the Golden Gate Bridge swung overhead. A few people up there waved and gave the peace sign. The Bay was grey like the pewter-colour rocket launchers bolted to the decks. For a frantic second the brother wanted to turn the ship around. It was like a moving island of planes and jeeps and tanks. Maybe those khaki torpedoes and silver rockets were H-bombs. Or they were flares. He didn't know what an H-bomb looked like, perhaps a cassette or a crystal chip.

The officers announced that the ship was on its way to Subic Bay in the Philippines. Still not Vietnam, still not time to jump ship. Some men were disappointed that the Navy did not immediately send them to Vietnam. 'We're gonna miss the war,' they said. They should have joined the Army, they said, or the Marines. They were children themselves so would not recognize the Vietcong as children; they would think they were fighting short men.

The brother's favourite activity was to stand watch in the flight control tower. He volunteered for extra duty hanging over the sea, sighting dolphins and sea conditions. When the ocean went gold with what he thought were low-flying birds, he climbed down and saw flying fish for the first time. Another day, in the swaying air he sighted an airplane speck, which turned out to be an albatross come to follow the ship. The slop jockeys soaked the garbage with hot sauce; the brutes guffawed as the albatross ate it and its throat jerked. Still it followed near and far, black wings against the sky, against the sunrise.

A personnel officer had read the brother's records, and gave him the collateral duty of teaching English classes on board ship, Remedial Reading to grown men who were so ignorant they did not know where Indochina was or Sweden or the various states.

'What do you see when you read?' he asked. 'Describe what you see.' They were not seeing the stories or ideas.

'I see small, small words, and they get darker and darker.' Poor boys; they must have joined the Navy to get away from school, and here they were in school again.

'I see words, and the ink runs together. Then it's dark.'

'I see letters at first, but they turn into colours that jump around.'

'Colours. Blue, I think. Or purple.'

'The words look like they're melting in water. They float.'
'I see a mist. Like fog.'
'Dark like a tunnel.'
'Like in an elevator.'
'Dark. Claustro.'
'Like a tight cave. And I can hardly breathe.'
'Can't I stop reading now? I'm getting dizzy.'
'I have a headache.'
'My eyes are watering.'
'I can't breathe.'
'My eyes hurt.'
'Dark. Claustro.'

He taught writing by having them write home. They had a Navy textbook with sample letters. ' "Dear Mom," ' the boys printed. ' "How are you? I am fine. I hope you are fine too. We sure have a lot to eat here. They keep you busy in the Navy. The weather has been cool/warm. Lots of love. Yours truly, Your Name." ' Some of the students copied it out just like that. ' "Your name," ' they wrote.

They took so long copying, class ended before he could give them some spelling or literature. There were people who didn't know all the letters of the alphabet, or they knew them but out of order, yet they had passed intelligence tests to get in the Navy. 'The government lowered the standards to get our bodies,' he told them. He showed them where Canada and Sweden were on a globe.

'You speak English pretty good,' his students complimented him. When white people said that, he had figured out what to answer. 'Thank you, so do you,' but he was at a loss again. He did not feel like using sarcasm on these boys, nor would they understand it.

What he wrote to his own parents because his Chinese vocabulary was small was, 'How are you? I am fine. I hope you are fine too.' But when he wrote in English for his sisters to translate, he again said, 'How are you? I am fine.' He didn't want to worry them.

As the ship moved towards Asia, he dreamed fiercely. The dreams came more and more quickly; the land sent them: An army enters a city to free it from an enemy. A soldier of the rescuing army, he walks through a castle into the dungeons. Going down the stairs, he sees at face level – bodies hanging, some upside down, some brown and dried up, black hair and arms swaying, feet turning this way, then that, bodies with black hair in their middles, corpses with sections missing and askew, but mercifully all dead, hanging by hooks and ropes. Laundry tubs drain beneath the bodies. The live women and children on the ironing tables, the last captured, are being dissected. It has to be a dream or a movie, he thinks, but he blinks his eyes, and the sights do not go away. He takes up his sword and hacks into the enemy, slicing them; they come apart in rings and rolls. He grits his teeth and goes into a frenzy, cutting whatever human meat comes within range. When he stops, he finds that he has cut up the victims too, who are his own relatives. The faces of the strung-up people are also those of his own family, Chinese faces, Chinese eyes, noses, and cheekbones. He woke terrified. The live bodies he had cut up had not screamed or wept because their mouths had been gagged and eyes blindfolded. Scared awake, he looked at the underside of the rack above him and at the sleeping man across the aisle; it was only the closeness in these berths that had made him dream like that.

He went to sleep again, and another dream recurred: Armies crawl like alligators under barbed wire. They have been ordered to charge a beach like at Normandy – only the beach is as wide as the Sahara Desert or the Gobi or Death Valley. In a panic of attack all those miles, they crawl and charge for years. It is an army of burrowing animals, moles, groundhogs, prairie dogs, ostriches. Frightened by shadows and sounds, they dig deeper. Nursing cubs and kids wriggle beneath bigger animals. Turkeys burrow under one another and die in a pile. Administering first aid, he cuts open their chests and sees gross internal damage. He tries unstacking the animals, weaning them. The alligators, left arm and leg, then right arm and leg, crawl towards battle. Occasionally, a wild stallion rears up and is shot.

He woke again, wondering why he should have such disorderly animal dreams when the ship was a machine. These dreams must have come from his years of poultry chores. When he slept again, he dreamed that he was a barkless dog tied to a table leg in a kitchen equipped with a sink, oven, and operating table. Families

284

– mother, father, and one child – are in kitchens like this all over the world. A voice comes over the loudspeaker: 'Children, take up your knives; women, forks; men, spoons.' The fathers take the children's knives and stab them quickly. Then with their arms around one another, the wife picks up the fork, and the husband the spoon. The loudspeaker says for them to kill themselves by forking and scooping. 'Spoon, knife, or fork?' the loudspeaker asks the barkless dog, who knows that if he took the sharpest instrument, he would deprive someone else of a quick death. He chooses the spoon, but is not willing to gouge himself to death. Because he is a dog and not watched as closely as human beings, he runs out of the kitchen-surgery, but outside, the shooting war has begun. He runs in and out the door, unable to decide whether it is better to commit suicide or to kill.

His bunk neighbours told the brother he talked Chinese and yelled in his sleep, complaining even more in sleep than awake. Mornings in another life, his family had told their dreams while eating breakfast. He found some shipmates who listened, though he would have otherwise muttered to himself.

The people he had met in basic training or another base seemed old friends meeting again, homeboys. Bill, a hippie Pacifist, followed him around asking about Zen, macrobiotic diet, yang and yin, brush painting. Bill was often swabbing decks or peeling potatoes because his hair was too long or completely shaved off, or he saluted crooked, or he wouldn't stand at attention during 'Anchors Aweigh'. He questioned the cooks and officers about the chili, whether there was hamburger in it, whether the fish had been fried in lard or vegetable oil. 'Use peanut oil,' he suggested. He picked out the bacon bits from his salad in case they were really bacon instead of soy. Ordinarily the brother wouldn't have liked a person who had a thing for the Orient, a sinophile, but Bill badgered him. 'Tell me about Buddhism,' he said. 'Do you know kung fu? Tai Chi? I want to be a Buddhist Pacifist. When the ship returns to San Francisco, I'm joining the flower children. When we get to Asia, I'm going to find my guru or stand on a street corner and let my guru find me. Come on, say a few words in Chinese. Go ahead.' Bill spoke Chinese in a scholarly or citified or northern dialect. He was very annoying, but he liked listening to dreams and complaints. There would be no real friends in the Navy anyway; there people don't stick together – they were stuck with one another, assigned to one another.

The brother also spent time with a chubby tenor who had dropped out of a seminary and did not become a priest. Louder than the country-and-western records, the other men played, he sang Italian opera and Mozart, which filled the bunkroom, the showers, the corridors and flew out across the water to the albatross. The young sailors shunned him in case he was homosexual and contagious. He rummaged the ship for bits of history and showed the brother the bolt marks in their berthing compartment, where ten years ago the Navy had kept a small cell for gaoling one sailor as a warning. The tenor found a pair of foils, and he and Bill or the brother fenced across the decks pretending to be Errol Flynn and Basil Rathbone, leaping off hatches and swinging from guy wires like riggings.

Instead of carrying out his lists of projects, his reading lists, guitar lessons, correspondence, the brother, like the other sailors, wasted time sitting around, bullshitting, complaining, going to the nightly movies. In the sudden lights after a movie, the audience looked especially depressing.

At Subic Bay the Commander ordered two hundred sailors to go to a dance with one hundred girls in an outlying town. The mayor, a woman, had invited them, but not enough sailors volunteered. The brother danced with some of the one hundred, 'all schoolteachers', according to the mayor's speech. The food was plentiful, and he watched a cockfight in the middle of the dance floor. One of the one hundred schoolteachers promised that in case the brother went to Vietnam, she would write dates on his letters and periodically mail them to his parents.

The next port was Korea, the magic place, where the good ginseng comes from. The civilian workers read the brother's name tag and asked if he were Korean. They had that same last name. 'Chinese,' he said, 'American. Chinese American.' 'Chinese American,' the Koreans repeated. 'Lucky, huh? Lucky.' He bought ginseng, 'man's heart', the root of life, the root in the shape of a human being, and sent it to his mother. She kept writing for him to buy more, red and yellow ginseng and many different grades, also instants and concentrates.

On Thanksgiving, the sailors gave a party for local children, who ate very seriously. The children hid bananas and oranges inside their coats, into which they or their relatives had sewn enormous pockets. 'We'll give you a doggy bag,' the men, who sat in every other seat, said. 'Go ahead. Eat.' But the kids stored it away. 'Have another apple. Have some more cupcakes,' the brother said to the kids next to him. 'Take the whole bowl.' He handed one boy the potatoes. 'Say some Korean,' men said to the kids. 'Cat got your tongue?' 'They don't talk much, do they?' they said. 'Aren't they cute? Cute little fellas.'

Next the ship went to Taiwan, where he would be stationed. He watched the real China pass by, the old planet his family had left light years ago. Taiwan was not China, a decoy China, a facsimile. He would not find out if the air and flowers of China smelled sweeter than California and the sky filled with golden birds, whether promises would come true, time move slower, and life last long.

In Taiwan he was for the first time in a country of Chinese people. The childish dream was that he would find like minds, and furniture that always fit his body. Chinese Americans talk about how when they set foot on China, even just Hong Kong, their whole lives suddenly made sense; their youth had been a preparation for this visit, they say. They realize their Americanness, they say, and 'You find out what a China Man you are.' An ophthalmology student from the ship, an American of Japanese ancestry, who was proud of his 'double-lids', said that the eyes of ethnic Asians have a naturally faraway focus. 'If we lived in Asia,' he said, 'where everything is arranged according to our eyesight, we wouldn't need glasses.' Clarity was a matter of preference and culture. 'Americans zone cities and make billboards for Caucasian eyes,' he said. 'Blackboards are set so many feet from the students' desks, traffic signals at such a size and distance, newspapers and books in a certain size type. If we AJAs with our epicanthic eyes and peculiar focus went back to Japan, we wouldn't need glasses any more.' The brother had American 20–20 vision, but didn't notice things getting either blurrier or sharper in Taiwan. That eye doctor trainee was a crackpot.

The brother, Bill the Buddhist monk, the opera singer, and the ophthalmologist decided to live on the economy. They rented a prefab house next to rice paddies with water buffaloes; it had a fireplace though the climate was hot. The others looked for a houseboy to do the cleaning and cooking. 'We ought to clean up after ourselves,' the brother argued. 'A man ought to wash his own dishes and wash the clothes he wears. Like Truman. Truman washed his own socks. Cleaning up after yourself is the followthrough.'

His friends said he was blithering again. 'We're pumping bucks into the economy,' they said. 'We're paying top dollar and putting food in bellies. If we don't hire him, somebody else will make him work for less.' They hired an old man for houseboy.

The brother hoped Bill would not point him out to the old man, 'He's Chinese too,' unleashing a whole set of customs. The old man would scorn him for speaking the wrong kind of Chinese, scold and mock, turn him into a child, a bad Chinese who couldn't speak right. 'Ho Chi Kuei,' he'd scold. 'Ho Chi Kuei.' He'd call him names for who knows what. For being in the Navy, for living with a gang of white devils, for going out with girls, for drinking, for coming in late, for smoking dope, for the invasion and colonization of Asia. The old man leaned on his iron pressing their uniforms sharp 'inside out', as the sailors requested. The brother had pressed them this same way when he worked at the laundry. If he were living alone, he would have gotten rid of the old man. So the old man wouldn't see his father's Chinese writing on envelopes, the brother made sure his mail came to his office at the base.

Once he came home in the middle of the workday and found the old man asleep on the sofa, and left so as not to wake him. Another day while wandering in a market, he saw him with his wife and three children. When the old man introduced everyone, the brother felt surprisingly honoured, as if the old man were letting him have something special, personal. The brother resolved he would return after he got out of the Navy and say Hello to him. He'd look him up. He had a list of things to do after the Navy, after the war was over, the endless war not even officially begun yet, the beginning let alone the end not in sight: he would take a cruise ship from San Francisco to Asia; he would see the Philippines and Taiwan as a civilian.

The Chinese workers at the base were curious about him.

'What are you?' they asked. 'Chinese American,' he said. 'Lucky. You're lucky,' they said in English just like the Koreans.

Life was getting to be a routine when in the Chinese New Year season, which the Vietnamese and Americans were calling Tet, the brother was assigned to the USS *Midway* for an attack mission to the Gulf of Tonkin. There were nuclear weapons on board, sidewinders, matadors, six-hundred-mile-range rockets with atomic warheads. The men discussed cyanide in case of torture. 'If I were in the jungle, I'd carry cyanide.' 'But bringing cyanide is like having Thorazine on hand when dropping acid. Expecting a bad trip causes a bad trip. You set yourself up.' The hippies were doping themselves silly. A sister ship was supposed to accompany the *Midway*, but a kid had dropped a wrench into the engine. It wasn't sabotage, just an accident. Pilots ejected themselves inside of hangars, mechanics got sucked into the jets, flight deck crew sliced by guy wires. It did not require precision to deliver the massive tonnage.

The brother did not go AWOL to Sweden or Canada. He was, after all, only coming a few miles physically closer to Vietnam, and his job of flipping switches and connecting circuits and typing was the same as on land, the numbers and letters almost the same.

So here he was on an aircraft carrier from whose flight deck hour after hour corps of planes took off. He could not take naps, his bunk was directly beneath the rocket launchers. Even using binoculars, he did not see much of the shore. Hanoi was an hour away by plane. He did not see the bombs drop out of the planes, whether they fell like long white arrows, or whether they turned and turned, flashing in the sun. During loading, when they were locked into place, they looked like neatly rolled joints; they looked like long grains of rice; they looked like pupae and turds. He never heard cries under the bombing. They were not attacking the enemy with surprise bombings but routine bombings or 'air operations' in twelve-hour shifts. When the sister ship got there, there would be bombings through the night, round-the-clock bombings. The pilots flew out there, unloaded their quota, and came back. It took intelligence and imagination to think that they were in Vietnam in the middle of the heaviest American bombing. A man he'd eaten lunch with did not show up for dinner, and that meant the man's plane had gone down. He had to imagine his death because he saw no blood, no body. The pilots either came back or they did not come back. There were no wounded. Sometimes a pilot would say that he had returned with a dead co-pilot in the cockpit. The sailors did not mourn the pilots, an arrogant, strutting class who volunteered for the bombings. Nobody was drafted to drop bombs. 'Extra dessert tonight,' the sailors said. 'He asked for it,' they said. 'Hot shot.' 'Gung ho.' When the pilots returned alive, it was no different from a practice run. No celebrations and no mournings, just business, a job. An officer was assigned to sort the dead man's personal effects; he censored those things too embarrassing to send to the family, such as photographs of Asian women.

The brother did touch foot on Vietnam by visiting a base near Saigon. He did not explore the city. He met some infantrymen who told him that when they were ordered to patrol the jungle they made a lot of noise, clanged equipment, talked loud. The enemy did the same, everybody warning one another off. Once in a while, to keep some hawk officer happy, they fired rounds into the trees.

The brother was formally asked by his Commanding Officer to train as a pilot. He had the test scores, the potential, but he said no.

The pilots often invited their shipmates for the bombings. 'Want to come along?' 'Come on. Take a ride. Come along for the ride.' The brother said No, 'No, not me,' many times. Then one day he said, 'Sure. Why not? When? Sure, I'll come along for the ride.' He put on a parachute and walked with the pilot and co-pilot across the flight deck on to the plane. He felt overheated, his head crammed into the helmet and his body pulled backward by the parachute. He had to duck through the door. Stuffed into his low seat, which tilted towards the ceiling, he found with effort the seat belts and buckled himself in. The door slid shut. It was not to late to ask out. The plane was still lined up behind others waiting for takeoff. He could say he'd changed his mind and cause only a minor inconvenience. He wouldn't be embarrassed. The engine revved. He wasn't, after all, committing a worse act by riding on the plane than riding on the ship. The plane accelerated on its short runway, left the deck, and climbed over the water, the horizon slanting, dipping, and rising. Then there was the steadiness one feels riding in any plane, train, or car. The instruments, needles, dials, and lights made no alarming flashes or jumps. He put on a headset and heard familiar numbers and letters. He stood against the gravity and looked out of the windshield, which was narrow like a pair of wraparound glasses. All that he witnessed was heavy jungle and, in the open skies, other planes that seemed to appear and disappear quickly, shiny planes and their decals and formations. The bombs must have gone off behind them. Some air turbulence might have been a bomb ejected. He heard no explosion. There did seem to be some turns and banks like a ride in any small plane. The plane turned in the direction from which they seemed to have come – he could tell by the sun now on the other side – and they were descending and landing. The plane caught in the wires, not needing the net. The door opened, and he climbed out. 'Smooth run,' said the pilot. 'Yeah, smooth,' said the co-pilot. The brother felt no different from before, but he made a decision never to go again.

He got promoted and transferred back to Taipei. His Commanding Officer dealt out personnel papers: 'Communications Specialist. Q Clearance,' he heard. 'You've been run through a security check – ' (The brother's breath caught – his family deported.) '– and cleared. Congratulations. Secret Security.'

'Thank you. Thank you. I got something out of the Navy,' the brother blurted. 'I'm getting something good out of the Vietnam war.'

The government was certifying that the family was really American, not precariously American but super-American, extraordinarily secure – Q Clearance Americans. The Navy or the FBI had checked his mother and father and not deported them. Maybe that grandfather's Citizenship Judge was real and legal after all. So Uncle Bun's defection to Communism didn't matter, nor Father's gambling, nor Great Uncle's river piracy, second-storey work, and murder. And the government had forgiven whoever it was who had almost gotten caught stowing away, or he had covered his tracks so well that they overlooked him, missed him, impervious to investigation. The Communist grandmother, aunts, and cousins, potential hostages, were not hurting his trustworthiness as an American. Maybe Uncle Bun was dead, never got to China; maybe he wasn't even really an uncle. His grandfather's and father's papers had indeed burned in the earthquake, and it was all right that his mother was an alien. The government had not found him un-American with divided loyalties and treasonous inclinations. Though he was conveniently close to China, the US government, which could make up new laws, change the law on him, did not dump him there. While his services were needed for the undeclared American–Vietnam war, the family was safe. And the family had friends and neighbours who protected them during investigation.

His Commanding Officer said that the brother's record as a communications expert with language aptitude qualified him for the Monterey Language School. Wouldn't he like to study Chinese? Or Vietnamese? 'You studied French,' he said. 'You speak Chinese too, don't you?' A vision of Monterey leapt up like a mermaid out of the sea and lured him. He wanted that Pacific coast, that sunshine and fog, the red tile roofs in the dark trees, the fiery and white bougainvillaea, the walks on the streets leading to the ocean – and school again, to be a student a luxury. 'Let me think about it,' he said.

A letter came from his older brother, who had gotten a commission in the Air Force. He had just been given Top Security Clearance. Maybe he was the one who had prompted the security check, too ambitious to remain a private. The NAC had processed both of them at once. So they had not only been checked but double-checked, and cleared, doubly cleared.

The brother found some language books in the library. If he learned Chinese better, or if he let on how much he already knew, the Navy would assign him to be a spy or an interrogator. There was only one use the military had for Chinese language – war, the same use it had for raw materials and science. He would be assigned to gouge Vietcong eyes, cattle-prod their genitals. He would have to hang prisoners from helicopters, drop the dumb-looking ones, and tell the smart remaining ones to talk or else. It wouldn't be Chinese poetry he'd be memorizing but the Pentagon's *Vietnam Phrase Book*:

Welcome, Sir. Glad to meet you. How many are with you? Show me on your fingers.

Are you afraid of the enemy? Us?

Do you place faith in America? Will the people fight for their freedom? We are here to help them in the struggle on the side of (1) the free world (2) the United States (3) the Allies (4) freedom (5) God.

Would they (1) support (2) join (3) fight on the side of (4) work for (5) sacrifice their lives for US troops?

Your nickname will be —. My nickname is —.

Do you believe in (1) US victory (2) annihilation of Bolshevism?

Open the door or we will force it.

Is he your father? Village leader?

Are you afraid? Why?

If we cannot trust a man, (1) wink your right eye (2) place your left hand on your stomach (3) move your hand to the right, unnoticed, until we note your signal.

The Vietnamese call their parents Ba and Ma; *phuoc* means 'happiness', 'contentment', 'bliss', the same as Chinese; *lan* is 'orchid', the same as his mother's name; Vietnamese puns are like Chinese puns, *lettuce*, *life*; they probably also bring heads of lettuce home on holidays. *Study, university, love* – the important words the same in Chinese and Vietnamese. Talking Chinese and Vietnamese and also French, he'd be a persuasive interrogator-torturer. He would fork the Vietnamese – force a mother to choose between her baby with a gun at its belly and her husband hiding behind the thatch, to which she silently points with her chin.

'No,' he told his Commanding Officer. He had been given a choice, and he said No. 'No, thank you.' He would not be like the scientists making plasma bombs and supersonic brain scramblers for want of a better use of their abilities.

On days off and after work, he and friends went to museums, bars, the aborigine village, looked for girl friends, wandered about the Taiwanese countryside, shopped for stereo equipment.

Passing many Chinese faces made him feel vaguely rude for not greeting every last one the way he'd been taught to do back home. As happened every time he went out, he heard somebody shout, probably at him, but he did not understand the words. Once in the middle of the night, someone came out of an alley and jumped him from behind. An arm hooked around his neck. He broke loose and ran, got away. Later his throat remembered the choke-hold of that arm. It had probably been a mugger, not someone after him personally. Off duty, he wore a white shirt, baggy pants, and civilian shoes to blend with the crowds. Yet he had not 'returned'. Of course, the Centre was elsewhere. This island was not the Centre, its people emigrants, rejects, and misfits. He'd be more at home if he walked straight away from this Taipei street to a military base. Sailors and soldiers didn't blend into American towns either.

He had two weeks R and R and went on a vacation to Tokyo and Hong Kong. His parents had given him the names of relatives to visit. He liked Tokyo, where the Japanese were too busy to stare at strangers. They walked fast, had places to go, business to do. He bought Peace brand cigarettes for their packaging. Then, not able to delay any more, he went to Hong Kong, where he heard Cantonese almost like back home. Store keepers and waiters told him that they had hard lives. 'You're lucky,' they said. He took a train tour, which included a trip to the border of the New Territories. He saw a valley and distant hills covered with wild vegetation. 'There is the People's Republic of China,' said the guide. If he had not said that, the brother would not have known. A solitary guard stood here and there, also local policemen in British uniforms. The brother saw no man-made crossings, tracks, bridges, or fences, or anything to hinder or facilitate a crossing. No red wall, no curtain. He walked on the overpass above the railroad tracks for a better look at Red China. Just as Hong Kong had a Communist wharf among other wharves, Communist shops among other shops, he saw no Red distinction.

He boarded another train back to the city to look for the street where his relatives lived. Shopping, he tried to remember what to bring on the occasion of meeting after many years. Oranges, black bean cake, a roast duck might have been appropriate for a harvest blessing or a month-old baby, and his relatives would make fun of him and call him Ho Chi Kuei and *jook tsing*. But he would bring gifts upon entering a nightmare. His aunts and cousins would be poor, and live in a cave or shack. He would find a cardboard and tin shack full of people. Out of a grey rag pile, thin hands would grope and beg, and mouths stretch wide open. 'They will change my life,' he worried. Their faces would resemble brothers' and sisters' and parents' and his own. He would need to rescue them. He would not be able to leave them. Or he would leave at great cost, pain, and guilt. He would end up like his parents, pledging his salary for ever. The relatives would have no manners, no polite ways that would make his visit easy. But a cardboard box on a hillside was not the worst shelter; worse would be if he were a Vietnamese returning from Paris to his hootch or his hole underground.

Queen's Road led him away from the hills. He would rather have rich relatives, the kind who didn't notice beggars, the kind who said, 'Why, the hill people and sampan people are lazy. They choose to live like that. Yes, they prefer it.' They'd take him out to dinner and wouldn't let him pay. They'd say, 'I've never met a poor Chinese. We Chinese are raised with discipline. We make it.' He'd tell them his parents were well, and leave. He'd have no trouble leaving them. He came to apartment buildings or housing projects with balconies of laundry. As many little girls as little boys were out on the sidewalks.

But as he looked, the numbers on the doors skipped the one in his hand. There was a number higher and one lower. He was not shirking; he walked back. It was not there, no such number, his number missing. He went in the alleys and looked in the crates. He entered the buildings with addresses that were approximate. No one had heard of his relatives' names. Trying combinations of the numbers, he searched on parallel streets, searched an afternoon, and did not find the house or hovel or tenement where they lived. He left the perishable food in front of any door. The next morning he tried again. Finally he left the rest of the gifts by another door. Perhaps they did not live in one of the shacks upon the hill and had put a fake address for their relatives not to worry.

The brother decided that after his time in the Navy and after the war, he'd try again, and also ride into China and look for the ones there.

It was just as well he hadn't found them. The ophthalmologist had gone to Japan and found his village and his relatives, who were very hospitable and gave him the main bed and meat. But on the last day, before dawn, he heard the door slide open. Through his eyelashes, faking sleep, he watched his uncle tiptoe across the room and leave a piece of paper on his chest. (The brother pictured it on his breast, but he must have meant the chest of drawers.) It was a day-to-day running account of all he had eaten, down to the numbers of helpings of rice, a list of the laundry his aunt had washed and ironed, the number of times the little girl cousin had polished his shoes, each cup of tea, an itemized list of all the presents and loans, the bathrobe and slippers, the number of baths in the hot-tub, the number of days and nights in his room, totalled neatly in yen and dollars. He had paid it, of course.

When the brother took a cargo plane on standby home – CONUS, the Continental United States – there were no other passengers; it was a plane especially to take him home. At night in lonely parts of airports, he saw electric conveyors move coffins draped with flags on and off planes. A soldier stood guard in front of stacks of them.

Mustered out at Treasure Island, he rode a Greyhound to Stockton. He walked the few blocks to his parents' house, in front of which many cars were parked. A party was just ending. Some of the guests were leaving. 'He's back,' they said, typically talking about him in the third person.

'Well, so you've come back,' said his father, 'you've come back.' 'You're back home,' said his mother.

The chicken still sat whole on the table. Pieces of the roast pork from a whole pig, noodles, and lettuce remained. This was a very important, religious party, a thanksgiving that he had come back home, more than personal, not a party only for him, and that was why they hadn't had to wait for him to have it. He ate the rock sugar on red paper his mother handed him; he ate the leftover pork. She hacked the white chicken for him. No, his appetite hadn't come back yet; he'd have to do more duty-eating.

Three years after his return, the United States withdrew from Vietnam. For a time longer than that, the things people did seemed to have no value; nobody else saw this. But his appetite did gradually increase. He had survived the Vietnam war. He had not gotten killed, and he had not killed anyone.

The hundred-year-old man

There is a man who would be one hundred and seventeen years old now. He had a one-hundred-and-sixth birthday party in the Palolo Chinese Home in Hawai'i in 1969. He wore a wool cap. He told the guests he came to Hawai'i in 1885 on the SS *Coptic*. He brought with him pigs in cages, and chives and onions growing in cans. He had divided his ration of fresh water with the pigs, the chives, and the onions.

He worked in the sugarcane fields for four dollars a month, and his first job had been to clear the brush for planting. He lived in a grass house, but later moved into a dormitory, where he slept in a bunk covered with grass mats. He sent one half of his pay to his family in China. Here's how he spent the rest: He bought kerosene and wood; he paid off some of his debts, his passage to Hawai'i, and the twelve-dollar fee for processing his papers; he spent six dollars to join his Benevolent Association, which gave him room and board when he took his monthly trip to Honolulu on pay day. He rode to town in a horse cart for thirty cents; it carried five passengers. When he could not afford the thirty cents, he walked.

He rested by smoking opium, which the plantation foreman sold. A half-hour's worth of high was called a dragon seed and cost fifty cents. When Hawai'i outlawed opium, he switched to cigars.

He saw King Kalakaua and Prince Kuhio. In 1893 he did not go to town because of the American revolution against Queen Lili'uokalani, who was 'big and friendly', he said. 'I was for the Americans,' he added.

Since 1885 he has left the island twice, once to go to Maui and once to Kaua'i.

On this one-hundred-and-sixth birthday, the United States was still fighting in Vietnam, and people asked him how to stop the war. 'Let everybody out of the army,' he said.

'In one hundred and six years, what has given you the most joy?' the reporters asked.

He thought it over. He said, 'What I like best is to work in a cane field when the young green plants are just growing up.'

'In the end,' said Tu Fu, 'I will carry a hoe.'

On listening

At a party, I met a Filipino scholar, who asked, 'Do you know the Chinese came to the Philippines to look for the Gold Mountain?'

'No,' I said. 'I know hardly anything about the Philippines.'

'They came in a ship in March of 1603,' he said. 'Three great mandarins landed at the Bay of Manila. The Filipinos were amazed to see them riding in ivory and gold chairs. They were higher class than the thirty thousand Chinese who were already living in Luzon. They had with them a Chinese in chains, who was to show them where to look for a gold needle in a mountain.'

It was past midnight, or it was his accent, but I could not hear if he was saying that looking for the Gold Mountain was like looking for a needle in a haystack. 'No. No,' he said. 'A gold needle.' To sew the sails, was it? A compass needle, was it? 'The mandarins asked for more ships, which they would fill with gold, some to give to the Filipino king, some to take back to the Queen of Spain, and some for the Emperor of China.'

A group of Chinese Americans were gathering around the Filipino scholar. 'Oh, yes,' said a young man, 'a Chinese monk went to Mexico looking for that mountain too, and either he came there with Cortez, or it was before that.'

'And the Filipino king,' continued the Filipino, 'who had met conquistadores and knew about seven cities of gold and a fountain of youth, sent them to the town of Cabit.'

'And they went to Weaverville, California,' said another. 'And in Weaverville, Cantonese labourers built a replica of their village in China.'

'No, no,' said someone else. 'The way I heard it was that some cowboys saw mandarins floating over California in a hot-air balloon, which had come all the way from China.'

'Now, these Chinese who were looking for the gold needle,' I reminded the Filipino man, 'what happened after they got to Cabit?'

'They sailed up a river farther and farther inland.' And they built roads and railroads and cities on their way to this mountain. They filled swamps. They had children. 'And on a certain mountain they sifted rocks and dirt looking for a gold needle. They asked the man in chains where the gold was, and he said that all they saw was gold.'

Because I didn't hear anything, I asked him to repeat the story, and what he seemed to say again was 'They found a gold needle in a mountain. They filled a basket with dirt to take with them back to China.'

'Do you mean the Filipinos tricked them?' I asked. 'What were they doing in Spain?'

'I'll write it down in a letter, and mail it to you,' he said, and went on to something else.

Good. Now I could watch the young men who listen.

Bruno Schulz
Sanatorium Under the Sign of the Hourglass
£1.50
Introduction by John Updike.

By the author of *The Street of Crocodiles*, this collection, while very much a work in its own right, returns to and extends many of the earlier book's themes. The narrator, Joseph, continues his precise and poetic exploration of life with his family in a small town in pre-war Poland, a portrait infused with magic, vision, and the sheer exhilaration of his art.

'A writer of a real, imaginative vision' ROBERT NYE

'One of the most remarkable writers who ever lived'
ISAAC BASHEVIS SINGER

Peter Matthiessen
The Snow Leopard £1.95
Winner of the US National Book Award.

In autumn 1973 Peter Matthiessen and biologist George Schaller made the dangerous 250 mile trek from Katmandu to the Crystal Mountain in Tibet, one of the holiest places in Buddhism. While Schaller studied the Himalayan blue sheep, Matthiessen sought a glimpse of the near-mythical snow leopard, seen by only two westerners in a quarter-century. And as a student of Zen, he wanted to consult the revered Lama of Shey Gompa, who had been in seclusion for years. This is both an exciting epic of wilderness travel, and an inspiring account of a 'journey of the heart'.

'A beautiful book' PAUL THEROUX

'A masterpiece' JOHN HILLABY

Picador

☐ **The Beckett Trilogy**	Samuel Beckett	£1.95p
☐ **Willard and His Bowling Trophies**	Richard Brautigan	£1.25p
☐ **Bury My Heart at Wounded Knee**	Dee Brown	£2.75p
☐ **Our Ancestors**	Italo Calvino	£2.95p
☐ **Auto Da Fé**	Elias Canetti	£1.75p
☐ **Hidden Faces**	Salvador Dali	£1.95p
☐ **Nothing, Doting, Blindness**	Henry Green	£2.95p
☐ **Household Tales**	Brothers Grimm	£1.50p
☐ **Meetings with Remarkable Men**	Gurdjieff	£1.50p
☐ **Bound for Glory**	Woody Guthrie	75p
☐ **Roots**	Alex Haley	£2.50p
☐ **Growth of the Soil**	Knut Hamsun	£2.95p
☐ **Meanwhile**	Max Handley	£1.50p
☐ **When the Tree Sings**	Stratis Haviaras	£1.95p
☐ **Dispatches**	Michael Herr	£1.75p
☐ **Earth Magic**	Francis Hitching	£1.00p
☐ **Kleinzeit**	Russell Hoban	£1.00p
☐ **The Greenpeace Chronicle**	Robert Hunter	£2.50p
☐ **Three Trapped Tigers**	G. Cabrera Infante	£2.95p
☐ **Man and His Symbols**	Carl Jung	£2.50p
☐ **The Other Persuasion**	edited by Seymour Kleinberg	£1.75p
☐ **The Act of Creation**	⎫	£1.95p
☐ **The Case of the Midwife Toad**		£1.25p
☐ **The Ghost in the Machine**	⎬ Arthur Koestler	£1.75p
☐ **Janus**		£2.25p
☐ **The Roots of Coincidence**		£1.00p
☐ **The Thirteenth Tribe**	⎭	£1.50p
☐ **The Memoirs of a Survivor**	Doris Lessing	£1.50p
☐ **The Road to Xanadu**	John Livingston Lowes	£1.95p
☐ **The Snow Leopard**	Peter Mattiessen	£1.95p
☐ **The Man Without Qualities, Vol. 1**	⎫	£1.95p
☐ **The Man Without Qualities, Vol. 2**	⎬ Robert Musil	£1.75p
☐ **The Man Without Qualities, Vol. 3**	⎭	£1.75p
☐ **Great Works of Jewish Fantasy**	Joachim Neugroschel	£1.95p
☐ **Wagner Nights**	Ernest Newman	£2.50p

☐ The Best of Myles	⎫	£1.50p
☐ The Dalkey Archive	⎪	£1.50p
☐ The Hard Life	⎬ Flann O'Brien	80p
☐ The Poor Mouth	⎭	90p
☐ After My Fashion	⎫	£2.50p
☐ A Glastonbury Romance	⎪	£2.95p
☐ Owen Glendower	⎬ John Cowper Powys	£2.50p
☐ Weymouth Sands	⎭	£2.95p
☐ The Crying of Lot 49	Thomas Pynchon	£1.50p
☐ Hadrian the Seventh	Fr. Rolfe (Baron Corvo)	£1.25p
☐ On Broadway	Damon Runyon	£1.95p
☐ Snowblind	Robert Sabbag	£1.25p
☐ The Best of Saki	Saki	95p
☐ Sanatorium under the Sign of the Hourglass	Bruno Schulz	£1.50p
☐ Miss Silver's Past	Josef Skvorecky	£1.95p
☐ The Bad Sister	Emma Tennant	£1.50p
☐ The Great Shark Hunt	Hunter S. Thompson	£2.95p
☐ The Forest People	Colin Turnbull	£1.50p
☐ The New Tolkien Companion	J. E. A. Tyler	£2.95p
☐ From A to B and Back Again	Andy Warhol	£1.25p
☐ Female Friends	Fay Weldon	£1.50p
☐ The Outsider	Colin Wilson	£1.75p
☐ Fairy and Folk Tales of Ireland	edited by W. B. Yeats	£1.95p

All these books are available at your local bookshop or newsagent, or
can be ordered direct from the publisher. Indicate the number of copies
required and fill in the form below

Name _____
(block letters please)

Address _____

Send to Pan Books (CS Department), Cavaye Place, London SW10 9PG
Please enclose remittance to the value of the cover price plus:

25p for the first book plus 10p per copy for each additional book ordered
to a maximum charge of £1.05 to cover postage and packing
Applicable only in the UK

While every effort is made to keep prices low, it is sometimes
necessary to increase prices at short notice. Pan Books reserve
the right to show on covers and charge new retail prices which
may differ from those advertised in the text or elsewhere